Gerhard Oberleitner

You Up There – We Down Here

AA Assistants vs. Allied Bomber Crews

To my Mother

Gerhard Oberleitner

You Up There – We Down Here
Anti-Aircraft Assistants
vs.
Allied Bomber Crews

Oberleitner, Gerhard : You Up There – We Down Here · Anti-Aircraft Assistants vs. Allied Bomber Crews : Time Capsule : Andelfingen 2010 : History Facts : ISBN: 978-3-9522968-7-5

Research and Texts: Gerhard Oberleitner, Ybbs an der Donau, Austria
English Translation: David Kosh, Polyvox, Jona, Switzerland
Maps: Rick Britton Cartography, Virginia, USA
Editing: History Facts, Andelfingen, Switzerland
Cover and Layout: History Facts, Andelfingen, Switzerland
Print and Binding: MV-Verlag, Münster, Germany

This title was originally published in German as: Oberleitner, Gerhard : Ihr dort oben – wir hier unten : Flakhelfer gegen Bomberbesatzungen : Zeitzeugnis : Andelfingen 2010 : History Facts : ISBN: 978-3-9522968-6-8

Translator's note:

Where dates have been given in the original German-language format, e.g. 21. Oktober 1944 (dd.mm.yy), we have applied the American usage October 21, 1944 for reader convenience. To denote diary entries, the author stated the month of the year in Roman numerals: 25.VII.44 for July 25, 1944 – a popular method at the time. However, when dates relating to footnotes, reports or official documents are given in the conventional European manner, e.g. 15.11.1944 (15th November, 1944), we have retained that style for authenticity and ease of cross-referencing with original documents. [Any explanatory comments made by the translator are shown in brackets.]

Publisher's Note

This volume is very special from various aspects: it describes a period in the life of a youth who, still a high school student, is drafted to defend the biggest tank assembly plant in the armaments industry of the Third Reich. The artlessness of the boy and how he perceives his own wartime experiences is unique. It is more than just a stroke of luck that this Luftwaffe Anti-Aircraft Assistant not only kept a diary, but also recorded his time as a serviceman with his beloved camera. No autobiography can ever be totally objective, indeed, such records can, may and should be objective. In this book, the author devotes three chapters covering the perspectives of his wartime opponents at that time, thereby creating a far more comprehensive overview of the conflict. When reading this publication, three aspects in particular need to be taken into account:

- The diary extracts cited in this book reflect the original voice of a 16-year old Austrian youth of the WWII period. To have eliminated some of the expressions and formulations of the day, many nowadays frowned upon, would have destroyed the authenticity of the text. To maintain their authenticity, we have reproduced the diary extracts just as the author noted them down.

- When war is described by a naive, 16-year old trooper, it is obvious that many elements of the „big picture" that are readily accessible to us nowadays were carefully concealed from his generation. And, it would demean this research to repeatedly point out that the author knows more today than he did then. It is evident from his diary entries, however, that even at that tender age, the critical attitude of his family towards the Nazi regime indicates that he certainly understood more than did the majority of his comrades.

- The photographs taken by the author and reproduced in this book are not always of immaculate quality, but they do clearly show what interested a young man of his day. Any photographic material that does not originate from the author is marked to denote the source: Johannes Kreutzer (JK), Richard Pazelt (RP), Hans Rechenberger (HR), 461st & 484th Bomb Groups Association via Gunter Wiesinger (BGA), and the archives of History Facts (HF).

- Official documents or text extracts are cited, with original documents reproduced for ease of understanding the contexts, problems and mood of the times, or to indicate the sources of the material researched.

In his book „Ketzergedanken im Dritten Reich" [Heretical Thoughts in the Third Reich], Josef Radermacher provides a graphic insight into the period towards the end of World War II – a citation from it is highly appropriate to the tenor of Gerhard Oberleitner's own diary:[1]

»October 1944! On the Eastern Front, the Russians have entered East Prussia; in the West, the Americans have reduced Aachen to a pile of rubble; the British have reached the Maas; in the south, too, the front is approaching the frontiers of the Reich…

Thousands of enemy aircraft fly over Germany without meeting any opposition worth mentioning; at will they drop their bomb loads weighing uncountable hundredweights on our home towns and cities. Millions of Germans are wandering throughout the nation without a roof over their heads, having lost their homes and possessions. For the past two years, the Army High Command has been reporting nothing but defensive successes, which simply means being beaten back. Sixteen and seventeen-year olds are already taking part in the fighting. How a German victory is to be achieved becomes increasingly beyond comprehension by the hour. Only the hope of a miracle is being fanned among the population, the hope of a miracle weapon that is still being invented, or is almost ready, or is not yet being deployed because the Führer still expects the enemy to stop bombing us voluntarily.«

---

[1]   Radermacher, Josef : Ketzergedanken im Dritten Reich : Krefeld 1946 : Scherpe Verlag, pages 151 et seq.

Contents

Preface

After accompanying me to the railroad station on that morning of January 5, 1944 my mother was weeping as we said our goodbyes – I could not understand why.

Admittedly, I was not traveling back to school in Amstetten, just 20 km away, as I normally did after the Christmas vacation. This time I was journeying with my classmates to the Wegscheid Anti-Aircraft Training Camp near Linz, and that was another 60 km further down the line.

In common with virtually every other male high school student born in the German Reich in 1928, I had been drafted for service with the anti-aircraft defense service and today was the beginning of a huge adventure. That was my reaction as a 15-year old – surely it could not be that dangerous!

Mother knew better. 1943 had been a ghastly year for her: in May, my father had been arrested by the Gestapo and shunted from jail to jail, ending up as far away as Poland in a satellite of the Majdanek concentration camp in Lublin. In that same period, my brother, then a 19-year old armored engineer, had lost his right foot at Welikije Luki in Russia. By November, the family had finally been reunited but now, just two months later, at the beginning of the second to last year of the war, it was my turn – and Mother's worries were to begin all over again.

Naturally, given the political attitudes at home, I was also mentally a "dissenter" and any belief in the Ultimate Victory, if it had ever existed, had long been replaced by a critical frame of mind. Despite all this, it never entered my head to avoid doing my duty, particularly in combat situations. "They up there" were our opponents and we had to defend ourselves against them. Because they did not differentiate whether "we down here" were politically for or against the Nazi system.

Somehow, the regulated military lifestyle with its strict observance of orders and discipline suited me, provided those orders given by our superiors did not degenerate into bullying.

In any event, my time with the AA proved to be tough schooling that was to influence the rest of my life, and was unique to my generation. To what extent it affected me and my comrades is difficult to say, but somehow I have the feeling that ultimately it was not to our disadvantage.

I would even venture to say that our relatively good physical condition at a now advanced age can be attributed to the rigors that we were subjected to as fifteen and sixteen-year olds.

At school I had kept a diary and continued to do so when I joined the AA. I also wrote two pamphlets and took quite a few photographs. Now, more than sixty years later, those records that I was able to preserve during the eventful postwar period have proved useful as reference sources when writing this book and are the basis of its authenticity.

I also informed my classmates and wartime comrades about the origins of my research, and that I was writing a book based on it. Many of their opinions and innumerable memories have been integrated into it as a result.

Representing our many comrades born in 1927, and those from other high schools who were temporarily stationed with us, the Reverend Josef Lammerhuber, also an AA Assistant from Waidhofen, read the manuscript and contributed his own recollections.

I am indebted to Günter Wiesinger from Linz, who made photos, documents and articles on the American and German air forces available to me, and also to Leopold Banny from Lackenbach, author of the book about the operations of the Austrian AA Assistants „Droning Skies – Burning Earth", for the American reconnaissance photographs and Interpretation Reports.

I feel particularly close to Richard G. Yerick from Wickliff, Ohio. I got to know him in the course of his investigations about his uncle, Martin Yerick, who lost his life when the Liberator in which he was flying was shot down close to us on February 23, 1944. The opportunity of describing what was happening on the other side, both in the air and on the ground, is all thanks to his photos, documents and anecdotes.

Those bomber crews were also young men, barely much older than we, whose mothers worried terribly about them and who mourned when they lost their lives over our territory and through our actions.

Only the time that has elapsed since those events – a lifetime – allows the mind to become conscious again of the unbelievable external coercion under which family life was lived. And also the risks of dictatorship and war that people at home were subjected to, not to mention those who were permanently exposed to the dangers of the hostilities – sometimes not even conscious of the situation and often perceiving it as normality. From a modern perspective, in a time when we live in peace and prosperity, all that is impossible to understand. This applies to those who experienced it personally and even more so to those born later.

Researching this book frequently touched me personally. Events long forgotten resurfaced, innumerable memories, particularly of friends and comrades, but also of my family, came alive again.

From all this, a very personal but authentic record has been created. Today, I understand my mother's tears when we parted on that cold morning of January 5, 1944. She still did her best to take care of me and was the most important person in my life during that that dreadful period.

Gerhard Oberleitner, Ybbs, Austria, 2011

The author as an AA Assistant with his mother

Foreword by Richard G. Yerick, Ohio, USA

Friends through Fate

I was just a boy when I had a dream that someday I would learn how my uncle Sgt. Martin Yerick fought and was killed during the Second World War. He was a gunner on the B-24 Liberator Bomber piloted by Lt. Benjamin B. Chase, Ship #33, that crashed near to the Flak Battery 1./695 in St. Valentin, Austria.

I began my research in 1991, studying de-classified government records, war diaries, and interviewing veterans. Later it was decided that in 2003 I would make my first of six trips to Austria to continue my research. Even as a foreigner trying to overcome the language barrier, I was welcomed like family, helped by all I came in contact with to learn more facts, collect photographs of the crashed bomber, and even bring home relics from the plane.

But greater things were in store for me. Some of these photos were taken by a 15- year old boy who was a Luftwaffen-Helfer in the battery, and also a witness to the event itself. With the help of an air war enthusiast Günther Wiesinger of Linz, I found this photographer, self-appointed historian, writer and now author, Gerhard Oberleitner of Ybbs, and he made the day of the crash February 23, 1944 come alive.

His notes and memory tell of an Me 109 German fighter attacking the American B-24 bomber with parts of the plane falling into the battery, along with the co-pilot landing there with his parachute, an interesting account, that makes up only a small part of the story told within this book.

The operation of the flak battery itself is well documented, an effective weapon that chose its victims indiscriminately. I was interested to know their „secrets of success" and so I met his comrades. Such fine men, they gave no indication of the young soldiers they once were some sixty years earlier.

This experience may be one of my life's greatest accomplishments, but this American from Ohio, USA realized that he came to Austria not only to fulfill his own legacy, but to convince his friend Gerhard to fulfill his.

Now he has done just that, and this book is the proof. His words speak on behalf of all who were caught up in the air war over Europe, whether on the ground or in the skis.

This is a different Generation. We can meet as friends and we make history. I am proud to call this honorable man Gerhard Oberleitner my friend, and his story captivates me. He helped me to fulfill my dreams, and for that I am forever grateful.

Foreword by Richard G. Yerick, Ohio, USA

To keep a written diary and take photographs during wartime as he did was
"risky business". You might say, "He was walking on very thin ice". And he was.

For this he has my respect...

Richard G. Yerick, Ohio, May 2010

Eight schoolboys

Backdrop

In 1943, fighting on all fronts transformed the German war of aggression into a defensive one. The increasing strength of British and American air raids resulted in a virtual doubling of the number of anti-aircraft batteries protecting residential areas and armaments facilities within the territory of the Reich. At the same time, troops were withdrawn from these batteries to fill the ranks of the newly formed Luftwaffe Field Divisions.[2]

To close the resultant gaps in AA manpower, the Luftwaffe, commanding all air defenses, responded immediately: negotiations between the Reich Air Ministry and the Reich Education Ministry ultimately led to a decree dated January 22, 1943 relating to the "Wartime Auxiliary Service of Youth with the Luftwaffe", followed by a service regulation dated January 26, 1943. This defined the school classes that could already be drafted, registration of the students, medical examinations, structure of the curriculum and other details – an AA militia was to be set up using school-age boys.

The "LuftwaffenhelferLwH (HJ)" [Anti-Aircraft Assistants] were assigned to the Luftwaffe and the German Navy, but were to report to the Hitler Youth (HJ) organization. Externally, this was to be demonstrated by wearing the Airman HJ uniform and a swastika armband. Evening propaganda meetings, appeals and the like were intended to increase the influence of the HJ on young people.[3]

Pretensions and reality, however, were two different things. We AAA [Anti-Aircraft Assistants] totally rejected the HJ and their efforts to exert control over us. The minute we left the battery, we took off the armband, exchanging the HJ insignia for the Luftwaffe Eagle and making similar changes to our uniforms. This procedure was not unique to the school group from Amstetten, but was adopted without exception by all Luftwaffe and Navy Assistants. The HJ and their leaders in the AA battery left us in peace: no raising of the flag, instead „falling in to receive

---

[2]   Führer Decree of September 20, 1942
[3]   See Appendix, page 275

orders" for us; while the HJ had evening indoctrination meetings, we replaced these by parties in the battery!

Our school

According to the annual report for the 1943/44 school year, the State High School for boys, with classes for girls, (nowadays Bundesgymnasium) in Amstetten, at the time Lower Danube (now Lower Austria), was made up of eight classes of which the first four grades were taught in two parallel classes with the fifth grade having three parallel classes.

Temporary High School Building, first published in „50 Years of Amstetten (1948)"

Classes were taught by as few as 16 teachers, primarily young women and older male high school staff as the younger men were either at the Front or assigned to other wartime duties. The Head Teacher of our school was a dyed-in-the-wool National Socialist, or in the slang of the day, a "Nazi".

In the highest grades, i.e. the seventh and eighth, there were no longer any of the boys born in 1926 and 1927; they had been drafted into the AA in February or September 1943. Now, in January 1944, it was our turn, the 1928ers.

Our school

Class teacher Dr. Berta Scheffelbauer
(German, English)

Dr. Schadauer (German, History)

Dr. Friede Schwab (Latin)

Herr Bsteh (Maths, Physics)

The sixth grade

In the school year 1943/44, nine girls and ten boys were receiving their "wartime restricted" education; according to the annual report, 86 term hours were devoted primarily to physical exercises and art.

Class excursion to the St. Florian monastery

From January 1944 onwards, the number of boys in our class was reduced to two who had been exempted from wartime service with the AA. For us eight „men", who had been drafted, the girls organized a modest party just before the Christmas vacation[4] when we received our final school reports of the year. They had taken the trouble to write and recite a poem in which each of us boys and the teachers were briefly parodied, including happy memories of school excursions and hikes:

---

[4] The school year was made up of three "trimesters". Before Christmas and Easter there were reports for each trimester that included a brief account of the student's character. There were six different grades (nowadays five) and a "poor" between satisfactory and unsatisfactory was already considered worrying.

»You are now departing from our midst,
we have but one request to you all:
Behave well, forget us not,
comradeship demands it.

Do your duty, shield us well,
defend us with hearts of lions!
How dangerous it will now be,
that we nine girls are left alone.

But one defender stays,
hurrah, it is Steiner.
On his head repose all duties,
that Zehti once fulfilled.

The next is now called *Bast*,
well known as Rustan, Hermann, Ottokar.
He leads the way through fine example,
as Social Worker and Recycling Enthusiast.

With childlike expression,
his four eyes wander to *Senker*.
Who in turn returns his gaze as so oft,
his fortune in Bast's chemistry book rests.

His English speeches are very nice,
but nobody has yet to discern the joke.
Hence as a canny youth,
he announces his wit in advance.

Between this pair of friends,
sits our doctoral specimen.[5]
A precious boy, smart and sly,
he is meticulous in all.

The street plan, refuge of the helpless,
is ever in his hand.
But still it has occurred that our,
›lost child‹ has gone astray.

Frau Dr. Schadauer mistakes him oft,
for *Schmutz,* that all too shy a personage.
Approvingly nods our Chief,
as her glance falls upon ›Mister Smuts‹.

---

[5]   Spindelberger (Spindi)

Bast

Senker

Spindi

Schmutz

The sixth grade

Oberleitner the sales agent,
sits on the 2nd bench at the end.
Worldly, sports and oratorical genius,
he is our Montgomery.[6]

Latin tests reveal,
what true camaraderie is.
While *Wieser* silently curses Caesar,
Willi[7] seeks him in the crib sheet.

Now absent from this horde of heroes,
is one last pair of comrades:
Peperl Wallner is the one,
Nordic slender, with endless shanks.

The other they call Zehti,
we know him as our class leader.
His favorite subject is history,
but ne'er forgets he a math formula.

...

For all of you that is now behind,
step out in life with cheery courage.«

Oberleitner

Wieser

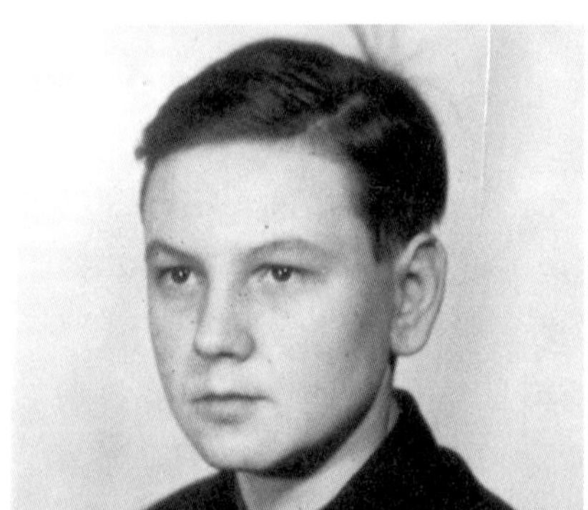

Willi

School trip to the Ötscher, fall 1943

Peperl

---

[6]   Not the British General Montgomery, but the figure in "Joan of Arc"
[7]   Reichebner

School excursion to the Taminschbachturm im Gesäuse 1942

My diary

I was 13-years old when, on January 5, 1942, I started to keep a diary. For the life of me, I cannot recall why I imposed this daily chore upon myself. Maybe it was to impress someone, but certainly not for my own pleasure, or to be able to read about what a heroic time we were living in over sixty years later. Newspaper clippings that I pasted in show that, at the beginning of 1942, the war was still progressing. The military setbacks in the Soviet Union during the severe winter months of 1941/42 were being played down in the daily bulletins of the Wehrmacht.

The first effects of the hostilities felt at home were not so unpleasant after all. We were able to spend the newly introduced "coal-saving vacation"[8], at home rather than in school.

My first diary entries did not last long – they stopped on Wednesday, April 22, 1942 with a brief description of my visit to the Variete Ronacher in Vienna „...I particularly liked Charly Rivel. His children (1 girl, 3 boys) were very good."

---

[8]   Known nowadays in Austria as "Energy vacations"

My next entries were made in a thin notebook during a skiing course from April 4 to 11, 1943 in the Ennstaler Alps where we stayed in the Edelraute hut near Hohentauern. It was not until September 1, 1943 that I finally decided to regularly record the day's events. There was plenty to write about: in May, Father had been arrested by the Gestapo, my brother was serving as an armored engineer on the Russian front where he lost his right foot, my mother had to run the carpentry business alone and I traveled daily to the high school in Amstetten.

The diary stops again on January 5, 1944, the day when I left to join the AA, the German anti-aircraft defense. The following three months of the New Year 1944 were highly eventful. Faced with the totally different living conditions, basic training in Wegscheid and with the battery, I simply did not find the time or leisure to keep up my diary. It was not until March 30, 1944 that I got started again. Every evening from then on I sat down and recorded what had been going on. And, there was no lack of events to report.[9]

Today, I am extremely pleased that I made that effort for the full duration of our assignment. Those notes, photos and documents are now the framework around which all the other anecdotes are constructed. Quotes from the original entries are repeated in *italics*, whereby the worst expletives are denoted by (…).

My photos

I took all the pictures with my medium format „Voigtländer-Bessa" folding camera. I always carried it with me, whether I was in the battery position, traveling, or at home. Not having either a range finder or light meter, all camera settings such as distance, aperture and shutter speed were manual and based on intuition or experience. Consequently, the number of poor exposures was high, which was particularly frustrating considering how scarce roll film was. I used the popular Agfa 6x9 cm, black and white 8 exposure roll film of the time with a light sensitivity of 18/10 or 17/10 DIN. The roll of film was inserted into the back of the camera

The author's camera together with his diaries and sketchbooks

---

[9]   See Appendix, page 252, for an extract of the original diary

and advanced manually after each exposure. Double exposures were the result when I forgot to wind the film and the pictures would be ruined.

I kept a carefully tabulated record of all the photos in a dedicated notebook.[10] In addition to the chronological number and the type of film, I recorded: the date the photo was taken, the camera setting, the location and light conditions, the subject and finally, the result, which was not always satisfactory.

Basically, I took photos of everything that got in the way of my lens: above all my comrades, life in the battery, our equipment, the battery position, including the nearby tanks that thundered along the ploughed-up ”Panzerstrasse” during their trials. One day I was standing beside that road and pointed my lens at the approaching tank. It roared past me, stopped suddenly and out climbed a tanker in his greasy uniform. He jumped down off the vehicle, came close, drew himself up to his full height in front of me and demanded:

„What are you doing there?”
„I'm taking photos!”
„Of the tank?”
„Yes, – why?”
„Don't you know that it's forbidden?”
„No, – why?”
„Don't ask such brainless questions!”

The author got some shots of the tank anyway. Here a shot of a Mark IV Tank, Variant H, taken on 5.VI.44.

---

[10]   See Appendix, page 252

My photos

He took the cocked camera from my hand, flipped open the rear cover, ripped out the film and threw it into the mud. Then he remounted and drove off. I stood there feeling sheepish and had to be thankful that the tanker did not report me to anyone or any authority.

Eight comrades

Basic training

To replace the young men born in 1926 who had to report for duty with the Reichsarbeitsdienst (RAD) [Reich Labor Service] in the middle of February 1944, all 5th and 6th grade high school students in the Reich born in 1928 were drafted to serve as Luftwaffe Anti-Aircraft Assistants (AAA), and as Navy Assistants on the northern coast of the Reich.

Thus, on January 5, 1944, we eight boys from the 6th grade of Amstetten High School, together with those from the 5th, traveled as a group by train from Amstetten railway station to Linz-Wegscheid. There, we joined the camp of the Heavy AA Replacement Battalion 38 where, over the next four weeks, we were to be inducted into military life. As we were still students and always had to bc under adult supervision when moving from one place to another, we were accompanied by a member of the teaching staff of our school. This still applied when we had become student-soldiers, only then it was someone with a military rank from the Luftwaffe who accompanied and supervised us.

With numerous other students of the same age from Gau Oberdonau[11], nowadays once again Upper Austria, we moved into hut 4 of barrack no. 9 of the apparently huge training camp. It was equipped with wooden bunks for straw mattresses and lockers, tables and stools for 12 to 16 men. There was also a wood-fired stove with chopped billets stacked at the end of the center gangway. At the front end of this gangway, close to the main entrance, stood the rooms of our three non-commissioned officers Sinn, Wengel and Weddehage. They had all been detached from the batteries of AA Group Linz-Steyr to train us.[12] In all there were 15 corporals and one sergeant supervising some 480 AAA, split into 4 batteries, each with around 120 men.[13] We were assigned to 1st Battery under Lieutenant Werkhausen.

---

[11]   Apart from the boys from Horn, we Amstetten youths were the only ones from Lower Danube; the other students, e.g. those from Melk or Waidhofen were sent to Vienna/Küniglberg.

[12]   PFC Sinn who was popular with us; he was later assigned to our neighboring battery Kronstorf, 3./695 (o).

[13]   According to Banny/Rappersberger, the total was 479.

In the middle, our Instructor, NCO Sinn

In addition to the living quarters there were kitchen and mess wings where we ate cooked lunch, or picked up sandwiches and the like, as well as the ghastly coffee, to consume in our hut. There were also barracks for ablutions as well as latrines. Neither area was heated but this did not dissuade the tougher elements among us from washing stripped to the waist. In those January temperatures, however, many of us, including myself, preferred to take a walk unwashed around the facilities and stare in admiration at our more hygienic comrades.

With the exception of our dress uniforms, we, the most recent draftees, were equipped entirely from Wehrmacht inventories. It seems that our dress uniform, consisting of a battledress blouse, trousers, overcoat and forage cap, cut in the style of the Luftwaffe HJ uniform and made of a fine gray-blue cloth, had been tailored specifically for us. We looked quite smart, the only annoying features being the swastika armband and the HJ cap badge.

Items originating from the Wehrmacht quartermaster's stores were:
- The spare, gray-blue fatigues with a forage cap as headgear
- Dungaree blouse and trousers including one pair of jackboots
- Long underpants, sports trunks, socks, handkerchiefs, vests etc.
- Bread bag, mess kit, field flask, steel knife and fork that left an unpleasant aftertaste
- Rucksack, blanket, padlock, cleaning kit and dog tags
- Gas mask with container and steel helmet were issued later in the battery position.

Basic training

The first days were taken up with writing postcards informing the folks at home that we had just arrived at our destination, were about to undergo a medical examination and that we were busy drawing our uniforms and equipment.

Postcard from one AAA Hans Müllegger to his parents.

The author Gerhard "Gertl" Oberleitner.

Full muster on the big drill square.

Condition and completeness of equipment were occasionally checked at kit inspections both in the battery emplacement. It was important to have any short issue confirmed immediately, as was the case when I did not receive a boot brush:

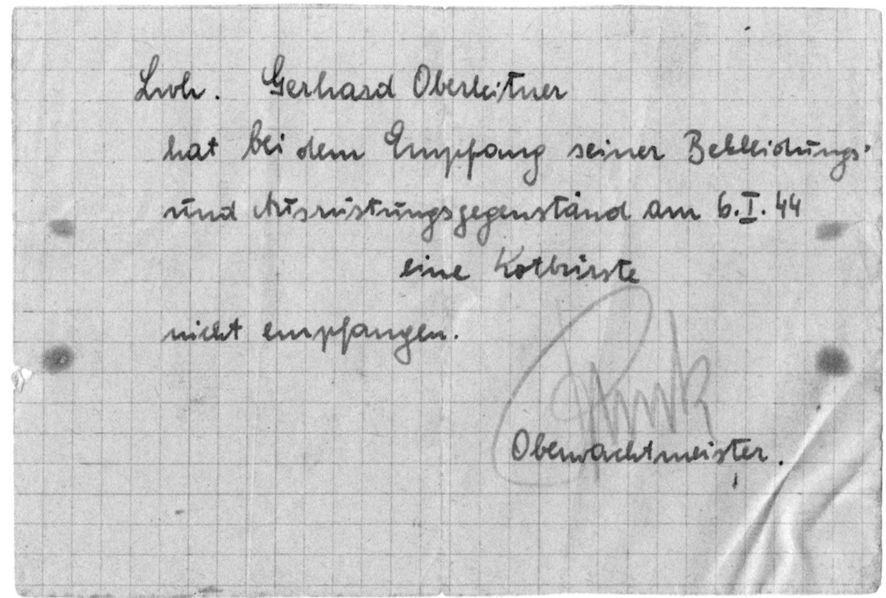

Confirmation signed by the Top Sergeant that AAA Gerhard Oberleitner has not received his boot brush.

Then things became strenuous: endurance drills in large groups, e.g. „Form up in rows of three", „Down!", „On your feet - at the double!", „Dismiss!", „Attention!" and so on and so forth, all accompanied by encouraging instructors' comments such as „Hopeless!", „You wimps!" and the like – all expressed as loudly as possible.

Saluting superiors was practiced to perfection. Everyone had to march past the instructor individually, eye contact made by a perfect turn of the head and a smart upswing of the right arm to give the "German salute"[14]. That part was still harmless.

When for some unexplained reason something had upset the instructors, there were knee-bends until we toppled over, countless press-ups, endless sprinting around with intermittent: „Full cover!", „On your feet - at the double!", „Down!" and whatever else entered their heads. That was the pitiless and loathed "square-bashing".

A lighter version of what was drilled on the barrack square was repeated during internal duties: familiarization with military regulations and the ranks of the three sections of the Wehrmacht [German Armed Forces]: Heer [Army, excl. Waffen-SS], Marine [Navy], and Luftwaffe [Air Force], from private to Field Marshal, and of special interest to us, decorations for valor!

Order of the day: unit has fallen-in together with the instructors. Photo taken from the second row and hence on the left, the sleeve of the man in front.

We already knew some of the marching songs that were part of the HJ repertoire, but had to learn others such as the inevitable „Westerwald" that is so damned cold. On the other hand, we already knew „Erika" or „A Penny and a Dime" and other songs that we sang at the top of our voices, much to the satisfaction of our superiors. What we had learned indoors was then practiced on the march, it usually came off nicely – our voices were young and strong.

---

[14] »AAA are only required to salute the officers, Wehrmacht officials and NCOs of the units they are assigned to. Otherwise, the saluting regulation of the HJ apply. AAA salute with the German Salute.
All AAA are to be addressed in the formal ›Sie‹.« [as opposed to the familiar ›Du‹]
The Reich Minister for Aviation and Commander in Chief of the Luftwaffe, Az. 11b Nr. 1/43 (Chef d. Lw./I Wehr 1 III) : AA Assistants : 26.I.1943, Item 9 (reproduced from Nicolaisen, pages 262 et seq.)

Next came weapons and equipment theory including anti-aircraft ballistics; practical training followed later when we were assigned to our batteries. One thing we did not get was political indoctrination which would have been the responsibility of the HJ, but they never came into camp.

The eight boys from the 6th grade (left to right): Josef "Sepperl" Wallner, Walter "Spindi" Spindelberger", Fritz "Spitzi" Senker, Gunter "Basti" Bast, Otto Walter[15], Walter "Schmutzi" Schmutz, Wilhelm "Willi" Reichebner, Franz "Franzl" Wiesner. The author taking the photo is obviously missing.

In the course of a day's training there were occasional „clean and mend sessions" when we attempted to remove the accumulated crud of the parade ground from our uniforms and boots. In addition to the standard issue brushes we also used cleaning agents that could be purchased from the camp store. They let off some kind of vapor because one day, during a heroic cleaning effort, Willi fell off the bench as if intoxicated.

Keeping order in the hut, making up our beds and folding our uniforms precisely on a stool before lights out were other disciplines to be learned. The Napola [National Political Institutions of Education] boys from the adjacent hut were outstanding models of orderliness – they had been subject to barracks drill since they were ten years old. Repeated inspections checked that all orders relating to cleanliness and order were being followed.

---

[15] Otto Walter had been with us up to the 5th grade and then transferred to a school in Horn, he rejoined us in Wegscheid.

The long and the short and the tall of 1. Battery of AAA
Training Unit Linz/Wegscheid on 1.II.44.

1. Battery of the Training Unit, around 100 strong, fall in for the author to take photos on 1.II.44.

What little spare time we had was spent with reading and games. After lunch in the canteen, we were under strict orders to take a nap and there were the inevitable checks to ensure those orders were obeyed. We neither needed nor wanted this enforced rest period[16], but "orders are orders".

---

[16] This mandatory rest period after lunch continued even once we were assigned to a position. By then, it seemed more like a welcome break.

Occasionally we were allowed to watch PG-rated films in camp. Others were X-rated and consequently prohibited, leading to loud protests from our side. That in turn resulted in countermeasures from our instructors: „*...Unit, three times around the block, at the double!*".

There was never any furlough, and nowhere to go anyway.

Visit from the family on 23.I.44 (right to left): Father, Mother, Brother, Cousin, Author.

Our parents were allowed to visit us on Sunday, January 23; and again on February 3, 1944 when all four batteries of AAA marched from Wegscheid to the Volksgartensaal Linz where, after speeches by a senior HJ-Führer and an even higher ranking Luftwaffe officer, we swore our AAA oath:[17]

> »I swear as a Luftwaffe Assistant to do my duty, to be loyal
> and obedient at all times, as behooves a Hitler Youth.«

---

[17]   The Reich Minister for Aviation and Commander in Chief of the Luftwaffe, Az. 11b Nr. 1/43 (Chef d. Lw./I Wehr 1 III) : AA Assistants : 26.I.1943, Appendix 2 (reproduced from Nicolaisen, pages 262 et seq.)

Basic training

Personnel of Barrack 49, Hut 4, with instructor Cpl. Sinn in the middle.

Now, after over four weeks of basic training with AA Replacement Battery 38 in Linz-Wegscheid, we were AAA and assigned to different AA batteries to relieve our comrades of the 1926 year in the Linz-Steyr-St. Valentin area.

On Wednesday, February 5, 1944, we 5th and 6th grade Amstettner were picked up by Lieutenant Höfer, the second officer of the 88 mm Heavy AA Battery 1./805. The night before a major fight had broken out between the various huts. The remaining logs stacked in the corridor of Barrack 49 were used as projectiles with the result that several panes of glass in the skylights were smashed.

Lieutenant Höfer of 1./805 picks us up.

Our battery in St. Valentin-Langenhart

The Heavy AA Battery to which we were assigned and which would be home to us eight students from the 6th grade of the Amstetten high school for more than a year was designated 1./805 (o). In other words, it was the No. 1 Battery of Heavy AA Battalion 805 (static), AA Brigade 7, of AA Regiment 128 in the 24th AA Division in Luftgau [Air District] XVII.

Gun platoon of 1./805(o), later 1./695(o), in St. Valentin-Langenhart. Visible in the background are the church spire and to the left, the water tower of the railroad station. Taken in the summer of 1944.

On April 21, 1944 there was a restructuring and redesignating of the AA units in Luftgau XVII: the 1., 4. and 6./805 became 1.-3./695 , i.e. we remained the No. 1 Battery of Battalion 695 with the locality name St. Valentin-Langenhart and positioned some 2 km west of the village center (church) and 2 km north of the object we were defending, the "Nibelungenwerk".

Our neighboring battery 2./695 (o) was positioned on a hill near Weiler Seggau, some 4 km south of the village center, while the 3./695 (o) was located close to Kronstorf, around 6.5 km to the southwest, on the opposite bank of the Enns River.

At the north end of the St. Valentin marshalling yard there was a 10.5-cm battery of the Railroad AA Regiment 114, commonly known as the "Eis-Flak".

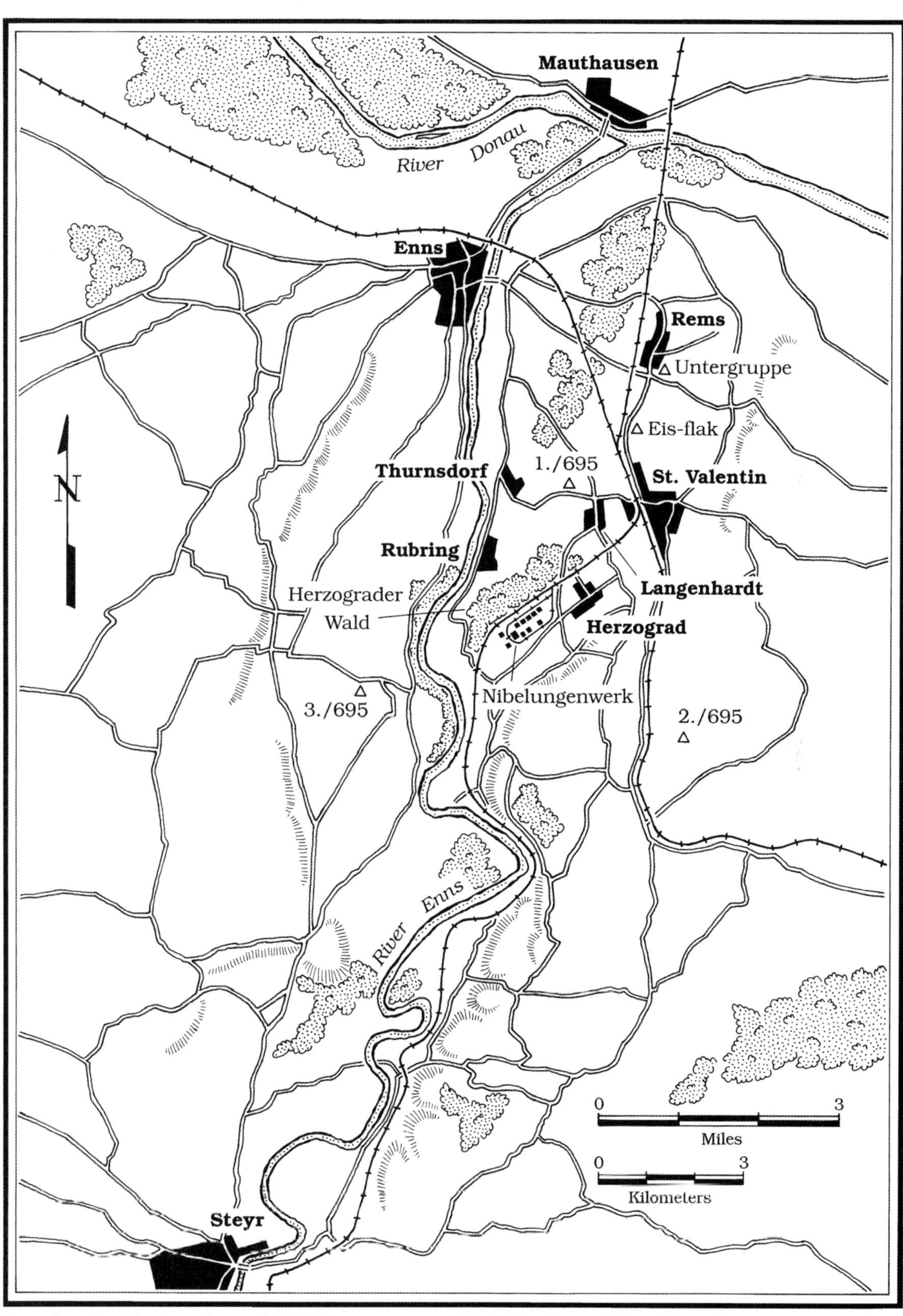

Map showing the locations of AA defenses around St. Valentin and the object they were protecting, the "Nibelungenwerk" of Steyr, Daimler Puch. Based on the Army Ordnance maps 1 : 75000 of 1937 and 1943; archives of the Federal Office for Calibration and Measurement, Vienna. (Britton)

Our battery in St. Valentin-Langenhart

Two postcards of the day show the village of St. Valentin and the surrounding countryside:

St. Valentin in Lower Danube: view towards Enns, which lies to the northwest. The watchtower of Enns is visible in the center, with Castle Ennsegg to the right. The distance between the St. Valentin church and the Enns watchtower is around 4 kilometers; in between is the west railroad track Vienna-Linz-Salzburg. Herzograd and the Nibelungenwerk were built later and would have been outside the photo to the left. (Photo 1938: Ledermann)

View of main street coming from the railroad station towards the church and crossing the Erla river. (Photo 1935: Ledermann)

Our battery in St. Valentin-Langenhart

Railroad AA on the St. Valentin rail site

The barracks of the next higher authority, the „Untergruppe" [AA battalion], were located at Rems village, directly on the Reichsstrasse No. 1, nowadays the Federal Highway, just over 2.5 km distant. That is where we reported, on foot of course, if we had any problems with our health or the guns; a junior medical officer and an armorer were stationed there.

Now to „our" battery: like all heavy AA batteries it was essentially organized into a tracker crew and a gun platoon. The barracks and the range-finding and fire-control equipment of the fire-control team, the so-called "B1" were situated each side of the road leading from Langenhart to Thurnsdorf.

The barrack road of the tracker crew looking towards Langenhart, to the rear left, the three "shacks". Not the cable gulley at right angles to the road.

Our battery in St. Valentin-Langenhart

The tracker crew of our battery with the fire-control system, partially protected against shrapnel. Some of the team can be seen at the left rear. Clearly visible for everyone is the diagonally positioned square alarm panel, Alarm Level II, also known as "foreplay". Note the cables laid under the road that connected us to the position to which we reported.

Spindi on the muddy "road" linking the fire-control and gunnery crews.

The equipment of both teams was connected by a cable trench running from the command system of B1 to the guns and via an earth track from barrack to barrack. That track also provided access to all three individual latrines "shacks".

The gunners, with their six 88 mm guns named Anton, Bertha, Caesar, Dora, Emil and Frieda, lay around 200 m to the north of us in middle of the wheat fields. Close to the guns and adjacent to the living quarters were the cookhouse and mess, including the shop for personal items, plus the clothing stores and armory, as well as a circular wooden shack commonly known as a "Finnenzelt" [Finnish shack] for the Russian "HiWi"[18] volunteer auxiliaries. Military theory lessons and also the film shows were held in the mess, as were the battery parties and other events.

The cable trench, looking towards the gunnery crew.

The weapons and equipment of the battery were not yet top notch: the gun crews had to make the best of captured Russian 85 mm guns that had been bored out to 88 mm caliber and were carriage mounted.

The Russian 88 mm AA gun with elevation zero (85 mm, opened to the German caliber). The weapon is statically mounted on its cross-carriage. Note the wheels that have been removed.

---

[18] "Hilfswillige" or Russians from prisoner of war camps who had volunteered to serve in the German Wehrmacht. They were employed for simpler jobs such as ammunition bearers. They always brought water to our barracks in cans, and our relationship with them was an easy and friendly one.

The tracker crew was also lacking the latest equipment. Whereas they did have a modern radar unit (FuMG) and a 4 m stereoscope for range finding, there was not as yet any automatic fire-control system. Once we had arrived, however, the situation improved week by week as soon as brand-new German AA guns could be fitted and „Kommandogerät 40" fire director units became operational.

The FuMG 62 "Würzburg" radar of our battery and its five victories painted onto the parabolic antenna.

Our battery in St. Valentin-Langenhart

6.II.1944: the new, German 88 mm Flak 36 guns had arrived and were dragged into position by the men. Note the marking „SU" (Soviet Union) on the coat of the fifth man from the left.

Mission accomplished: the German AA gun is in position (left) and the obsolete Russian one limbered ready for towing away (right). The barracks of the gun crew are visible in the background.

Our battery in St. Valentin-Langenhart

During the time we were there, the strength of our battery was around 70 to 80 men, made up of two officers, 15 NCOs, about 35 troopers and 25 AAA or Flak-V apprentices. Later on, female AAA replaced us when, before the end of hostilities, we were called up and had to, or rather were supposed to, serve with the Reich Labor Service (RAD) or the Wehrmacht, but more of that later.

The 1./805 (o) has fallen-in on 1.V.44 for a group photo. There were two officers (Captain Ludwig, far left; Lieutenant Höfer, second from the left), 10 NCOs, 26 soldiers and 18 AAA. The author does not appear as he was acting as photographer.

The officers of our battery:

Left, Captain Ludwig, Battery Commander until summer 1944; center, his successor Lieutenant Göttinger; right Lieutenant Höfer or "Lofty" holding a copy of the „Völkischer Beobachter" – who, because we were not seeing enough action, volunteered for the paratroops in spring 1944. That same summer he was killed in action in Italy.

Our battery in St. Valentin-Langenhart

I also recall some of the Acting Corporals: Ochs, Bähr, Malke, Seidenspinner. These comrades, a fair bit older than we, came from many districts of the Greater German Rcich. With time, we became familiar with all their different dialects, and they got to know ours.

NCO Fip, Acting Cpls. Seidenspinner and Wahl

Thc Russian "HiWis" (volunteer auxiliaries)

In late summer 1944, assembly of a huge radar installation began. It was located at the side of the road, about 100 m to the west of B1. Known as a "Giant Würzburg", it could locate enemy aircraft formations at up to 200 km range. It

Our battery in St. Valentin-Langenhart

was not part of our equipment but belonged to the Luftnachrichtenorganisation [Air Signals Organization] of the Luftwaffe and was used in the AA alert system known as "Venus".

Building the FuMG 65 "Giant Würzburg" radar: base and pivot are already installed, elements of the antenna dish are still on the ground awaiting assembly, and the command hut has not yet been positioned.

The completed assembly; building materials have not yet been removed from the emplacement.

Our battery in St. Valentin-Langenhart

Our battery in St. Valentin-Langenhart

My diary mentions a number of men, some of who remain in my memory: the Company Sergeant Major Christiansen, in civilian life a forwarding agent from Hamburg; Sergeants Siemers, Josten, Bohne, Beitz, Panhorst; Corporals Pöppler, with who we had most contact, Wengel (Instructor in Wegscheid), Umland (drummer in the band "cheery and lighthearted"), Fip, Bleicher, Metzger, Sachtler, Tubert ("Radar"), Schellschmied, Scherweit, Bauschatz and Eggert (Quartermaster, Store Chief and Mess Manager). We did not have much to do with him, but he was more or less agreeable. Because of the diary entries they reappear frequently.

The NCOs of the gun battery, here still with the Russian AA gun.

NCOs Pöppler and Tubert

NCO Umland

The area about 100 m to the east of the first accommodation hut of the tracker crew was crossed by the Thurnsdorferstrasse. At the time, it was officially the „Rüstungsstrasse" [Armaments Road], but was known to us as the previously mentioned "Panzerstrasse". It ran from the Nibelungenwerk to the direction of Ennsdorf. Brand new tanks coming from the plant were run in on this road. Constantly torn up by the tank tracks, it was invariably in terrible condition. We had to cross it if we were headed to or returning from the village or the railway station. Tramping through the knee-deep mud was unavoidable and in summer, when there was wind from the east, the tanks threw up dense clouds of dust that settled all over the battery grounds. Nowadays, the road is asphalted and free of dust, carrying an increasing weight of traffic. Interestingly, the locals still call it the "Panzerstrasse".

Panzers, the bane of the AA emplacement – clouds of dust on the Panzerstrasse – PzKpfw IV Ausf G built by the Nibelungenwerk.

Nibelungenwerk

Our battalion was deployed to protect the tank production plant "Nibelungen-werk", operated by Steyr-Daimler-Puch AG, against attacks from the air. It was located in the Herzograd Forest, some 3 km southwest of the village center, fairly close to our position and visible to enemy air reconnaissance.

The plant was a project of the Third Reich. Immediately after the 1938 annexation of Austria into the German Reich, preparations to build the "Ni-Werk" began. The Bauernwald Forest and a major part of the Herzograd Forest on the estate of Castle Ennsegg, then owned by the Fürstenberg family, was purchased.

First, a Reich-owned residential estate was built for the administrative employees and engineers of the plant. Next followed the "Tausendmannlager" [Thousand

Man Encampment] that lay to the east of Altlangenhart: today's housing settlement for the workers, with streets named after heroes of the Nibelung Epic, including a House of Allegiance, a plant surgery and a company training center. Worth mentioning is that the plant apprentices, the same age as us, i.e. all born in 1928, also lived in that settlement. In the language of the day, they contributed to the "Endsieg" [Ultimate Victory] by manning the workbenches, whereas we "manned the guns".

The apprentices of the Nibelungenwerk in 1944. (FK)

Whereas we youthful AAA were indifferent to the HJ and consequently left in peace by them, the apprentices were completely subjected to their regime, which included propaganda evenings, exercising, sports competitions and the like. Of course, they also had to take part in party events. We AAA were spared all that as we had other things to accomplish. No doubt, the manual skills those boys of our age developed were first-rate. By contrast, our AA training would be completely useless in our later careers.

Some of the apprentices had been issued uniforms – but ours were more dashing. (FK)

1942/43, the Ni-Werk welcomed prominent visitors: Adolf Hitler, Hermann Göring, Albert Speer, the two Gauleiters Eigruber (Upper Danube) and Dr. Jury (Lower Danube). Professor Ferdinand Porsche was a frequent visitor; he was the designer of the "Porsche Tiger" and "Ferdinand" tanks that were produced here in small numbers. Of the around 8 000 PzKpfw IV tanks that were built, more than one half were assembled by the Ni-Werk.

It was obvious that tanks were being built at this plant. However, the majority of the population, and certainly not we AAA, knew just how many of those vehicles, the object we were assigned to defend, was actually producing. The workers were not allowed to talk about the subject. Only after the war did we learn that, in addition to St. Valentin, there were other major tank producers, e.g. in Magdeburg and Henschel in Kassel.

Daily, completed tanks roared past our position during their test runs on the nearby "Panzerstrasse", but that was nothing unusual for us – we were at war and obviously, tanks were needed at the front.

Apart from the apprentices, men and women from the surrounding villages were "mobilized" and sworn to strict secrecy. Ever increasing numbers of foreign workers, forced laborers and prisoners of war, housed in separate camps, were also drafted in.

Towards the end of the war, around 10 000 workers from 14 nations were laboring at the plant – an incredible number. Mostly they were prisoners of war from France, Holland, Belgium and Norway. The mobilized workforce also included Italians, Czechs, Poles and other nationalities such as Spaniards who were helping, or rather forced to help, Germany win the war.

Training in the battery

The majority of us from Amstetten were assigned to the tracker crew (B1). Because they were robustly built, Gunter Bast and Franzl Wieser joined the gun squad, where they were deployed as gun layers. Later, Franzl became a loader-gunner, inevitably earning him the nickname of "K3-Franzl".

As mentioned earlier, when we arrived in Langenhart, the 1./805 had not yet been issued with state-of-the-art weapons and systems; above all, no AA director. Instead, all ballistic data for the guns had to be obtained from the Malsi AA converter (named after Major Malsi). The first piece of equipment that we tracker crewmen encountered was the Malsi – „...a simple, yet complicated device..." It consisted essentially of a circular, rotating table around which several men stood. Three of them, each wearing headphones, received the input data from the detection devices; the radar (electronic plotting) or the 4 meter stereoscope (optical plotting), i.e. azimuth, elevation and range. They entered these data into the converter, e.g. the azimuth man who rotated the table with a crank. Once given the range of the target, an instrument attached to the table drew the course of the aircraft being plotted on the table.

Using another device, the fourth man on the table could calculate the estimated ongoing course of the target. We had to lead aim the guns because there was a time lag before the projectile exploded at an altitude of around 6 000 m during which the enemy aircraft continued on course.

Basic equipment of the tracking crew: left, 4-m stereoscope (optical range finder), foreground, AA director, and at the far right, the "Malsi" converter table.

Based on the course measurement and with the help of other useful devices, the converter calculated the settings for the guns: azimuth, angle of elevation and the timing for when the fuze should cause the projectile to detonate.

These settings were read off from the corresponding instruments by another three team members and dictated through throat microphones to the gunners. It was important to speak at a steady pace, although this was not so easy because the speed at which the data were calculated changed constantly between faster and slower. For example, the man reading off the azimuth would dictate in a monotonous voice:

„...thirty-two... thirty-three... [degrees]" etc.,

and the man reading off elevation:

„...fifty-siiix...sixty-five-four...eight...two ten...sixty-siiix...four—eight" etc., and then came the fuze settings:

„...one hundred fifty...one hundred eighty four ...one hundred sixty-four..." and so on and so forth. Taking the readings and dictating them steadily was constantly practiced and battery exercises conducted until the sequence of speaking and listening, from locating the target to readiness of the guns, and right up to the command "Open fire!" when combating bomber formations or single aircraft was seamless. Very unpleasant was the sensation when the azimuth remained constant but the elevation figure increased rapidly upwards and the fuze setting became ever shorter – that meant a direct enemy approach and a potential attack on our position!

In addition to the six men for the input and output data, there were another two determining course and speed, plus the "technical fire-control officer", who relayed the commands „Fire salvo ... group" to the gun captain. And finally, the man operating the fire bell; in total a team of ten, including the two for the elevation and fuze data, who were sitting under the table. Hence, the bunker was pretty crowded and the continuous relaying of data and the loud commands of the "technical officer" generated quite a commotion.

The tracking equipment was a short distance away from the Malsi bunker in open positions but surrounded by a low wall of earth in the same way the living quarters. It included the „4 m stereoscope" for optical plotting and the FuMG – nowadays it would be classed as radar – for electronic target location. The latter was used at night or when visibility was poor and did not allow optical range finding.

AAA of 2./695 (o) manning their 4 m stereoscope. (HR)

Training with 1./695 (o) on the 4 m stereoscope in an open wooden emplacement reinforced by earthworks...

...Training on the radar system and...

...on the battery's AA fire director.

Whereas the FuMG radar was operated exclusively by soldiers, AAA were trained to use the range finder, i.e. primarily for measuring elevation and azimuth. They needed good eyesight and, extremely useful for estimating range, spatial vision. To acquire a target, it first had to be identified visually and then, following the initial command, e.g. „Aircraft direction six!" the device with its outstandingly powerful binoculars, directed at it. Next, following the report „Target acquired!" the values for azimuth, elevation and distance could be read off the system and relayed to the Malsi converter.

In the summer of 1944 our battery, now designated 1./695(o), received the most modern fire-control system of its day, the model 40 AA fire director. Even by to-day's standards, this device was a technological marvel. In modern parlance, the huge calculator under the range finder was a mechanical analog computer operating at twice the speed of many of today's advanced devices. The „Em 4 mR 40 blc"[19] was a masterpiece of shutters, mirrors, prisms and lenses. If it was not generating results with its own measuring devices, readings from the radar or the Malsi converters were transmitted to this fire director from where the ballistic data, derived from aircraft speed, course and height, were relayed to the AA guns.

---

[19] Abbreviation for: range finder with 4 m stereoscope length, year of build 1940; blc was the manufacturer's code, in this case Zeiss, Jena.

The newly arrived fire director Kommandogerät 40.

We Malsi or tracker crew were now instructed on this piece of equipment, its design, its functions and operating system, both theoretical and practical. It was really a huge improvement compared to the tedious Malsi converter.

Those of us who had already manned the 4 m stereoscope were stationed on one side of the system as azimuth and altitude trackers and, if considered to have the aptitude, also to train on the rangefinder using tables containing rows of measurements. On the other side of the installation, two men operated the switches and cranks: the B4 turned the hand wheel on the right to set the probable course of the target aircraft. To achieve this, he had to align a line drawn by a stylus on a sight glass with a curve on the internal and constantly rotating cylinder. It called for considerable practice to become proficient and fast.[20] On the left-hand side, the B5 operated the main switch and those for changing elevation and „range finding normal" or „last altitude fixed" or similar and coincided with the tachometer needle for the ground speed. Relaying setting data to the guns was now electrical using the follow-the-needle system and no longer by telephone.

Apart from the two systems described previously that we had to learn, B1 had another fire command auxiliary device, but it was rarely used or exercised. Any-

---

[20]   This was relatively straightforward if the target (e.g. the leading aircraft) was flying on a straight course, but difficult when it was weaving. Once on target, heavy bombers generally flew doggedly straight ahead at constant speed before releasing their loads.

way, it and the Malsi were soon to be replaced by the model 40 fire director. It was cube shaped with an edge length of around 80 cm to which different levers and cranks were attached. It is fair to say that it was universally unpopular.

Gun crew with 2./695 posing in front of their AA gun. (HR)

Training on all the operational functions of the heavy 88 mm AA gun was done with the gun crew:

- The elevation gun layer, or K1, elevation tracker had to learn the following text by rote and use it in practice: „K1 inserts the plug of the earphones into the telephone terminal box for elevation and continuously inputs the relayed data by turning the hand wheel." This was still valid when the tracking data were being received from the crew members on the Malsi.

- When relaying data from the fire-control unit, the azimuth tracker, or K2, learned the following instructions by heart: „With the aid of the azimuth tracking device, K2 continuously sets the data from the fire-control unit by aligning the tracking needle with the values shown on the gage glass."

- For K3, the loader, the drill was: „When the fire bell rings, K3 grasps the base of a round readied in the fuze setting machine with his right hand. With his left hand on the center of gravity of the round, he chambers the round in the barrel using his clenched fist. With a simultaneous left twist of the torso, he fires with the right hand."

Only the stronger boys among the AAA were selected as K3, e.g. our "K3 Franzl" – AA shells weighed around 14 kg and had to be lifted almost vertically upwards with barely a break during rapid fire.

This photo shows Max trying his hand as a gun loader.

- K6 sat at the fuze setting machine and had to learn this ritual: „K6 inserts the plug of the earphones in the telephone terminal box for fuzes and continuously sets the relayed data by turning the hand wheel with his left hand. With his right hand he operates the crank of the flywheel so that the needle settles in the center position."

- K4 and K5 made up the ammunition column, carrying rounds from the munitions bunker to the K7 whose task was defined as: „With a light twist, the K7 sets the shell vertically into the fuze setter cup and observes the indicator flap." Finally, there was the K8 as an ammunition bearer who did not have to repeat any instructions.

Responsible for the gun itself and the coordination of the gunners was the gun captain. As a rule, he was an NCO who stood to one side of the gun and was connected to the „technical fire-control officer" through earphones. He repeated the latter's orders, e.g. „Group fire - salvo!", then the firing bell on the gun rang for three seconds during which time the K3 removed the shell from the fuze set-

ter cup, chambered it and then fired when the bell stopped ringing. „Salvo"
meant the simultaneous firing of all six guns, which was not always successful
and led to sarcastic comments from the tracker crew like: „...your firing sounded
like a goat crapping on a drum...!"

The author, play acting the elevation tracker on a German 88 mm anti-aircraft gun model 36 the
day it was delivered. The gun has only been temporarily installed; the protective embankment is
also still missing.

Coordination between individual pieces of equipment and the guns was drilled in
battery exercises on an almost daily basis, whereby AAA were expected to master
various assignments. Regular exercises were also conducted with neighboring
batteries to test readiness under true combat conditions. At the beginning of exercises, but also during action stations in real attacks, „trial data" were relayed
to test communications between transmitters and receivers. At those times, ex-
changes of sassiness or foul-mouthed remarks were not uncommon: „Can you
hear me, you dork?"

Living quarters

Arriving from Wegscheid in the afternoon of February 5, 1944 we sixth-graders
moved into one of the barracks of 1./805 (o), located in the district of St. Valentin-Langenhart on both sides of the road leading to Thurnsdorf.

Our barracks, note the rapidly thrown up earth embankment to protect the building.

The external appearance of the barracks was totally in keeping with the meagerness of the times: unpainted walls made of weathered timber showing rivulets of rust from old nails, a simple wooden roof covered in cardboard with no guttering.

They were constructed from the typical wooden paneling of the day, sunk about 1 meter into the ground and surrounded by a crude earth wall that, at this time of year was covered in snow.

Walking down external wooden steps and through the front door, we entered a narrow, level entrance hall. From there, an internal door led to a large space that was divided in the middle by lockers to form a front living area and a rear dormitory. A small storage closet to the side of the entrance provided space for various utensils such as washbowls, water or coffee cans, mousetraps and the like. In summer, the stove was also stowed there. There was no vacuum cleaner or other cleaning conveniences, just brooms, pails and dusters.

During the day, four windows let in light to the forward living area and at night, several spherical lamps made of white, translucent glass provided illumination. The walls and the inner roof were painted white and a few pictures added a touch of color to an otherwise bare environment without shutters or drapes. In the sleeping area there was shelving for storing books, school implements and other bits and pieces.

The barrack road facing Thurnsdorf in winter and in summer.

The floor was made of planed, untreated softwood boards that were difficult to keep clean. It had to be scrubbed once a week during the general clean-up. Because of the numerous gaps between the boards it was not necessary to dry the floor after scrubbing; water consumption was correspondingly high.

Living quarters

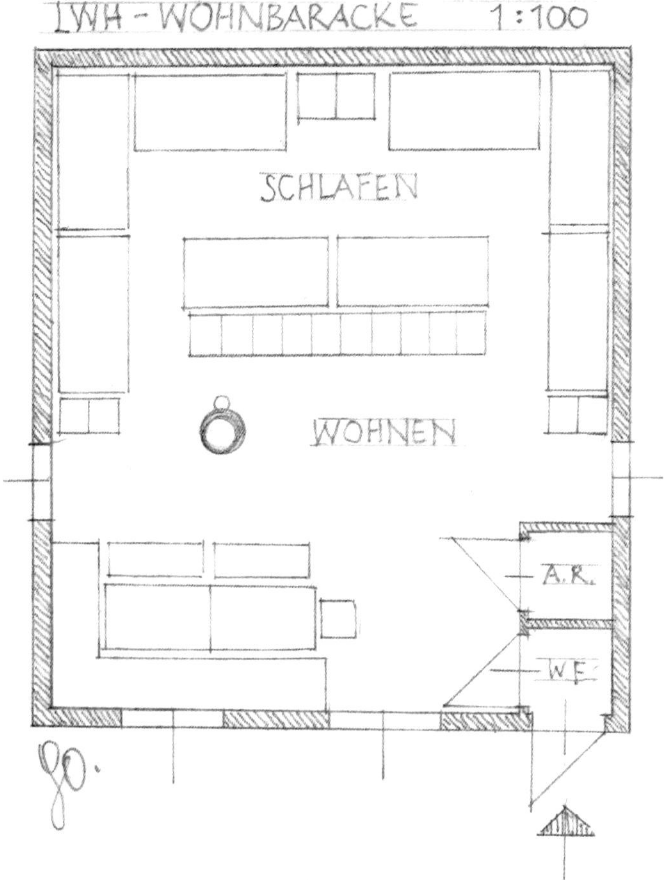

Layout of the barracks redrawn from an original sketch in the author's notebook.

At the rear there were wooden two-level bunks with paillasses, up front tables, benches and stools for 12 to 14 boys, or more in emergencies. A simple sheet-metal stove with a stovepipe straight through the roof provided warmth, provided it was stoked permanently and the stovepipe was cleaned out regularly, invariably causing a real mess. Insulation of the barrack walls, the roof panels and the single-glaze windows was totally inadequate; it was rarely warm inside during the cold months, but all the more so in summer.

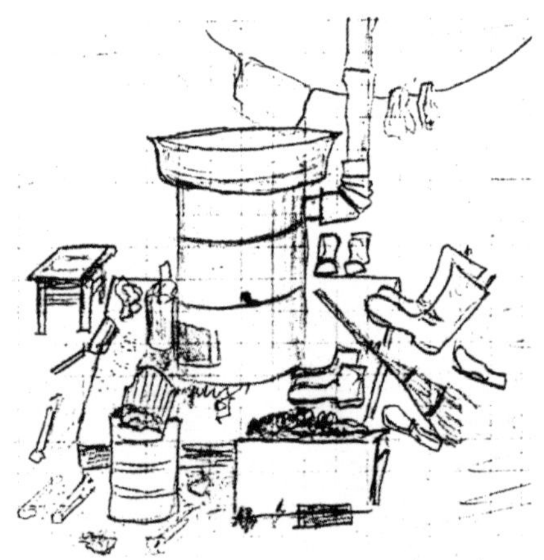

From the author's sketchbook: "All hopes and fears of the AAA depend on the stove."

The stuffing in the mattresses or rather jute sacks was not the common straw, but fine wood shavings. These were not unpopular because over time they molded themselves nicely to the body and did not have to be loosened or shaken up. Bed linen was changed at regular intervals; the white sheet and the blue checkered covers for the horsehair blankets and pillows. Underwear we took home to our mothers.

Barrack entrance and author. Note the defective cardboard roofing and crude construction.

Everything else was bare bones, spartan, functional – no feminine touch whatsoever! No flowers, no cushions, no covers – nothing! But at least, there was no lingerie hanging up all over the place.

Each one of us had a locker compartment around 50 cm wide to hang his uniform, washing gear and cleaning kit and snacks. Our gas masks, helmets and other bulky items also took up a lot of space and it needed a fair amount of discipline and routine to keep everything in order. It was important to pass the weekly and Sunday locker inspections and to avoid "attracting the attention" of our superiors.

The latrines for the entire battery consisted of three wooden shacks on the track between the tracker and gun crews. Erected over trenches dug in the ground, they obviously had no facilities for flushing. To take a leak we simply used the ground around the barracks. Washing and bathing facilities were limited to a number of washbowls and water pitchers. The bowls were placed on stools and water was fetched by whoever was on duty in the quarters. Mostly, however, it was the Russian auxiliaries who brought us the water. Disposal was straight through the window to the outside. If the situation in our airspace permitted, we were marched off in a column to shower in the workers' washrooms in nearby Langenhart. On average we had this opportunity once every two weeks and apart from this we were granted short or longer home leave where we could catch up on our somewhat perfunctory cleanliness. Despite the limited hygienic conditions there was never any outbreak of lice or the like, the only vermin were mice from the fields.

As we moved into these new quarters, we were welcomed by six comrades from a senior high school in Graz. For the first few days they briefed us on operations in the battery that were still unfamiliar ground for us. Shortly afterwards, however, they were relocated and our numbers were then made up by former schoolmates, all born in 1927, who had already been inducted in the fall of the previous year and assigned to other batteries in the Linz area. Next, the three AAA from Waidhofen an der Ybbs and later those from Freistadt joined our group in Langenhart. We stayed in this barrack standing to the left of the road and at the very front of the row accommodating the tracker crews throughout the summer and into the late fall of 1944. Then, in the course of reassignments and regroupings, and much to our irritation, we were moved to another barrack where, once again, I landed on the top level of a three-tier bunk. This had the benefit of not requiring such a tight regime of order as it was difficult to inspect, but the air was particularly bad and the alarm bell was located very close to my ear. It was to repeatedly frighten me out of my wits in the numerous night-time alarms to come.

This unpleasant situation did not last for long. Mid-January 1945, we were relocated again, this time to a concrete bunker set deep in the ground. It was a damp hole without windows, warmer than the barracks, but consequently unhealthier. The entry in my diary for 16.I.45 reads: „*...Then we moved into the bunker... had to go to B1 in order to write. Mud, damp and lousy pailliasses are doing everything except raise our spirits...*"

A number of Freistädter with K3 Franzl. Bottom left the entrance to the accommodation bunker.

On January 28, 1945, my diary reports that Fürst, a youth from Freistadt and known to us as the "Tomcat", has suffered an attack of rheumatism and, when the pain became unbearable, has to be sent to the sick bay for treatment:[21]
„*The Tomcat is having a tough time again: he is suffering badly from rheumatism. He is lying in bed groaning and wheezing, twisting, turning and cursing; he doesn't give a damn about anything else, and groans: there is a bear lying on my left hip!*"

There was worse to come as I noted on February 1, 1945: „*It had just started to thaw. In the middle of the night, Pepi Pichler, who was sleeping above me, woke me up and said that I should shine my torch on him; he and his bed were soaking wet. I shone the torch upwards and soon everyone is wide awake when I sound the alarm: ,Water!!*'" Not only was the thawing slush dripping and trickling through the concrete ceiling slab, but the thermal insulation panels made of wood shavings were coming loose from the ceiling and splashing into the water that was already ankle-deep on the floor. I was lucky not to have to help clean up this mess as that same day I was sent home on leave for two wonderful and comfortable weeks.

---

[21]   NB: on 23.1.45, I had the bright idea of writing my diary in poetry form, but gave up ten days later because it was too much of an effort and the results were unsatisfactory at best.

Rations

We had a really good cook. Apparently in civilian life he was a wine grower from Lower Austria and whatever he prepared from the basic rations for AA Assistants (see leaflet and meals schedule on the following pages) was well cooked and edible. Only the blood sausage on Fridays would turn our stomachs. It not only looked ghastly, but was virtually impossible to get down our necks. It could well have also been the fault of the butcher. Anyway, I instructed the food detail to immediately dump the disgusting brown something in the garbage pit on their way back from the cookhouse. The accompanying potatoes and sauerkraut had to be eaten „without" or complemented with sausage from canned rations.

Very tasty and available in sufficient quantities was the square bread ration. I recall the somewhat strange taste of the margarine and synthetic honey that we slathered on the bread. The jelly spread was actually very good.

We ate in our quarters from our mess kits and lids. The latter was also used to test our own cooking skills on the stove; for example, bread cut into small cubes and slowly fried in margarine, then enjoyed later with meat paste spread on it. The only beverage available was cold, clean water from the pitcher, nothing else.

Thanks to these supplementary rations for us adolescents – bread, milk, cereals and the like – plus the „provisions" from home, we always had enough to eat; there were even snacks from the Ostmark.[22]

Whereas the troops ate cold rations, we were given a sweetened milk soup in the evenings. We really appreciated this special treat from our cook. This once led to a complaint lodged with the battery commander (diary, Wednesday, 22.XI.): *„…We did not receive our milk soup. Crap. Spitzi complained to the Lieutenant, result: Duty NCO got chewed out. 2.) He came in and said we should not be upset, we would get our soup tomorrow. Talked to us like a father. Not like him at all. Normally he makes us do everything at the double…"* The following Friday, 24.XI.: *„… Again a ghastly blood sausage for lunch. Eckert[23] is being pig-headed since he got chewed out by the Lieutenant…"*

---

[22]   »The AA Assistants receive their rations free of charge in accordance with the troop provisioning regulations of the units they are serving with. They are not to receive alcohol and tobacco rations, instead, vitamin drops or candy are to be issued. AAA may only enter canteens and unit stores to make purchases. Selling them alcohol or tobacco is not permitted. Drinking alcohol in public houses or smoking in public and in their quarters is prohibited for AAA.« The Reich Minister for Aviation and Commander in Chief of the Luftwaffe, Az. 11b Nr. 1/43 (Chef d. Lw./I Wehr 1 III) : AA Assistants : 26.I.1943, Item 20 (reproduced from Nicolaisen, pages 262 et seq.)

[23]   The quartermaster, also responsible for the kitchens

Merkblatt
über die Verpflegung
der Luftwaffenhelfer

nach dem Stande vom 30. April 1944.

Dieses Merkblatt ist von den Lw.-Helfern mit den Ausweispapieren stets bei sich zu tragen.

Durch Änderung der Verpflegungsportionssätze sich ergebende Berichtigungen sind von den Lw.-Helfern eigenhändig vorzunehmen.

Bei Verlust des Merkblattes ist ein Ersatz durch Abschrift von den Lw.-Helfern selbst anzufertigen.

Lw.-Helfer erhalten die gleiche Verpflegung wie die Soldaten der Flakbatterien, bei denen sie eingesetzt sind. (Siehe Ziffer I.)

Darüber hinaus werden ihnen noch besondere Verpflegungszulagen gewährt. (Siehe Ziffer II.)

I.

Die **Soldatenkost** besteht aus der

Morgenkost:

Kaffee mit Brot und Brotaufstrich.

Mittagskost:

Von dem Wochensatz für Frischfleisch mit Knochen in der Höhe von 660 g, zusätzlich 80 g Bratlingspulver, das sind insgesamt 740 g, entfallen auf die Mittagskost 420 g.

Brot:

Tagessatz: 680 g Roggenbrot oder
625 g   „   und 50 g Weißbrot.

Brotaufstrich:

Im Monat 24 mal Fett je 39 g und 6–7 mal Marmelade je 200 g.

Puddings:

Im Monat 2 mal. Zur Herstellung werden verwendet:
20 g Puddingpulver oder
50 g Grieß,
20 g Zucker und zusätzlich
0,25 l entrahmte Frischmilch.

V-Drops:

Im Monat 4–5 mal je 20–35 g, je nach der Packung.

Obst:

Nach Anfall wie bei den Jugendlichen der Zivilbevölkerung.

II.

Zu dieser **Soldatenkost**

erhalten die **Lw.-Helfer** nachstehende **Zulagen:**

Täglich: 100 g Roggenbrot oder
70 g Roggenbrotmehl zur Zubereitung einer Frühstückssuppe,
1 l entrahmte Frischmilch, die in erster Linie zur Herstellung warmer Abendsuppen zu verwenden ist.

Wöchentlich: 60 g Frischwurst,
150 g Marmelade oder Kunsthonig.
Zur Herstellung warmer, gesüßter Abendsuppen, besonders an Tagen, an denen die Truppe keine warme Abendkost erhält:
100 g Mühlenerzeugnisse und 50 g Zucker oder
150 g Teigwaren und 50 g Zucker.

Für die Aufteilung der Lebensmittel auf die Mittagskost wird folgende Regelung als Anhalt gegeben:

An 6 Tagen je 70 g Frischfleisch mit Knochen einschließlich Bratlingspulver. Gemüse zu nachstehenden Tagessätzen:

Kartoffeln	Rohgewicht	1200 g	oder
Frischgemüse (Mohrrüben, Kohlrüben, Weiß-, Rot-, Grün- und Blumenkohl, grüne Bohnen, Spinat usw.)	„	1200 g	„
eingelegtes Gemüse	„	400 g	„
Sauerkraut	„	450 g	„
Mühlenerzeugnisse (Graupen, Grütze, Grieß)	„	100 g	„
Teigwaren	„	150 g	„

Diese Gemüsesorten werden in den Truppenküchen erfahrungsgemäß wie folgt ausgegeben:

600 g Kartoffeln und 600 g Frischgemüse oder
800 g „ und 400 g „ „
800 g „ und 150 g Sauerkraut „
400 g „ und 65 g Hafergrütze „

An einem Tag eine fleischlose Mittagskost aus einem Gemüsegericht.

Abendkost
(je Woche):

An 2 Tagen 80 g Frischwurst.
„ 4 „   warme Abendkost mit je 45 g Frischfleisch mit Knochen einschließlich Bratlingspulver und den halben Gemüsesätzen der Mittagskost, z. B. 75 g Teigwaren oder 300 g Kartoffeln und 300 g Frischgemüse.
„ 1 Tag   Käse (125 g Weichkäse oder 150 g Sauermilchkäse oder 250 g Quark) oder Fischkonserven, je nach Doseninhalt 120 g bis 180 g, bei Ölsardinen 90 g bis 125 g.

Die zubereitete Fleischportion ohne Knochen beträgt je nach Sorte und Güte des Frischfleisches 40–50 % der angeführten Mengen.

Monatlich: 250 g Keks oder ähnliche Backwaren und 100 g Zuckerwaren, wenn der Lw.-Helfer mindestens einmal im Monat bei einem nächtlichen Luftangriff eingesetzt war.

III.

Urlauberkarten.

1. **Übernachtungsurlaub** (z. B. über Sonntag). Lw.-Helfer, die bis zum Abend des nächsten Tages beurlaubt sind, erhalten von ihrer Einheit eine Urlauberkarte für 2 Tage, wenn sie nach Einnahme der Mittagskost den Urlaub antreten. Wird an diesem Tage kalte Abendverpflegung mitgegeben, dann erhalten sie nur eine Urlauberkarte für einen Tag.

2. **Kurzurlaub** bis zu 4 Tagen einschließlich Hin- und Rückreise: Ausgabe von Urlauberkarten durch die Batterie.

3. **Längere Beurlaubung:** Es werden von der Batterie nur Urlauberkarten bis zu 2 Tagen ausgegeben. Für die restliche Zeit des Urlaubes sind von den Lw.-Helfern selbst Urlauberkarten bei den Kartenstellen des Urlaubsortes zu empfangen.

4. **Anspruch auf zusätzliche Lebensmittelmarken** in der Höhe des Ausgleiches der für Jugendliche vorgesehenen Lebensmittelmengen:
   Dieser besteht bereits bei einem Urlaub von 2 vollen Tagen, nicht jedoch bei Übernachtungsurlaub.
   Bei Kurzurlaub oder längerer Beurlaubung erhalten die Lw.-Helfer diese Lebensmittelmarken ebenfalls bei ihren zuständigen zivilen Kartenstellen.

Herausgegeben durch Luftgaukommando XVII, Verw. A 6
(Mai 1944) — Wehrkreisdruckerei XVII, Wien ·3278)

With kind permission of Leopold Banny (first printed in Banny, p. 82).

Speisenzettel

Küchenverwaltung **Dienststelle L 21 954 Lg.Pa.Wien**

für die Zeit vom **1.Jänner** bis **5.Jänner** 194**4**

Tag	Morgenkost	Stück oder g	Mittagskost	Einheitssatz roh g	gekocht g	Abendkost	Stück oder g
1.44.	Kaffee	9	Rindsbraten Nudelsuppe Tomatensose Kartoffeln Aprikosenkompott	60 300 600		Frischwurst Butter Schwarzen Tee	85 40 2
1.44.	Bohnenkaffee (Preßkaffe) 125		Sauerbraten Grießsuppe Fischmehlsose Kartoffeln Pudding	60 300 600		Frischwurst Margarine D.Tee	85 40 4
1.44.	Kaffee	4	Pelkartoffelsose Haferflockensuppe Kürbisgemüse Kartoffeln	60 300 600		Apfel-Eintopf ~/Büchsenfleisch Marmelade Kaffee Lg.Helfer Milchsuppe Brot	150 40 200 4 300
1.44.	Kaffee	9	Frikadellen Graupensuppe Sauerkraut Kartoffeln	60 225 600		Sauermilchkäse Butter Suppe D.Tee	150 40 30 4
1.44.	Kaffee	9	Pichelsteiner- Eintopf (fleischlos) Kartoffeln Wurzelgemüse	 600 600		Gallicosen Kartoffeln Margarine Kaffee	45 600 40 4

Menu of a light AA battery; note the extra evening provisions for the AAA on the third day's evening. (Reproduced from Banny, page 81)

Coming back to our cook: his particular specialty was dessert on Sundays: „semolina pudding with apricot sauce" – a delicacy! And, in summer, when the entire crew criss-crossed the harvested fields in the vicinity and brought in sacks full of ears of wheat that the cook traded with the local miller for flour, there were dumplings in custard to eat.

After days or nights of action, there were also treats: cigarettes and alcohol for the troops and, for us, lemon drop candy and soda water.

The closer we came to the end of the war, the more often soup was served; at the very end that was virtually all we got, but always with plenty of bread. So much so, that if we pressed on our bloated bellies, all the liquid and the chunks of bread would be spewed up.

Even if we were not immediately suffering physically and always knew how to take care of ourselves, there was one lesson we did learn and have never forgotten to this very day: „always eat everything on your plate!"

Things get serious

Allied reconnaissance 1943

Up to the time of our arrival at the battery, there had only been sporadic attacks by the Allied air forces in the areas of Upper and Lower Danube. In the preparatory phase of the air offensives that were about to be launched, however, they undertook selective reconnaissance operations, particularly in the area defended by 7. Flakbrigade [7th Anti-Aircraft Brigade].

Reconnaissance aircraft P-51 Mustang C of the 1st Tactical Air Force located in Italy preparing for take-off. (HF)

It is clear from the archives of the Western Allies that, in addition to interrogating prisoners of war, reconnaissance was primarily conducted from the air. Evaluation of this aerial photography was summarized in „Interpretation Reports" that explained and detailed anything that seemed important. Subsequently, the photographs served to brief the navigators and bomb aimers of the operational bomber formations.

Interpretation of aerial photographs on an Italian airfield (HF)

In addition to the precise geographic position of the target, the Interpretation Report of October 18, 1943[24] contained the following details:

- Description of the location of the Nibelungenwerk, its extent and infra-structure in terms of traffic,

- Buildings and facilities of the plant and their structural status (finished or under construction) and, if discernible, their purpose,

- Details of plant operations: these are comparatively meager as these armaments activities took place inside the facilities and were not visible from the air. Hence, the report only mentions „a few vehicles on the site-internal roads", whose dimensions led to the conclusion of possible tank production,

- Details of AA defenses: in addition to eight light AA guns, some mounted on workshop roofs, plus four searchlights, a „heavy AA battery consisting of six guns, situated 2500 meters north of the plant buildings, is listed" – that was us, the 1./805!

---

[24] Interpretation Report No. D. 354 A : St. Valentin : 18.10.1943

Allied reconnaissance 1943

An F-5 Lightning "Rose Marie" of the 90th Photographic Reconnaissance Wing in Italy. (HF)

A British de Havilland Mosquito with American markings, used as fast bombers, fighter-bombers, pathfinders and reconnaissance aircraft. (HF)

In addition to aerial reconnaissance, the British and American intelligence services were collecting data on the Nibelungenwerk from every possible source available to them. For example, the transcript of a statement made by an Austrian P/W[25] who had worked in the plant's quality control department from June 1941 to March 1943. He was able to provide details of:

- The general organization of the armaments facilities in the Linz-Steyr-St. Valentin area and its links to the Hermann Göring Works in Linz,

- The physical condition of the building and facilities,

- Production of the Mark IV and Tiger tanks, of which four and two respectively were said to be rolling off the assembly line each week,

- The origins of subcontracted and semi-finished materials, for example Krupp-Essen, as well as,

- The manpower strength of 6 000 to 7 000 employees. He gave the names of management executives. It is interesting to note that the number of locals was as low as 20–25 % of the entire workforce; the rest being made up primarily of foreigners (Poles, Dutchmen, Italians, Russians and also Spaniards) operating as armaments workers in two 10-hour shifts.

In terms of defensive measures, he mentions an armed plant security force in black uniforms and the blue identity cards of the workers; also the air raid shelters in the nearby forests that, during his time with the company, were not yet needed or ever used.

Of course we had no idea of the level of knowledge of our opponents that vastly exceeded our own, and almost certainly that of our superiors too.

Certainly, we saw Mosquito or Lightning reconnaissance aircraft circling over our heads on an almost daily basis that later would observe and photographically record the results of the Allied attacks. As to the target itself, they already knew more than enough.

15th US Air Force (15th USAAF)

The victory of the Western Allies in the African theater of war[26] enabled the Americans, operating from airfields established in Libya and Tunisia, to finally

---

[25] For the Allies, Austria was still Austria and not the Nazi "Ostmark", P/W stood for Prisoner of War: see Appendix, pages 259 et seq.
[26] Capitulation of the German/Italian Army Group Africa in Tunesia on May 13, 1943

begin attacking German Reich territory from the south. The 9th USAAF flew the first attack on targets in the Ostmark [Nazi designation for Austria] on August 13, 1943. That following October, there were two further raids by the 12th USAAF.

Embroidered uniform badge of the 15th US Army Air Force in original scale: the background was blue, the wings, number and border gold; the star white and the dot in the center of the star black.

There were Allied landings on Sicily on July 10, 1943, which was rapidly seized, with others on the Italian mainland on September 3. These were followed by the assault on the Bay of Salerno that, despite fierce resistance by the 10th German Army, left the southern part of the Italian boot in Allied hands. Towards the end of 1943, the Allied advance stalled on the "Gustav Line" running from Rome to Naples and hinged on Monte Cassino.

This rapid advance of the Allied ground troops allowed the Americans to repair and extend the airfields abandoned by the Luftwaffe, thereby creating new airstrips for their heavy four-engine bombers. At the same time, a new air fleet, the 15th USAAF, was formed that began operations of November 1, 1943 while still based in Tunisia. Originally, it was made up of units from existing formations, primarily from the 12th AAF and, by November 1943, had already reached a strength of over 1 000 aircraft and 20 000 personnel. After transferring from Tunis, its headquarters were located in Bari from December 1, 1943. In the months of November 1943 to April 1944, this force was reinforced by additional bomber groups flying new machines from the USA. By May 1944, it had reached full combat strength and was structured as follows:[27]

---

[27] See page 77 for geographic locations, aircraft markings of the 15th USAAF are shown in the Appendix on pages 272 et seq.

5th Bomb Wing, headquarters in Foggia

Bomb Group	Initial ops.	Targets	Aircraft
2nd	11/43	Amendola	B-17
97th	11/43	Amendola	B-17
99th	11/43	Tortorella	B-17
301st	11/43	Lucera	B-17
463rd	03/44	Celone	B-17
483rd	04/44	Sterparone	B-17

47th Bomb Wing, headquarters in Manduria

Bomb Group	Initial ops.	Targets	Aircraft
98th	11/43	Lecce	B-24
376th	11/43	San Pancrazio	B-24
449th	01/44	Grottaglie	B-24
450th	01/44	Manduria	B-24

Crew tents on Torretta airbase – location of 764th Squadron, 461st Bomb Group. (BGA)

15th US Air Force (15th USAAF)

49th Bomb Wing, headquarters in Castelluccio

Bomb Group	First ops.	Targets	Aircraft
451st	01/44	Castelluccio	B-24
461st	04/44	Torretto	B-24
484th	04/44	Torretto	B-24

55th Bomb Wing, Headquarters in Spinazzola

Bomb Group	First ops.	Targets	Aircraft
460th	03/44	Spinazzola	B-24
464th	04/44	Pantanella	B-24
465th	05/44	Pantanella	B-24
485th	05/44	Venosa	B-24

304th Bomb Wing, Headquarters in Cerignola

Bomb Group	First ops.	Targets	Aircraft
454th	02/44	San Giovanni	B-24
455th	02/44	San Giovanni	B-24
456th	02/44	Stornara	B-24
459th	03/44	Giulia	B-24

305th Fighter Wing, headquarters in Torremaggiore

Fighter Group	First ops.	Targets	Aircraft
1st	12/43	Salsola	P-38
14th	11/43	Triolo	P-38
82nd	11/43	Vincenzo	P-38

306th Fighter Wing, headquarters in Fano

Fighter Group	First ops.	Targets	Aircraft
31st	04/44	San Severo	Spitfire, P-51
52nd	04/44	Madna	P-51
325th	11/43	Foggia	P-47, P-51
332nd	05/44	Ramitelli	P-47, P-51

Airfield of 463rd Bomb Group in Celone on 6.IX.44. (HF)

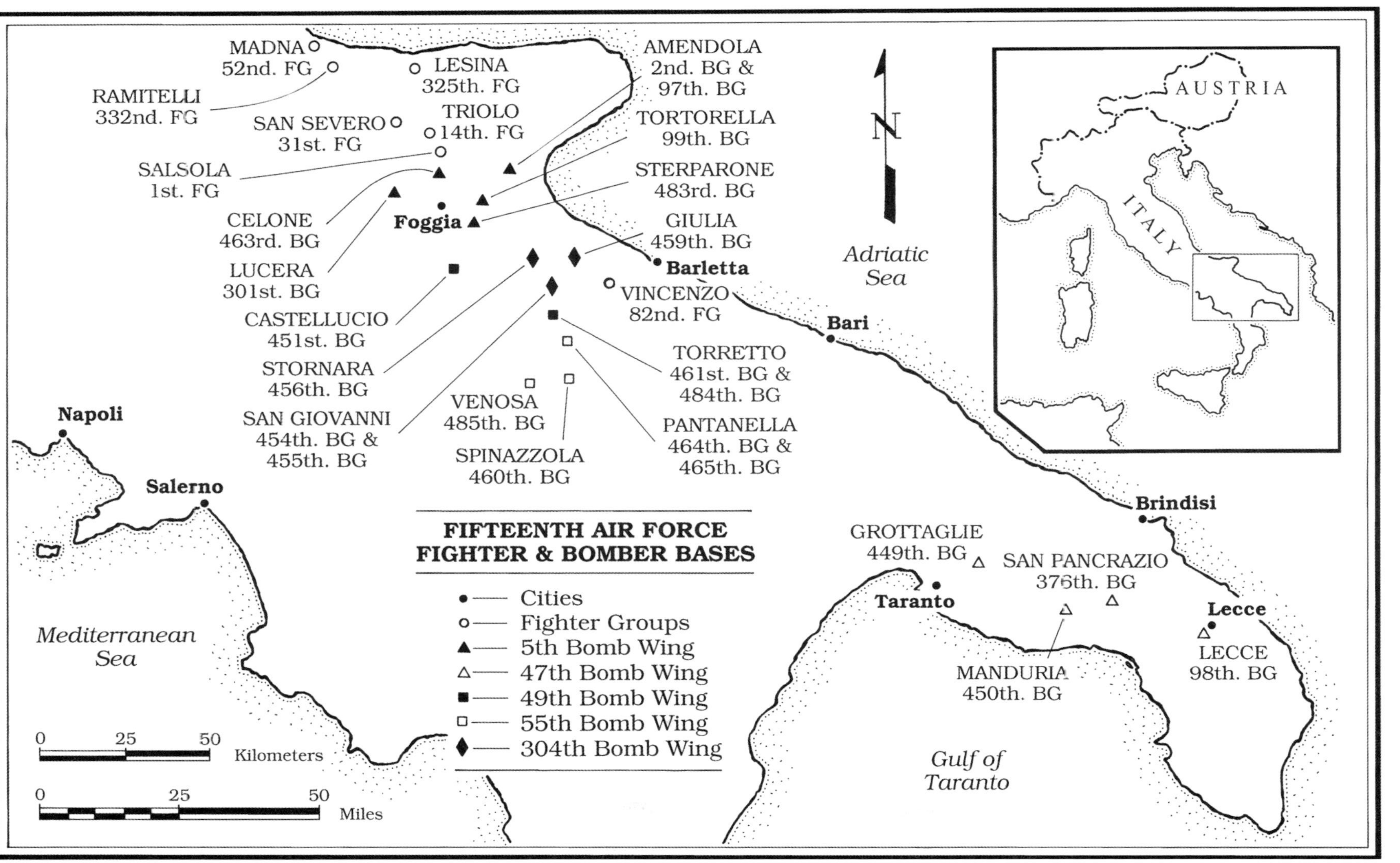

This map shows the locations of the squadrons in the southern part of the Italian boot. (Britton)

Conditions on the airfields could be more than precarious. "Sunny Italy" often failed to meet the expectations of the airmen and ground crews. In addition to rain and snow that were mainly just disagreeable, it was primarily water on the landing strips that caused serious concerns. Wire netting was used in attempts to overcome such problems – see photo right. (HF)

Generations encounter each other in Italy: a B-24 Liberator taking off from its airstrip for an operation over Austria, while donkey carts travel unimpressed along a sandy track. (BGA)

It was not always wet and uncomfortable: the airfield of 2nd Bomb Group, 20th Bomb Squadron, in Amendola on 19.IV.45 was an idyllic location with grazing sheep. (HF)

Prioritized, the 15th USAAF was ordered to fulfill the following tasks:

1. Destroy the German Luftwaffe, both in the air and on the ground.

2. Participate in the Combined Bomber Offensive "Point Blank". This was the definition of the cooperation between the American and British bomber forces aimed at crushing the German Reich: the British primarily attacked cities and the civilian population by night, the Americans bombed strategically important targets such as industrial and transportation facilities, refineries, armaments plants and the like by day.

3. Support ground troops in Italy, either directly – for example, by destroying the Monastery of Monte Cassino on February 15, 1944, a linchpin of the German "Gustav Line" – or indirectly by attacking German supply lines, in particular across the Brenner Pass.

4. Weaken German positions on the Balkans.

Fulfillment of those tasks was accomplished in an outstanding manner and we were to feel the effects; what Greater Germany was able to throw into the defense was pitiful.

The American concept for attacking Austria from Italy: support the advance of the ground troops with fighter-bombers and tactical bombers, and then to smash targets across the Alps in Austria, South and Central Germany with strategic bombers. (HF)

It was a massive challenge of logistics to supply and service this huge armada with fuel, bombs, ammunition and all other types of equipment; it was achieved in magnificent style and with growing intensity.

Standard maintenance work on aircraft of the 15th USSAF in Italy. On the left, engine maintenance on a B-17 G Flying Fortress on 28.II.45; on the right, ground crew are working on a P-51 C Mustang, its engine cowlings have all been removed to simplify the task. (HF)

Following a crash-landing in July 1944, ground crew are repairing this B-24 Liberator: a new engine „3" has just been fitted, its turbocharger is on the ground awaiting installation. (HF)

Bombs and tail fins were delivered separately and assembled prior to loading. These particular ones were used for the bomb loads of B-24 bombers. (HF)

Ground crew struggle to get their bombs to the aircraft despite the difficult ground conditions on 22.II.45. (HF)

Bombs being readied for a fighter-bomber operation by a P-38 Lightning. (HF)

On 7.X.1944 this B-17 of 483rd Bomb Group took a massive AA hit over Vienna but managed to fly more than 1 000 km to safety. The hit trapped the ball turret gunner in his turret; he only survived because the B-17 was able to land normally. (HF)

This B-24 Liberator was hit by anti-aircraft fire on 24.IV.44; despite damage to the wing and a feathered engine, the aircraft made it back to base. (HF)

On 15.III.44, German anti-aircraft fire took a huge chunk out of the left wing of this B-17 of 20th Squadron, 1st Bomb Group. (HF)

A crash-landed P-51 D Mustang is winched up to release its damaged landing gear. (HF)

When injuries to crew members were reported by radio, ambulances were already waiting when aircraft landed; on this occasion following a raid on Steyr by this B-17 D of 97th Bomb Group from Amendola on 2.IV.44. (HF)

This Liberator No. „34" was heavily damaged on 11.VII.44 by a rocket fired by a German interceptor fighter over Wiener Neustadt, but made its way home. The ball turret gunner succeeded in shooting down the attacking fighter. It was common after such spectacular damage for the crew to have themselves photographed with the surviving aircraft. (HF)

Our opponents, the aircraft of the 15th USAAF

Boeing B-17 Flying Fortress

This American long-range bomber Boeing B-17 "Flying Fortress" undertook its maiden flight in 1935. It was designed as the combat aircraft for patrolling America's coastline. It did not earn the title of "Flying Fortress" until the model „E" appeared. This type could be deployed as an offensive long-range bomber and featured improved on-board armament and armor. When production was terminated in May 1945, some 12 726 aircraft had been built, each costing 276 000 US dollars.

From model „E" onwards, all types are recognizable from the extended tail radius melding with the fuselage; characteristic for all B-17s is the elegant shape of the fuselage. From the fall of 1943, the model „G" was the most common type and is readily identified by the twin 0.5" caliber machine guns in the chin turret.

15th US Air Force (15th USAAF)

A B-17 G of 20th Bomb Squadron, 2nd Bomb Group on 20.VII.44, approaching its target and well concealed by cloud. (HF)

A B-17 on 6.VII.44 attacking a steel plant in Bergamo. (HF)

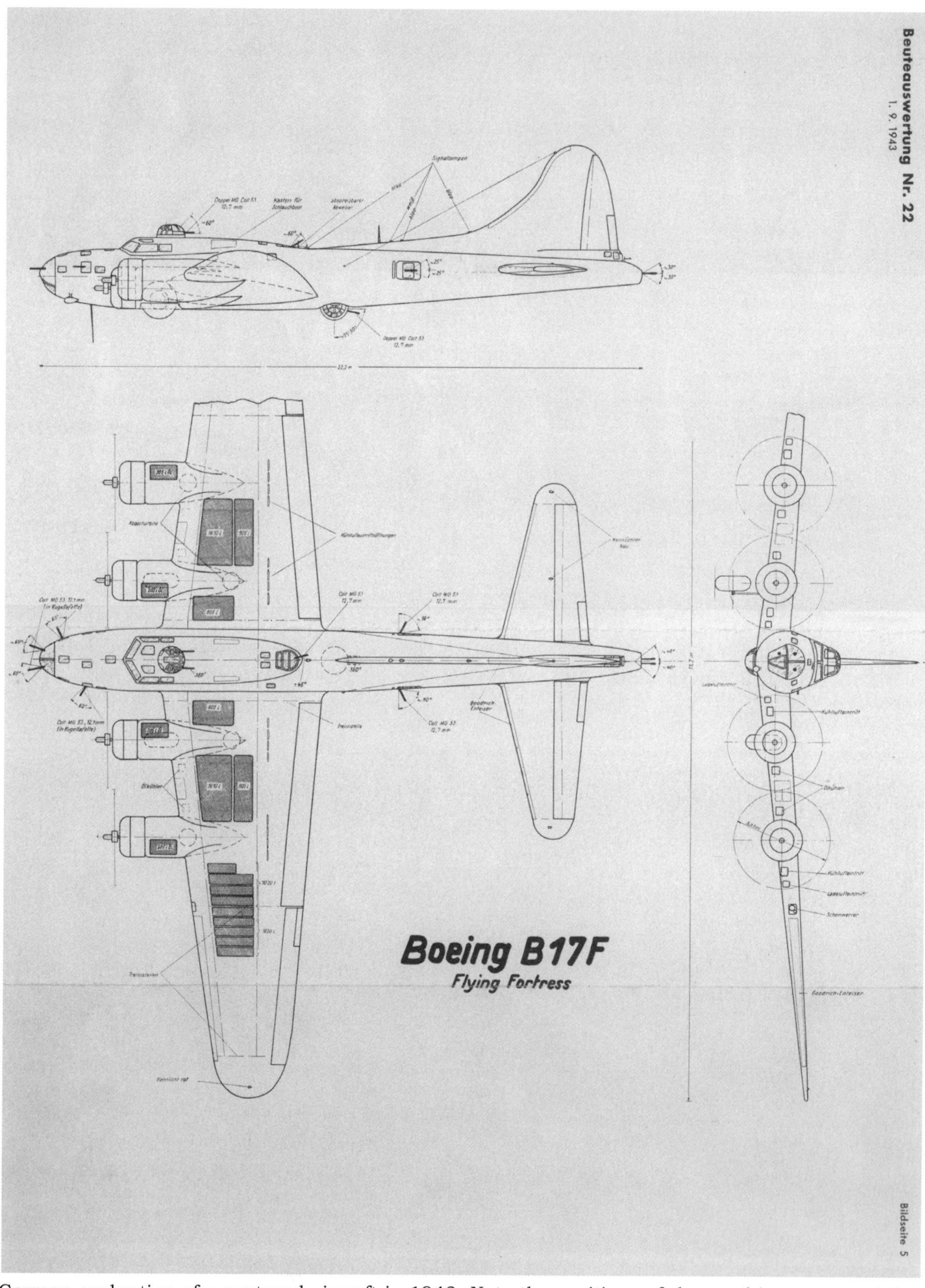

German evaluation of a captured aircraft in 1943. Note the positions of the machine guns and the fuel tanks. (HF)

Dimensions:
    Wingspan 103 ft 10 in (31.62 m)
    Length 74 ft 4 in (22.66 m)
    Height 19 ft 1 in (5.82 m)
    Net weight 36 135 lbs (16 391 kg)
    Gross weight 65 500 lbs (29 700 kg)

Equipment:
    Engines: four Wright "Cyclone" R-1820-97, each 1 200 hp (895 kW)
    Armament: 13 Browning M2 machine guns 0.5"-cal. (12.7 mm)
    Bomb load: 4 500 – 12 800 lbs (2 050 – 5 800 kg)

Performance:
    Top speed 287 mph (462 km)
    Cruising speed 182 mph (293 km)
    Range 1 800 miles (2 900 km) with 6 000 lbs (2 700 kg) bomb load
    Ceiling 35 600 ft (10 850 m)

Consolidated B-24 Liberator

The long-range Consolidated B-24 "Liberator" was designed as a day bomber with
the aim of outclassing the Boeing B-17 "Flying Fortress" in both range and bomb
load.

A B-24 Liberator over Italy on 21.IV.45 (HF)

15th US Air Force (15th USAAF)

Characteristic for this aircraft are its twin tail units, the slab-sided fuselage and its long, high aspect ratio Davis wings.

During WW II, more Liberators were produced than any other USA combat aircraft, a total of 18 188 in all – each one costing 336 000 US dollars.

First used operationally as bombers in 1941 by Britain's Royal Air Force to patrol the Atlantic. Together with the B-17, the majority of Liberators were used for the strategic bombing offensive over Europe and against the German Reich. Because of their different performances in flight, Liberators invariably flew separate operations from the B-17s. Logically, it was possible that individual machines joined up with units that were equipped with different aircraft for security reasons.

Following an attack on Vienna on 30.VIII.44, this B-24 Liberator of 451st Bomb Group flew back to base in Italy despite having a damaged left tail unit. The damage was caused by a 20 mm cannon fired by an opposing enemy fighter. (HF)

Dimensions:
    Wingspan 110 ft 0 in (33.50 m)
    Length 67 ft 8 in (20.60 m)
    Height 18 ft 0 in (5.5 m)
    Net weight 36 500 lbs (16 590 kg)
    Gross weight 65 000 lbs (29 500 kg)

Equipment:
    Engines: four Pratt & Whitney R 1830 each 1 200 hp (900 kW)
    Armament: ten Browning M2 machine guns 0.5"-cal. (12.7 mm)
    Bomb load: 2 700 – 8 000 lbs (1 200 kg – 3 600 kg)

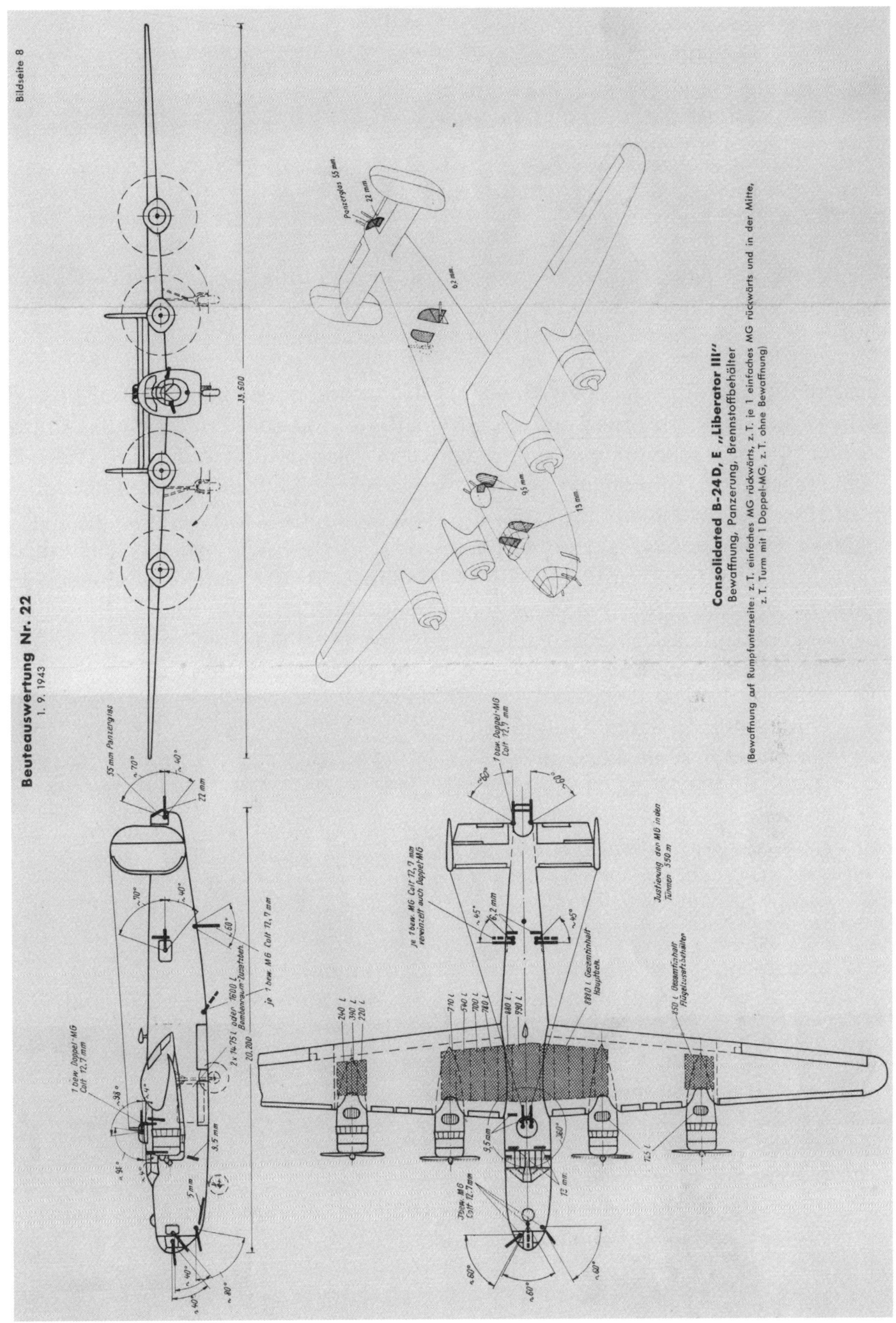

Bildseite 8
Beuteauswertung Nr. 22
1. 9. 1943
Consolidated B-24D, E „Liberator III"
Bewaffnung, Panzerung, Brennstoffbehälter
(Bewaffnung auf Rumpfunterseite: z.T. einfaches MG rückwärts, z.T. je 1 einfaches MG rückwärts und in der Mitte,
z.T. Turm mit 1 Doppel-MG, z.T. ohne Bewaffnung)
35.500
20.200
55 mm Panzerglas
22 mm
1 bew. Doppel-MG Colt 12,7 mm
je 1 bew. MG Colt 12,7 mm
2 x 14-75 l oder 7600 l Bombenraum-Zusatztank
1 bew. Doppel-MG Colt 12,7 mm
je 1 bew. MG Colt 12,7 mm verwinzelt auch Doppel-MG
Justierung der MG in den Türmen 350 m
0880 l Gesamtinhalt Haupttank
850 l Gesamtinhalt Flügelaußentanks
1 bew. MG Colt 12,7 mm

Performance:
    Top speed 290 mph (470 km/h)
    Cruising speed 215 mph (345 km/h)
    Range 2 100 miles (3 360 km) with 5 000 lbs (2 270 kg) bomb load
    Ceiling 28 000 ft (8 500 m)

Lockheed P-38 Lightning

The American single-seat fighter Lockheed P-38 "Lightning" undertook its maiden flight in 1939. The performance specifications called for a twin-engine aircraft, while the use of exhaust turbochargers led to the characteristic twin booms.

Initially the aircraft was deployed against Japan and subsequently from the end of 1942 also in North Africa and then from 1943 in Europe. Here, the Lightning became the first operational long-range escort fighter protecting the strategic bombers. In terms of maneuverability, the size of the aircraft rendered it inferior to Bf 109s and FW 190s of the Luftwaffe. As a result, the Lightning was gradually replaced by Mustangs or Thunderbolts; the 15th USAAF, however, kept their Lightnings operational until the end of hostilities. By the end of production in 1945, no less than 9 923 P-38s had been built, of which 1 400 were equipped for the photo-reconnaissance role; each aircraft cost 115 000 US dollars.

Dimensions:
    Wingspan (15.58 m) 52 ft 0 in (15.58 m)
    Length 37 ft 10 in (11.53 m)
    Height 12 ft 10 in (3.91 m)
    Net weight (5 800 kg) 12 800 lbs (5 800 kg)
    Gross weight 21 600 lbs (9 798 kg)

Equipment:
    Engines: two Allison V-1710 each 1 725 hp (1 194 kW)
    Armament: one Hispano-Suiza M2(C) cannon 20 mm
                    four Browning MG53-2 machine guns 0.5"-cal. (12.7 mm)
                    and und 12 rockets 5 in (12.7 cm)
                    or 4 000 lbs (1 820 kg) bomb load
                    or long-range fuel tanks

Performance:
    Top speed 443 mph (712 km/h)
    Range 1 300/2 600 miles (1 770 km/3 620 km with long-range fuel tanks)
    Ceiling 44 000 ft (13 400 m)

After protecting the heavy bombers from the Luftwaffe on 21.XII.44, this squadron is homeward bound to its base in Italy. (HF)

A formation of P-38 Lightnings over Italy. (HF)

Republic P-47 Thunderbolt

The American single-seat fighter P-47 "Thunderbolt" built by the Republic Aviation Company took off on its maiden flight in 1941. By the end of WWII, around 15 600 aircraft, each costing 83 000 US dollars, had been produced and assigned to every single theater of war.

This machine was rugged and fitted with a powerful engine. Compared to German fighters it was lacking somewhat in maneuverability, but this deficit could be offset by experienced pilots.

Republic P-47 D, here with the original cockpit layout, known as the "Razorback". (HF)

Dimensions:
    Wingspan 40 ft 9 in (12.42 m)
    Length 36 ft 1 in (11.01 m)
    Height 14 ft 2 in (4.47 m)
    Net weight 10 000 lbs (4 536 kg)
    Gross weight 13 500 lbs (7 938 kg)

Equipment:
    Engine: single Pratt & Whitney R-2800 with 2 535 hp (1 890 kW)
    Armament: eight Browning M2 machine guns 0.5"-cal. (12.7 mm)
              and ten 5 in rockets (12.7 cm)
              or 1 500 lbs (680 kg) bomb load
              or long-range fuel tanks

Performance:
    Top speed 433 mph (697 km/h)
    Range 800/1 800 miles (1 290 km/2 900 km) with long-range fuel tanks
    Ceiling 43 000 ft (13 100 m)

Long-range fighter Republic P-47 N Thunderbolt with 360° vision cockpit. (HF)

North American P-51 Mustang

The North American P-51 "Mustang" single-seat fighter completed its maiden flight in 1940. This aircraft was very fast, maneuverable and boasted extreme range. It was the ideal machine for flying fighter escort to the bomber formations. It was in this role that the Mustang began to appear over Reich territory from the end of 1943 onwards. This aircraft literally made the devastating daytime bombing raids of the American strategic bomber formations feasible.

Between 1940 and 1945 no less than 16 575 machines had been built, each costing 54 000 US dollars. Of these, almost 8 000 were P-51 Ds, recognizable by their „teardrop" style Plexiglas canopy.

P-51 C Mustangs of 31st Fighter Group in Italy preparing for take-off on 31.IV.44. When fitted with drop tanks, they were capable of escorting the B-17 and B-24 bombers all the way to the target and back, while fighting off the Luftwaffe. (HF)

Dimensions:
Wingspan 37 ft 0 in (11.28 m)
Length 32 ft 3 in (9.83 m)
Height 13 ft 8 in (4.17 m)
Net weight 2 465 kg (7 635 lbs.)
Gross weight 12 100 lbs (5 490 kg)

Equipment:
Engine: single Packard V-1650-7 with 1 720 hp (1 282 kW), built under Rolls-Royce "Merlin" license
Armament: six Browning M2 machine guns 0.5"-cal. (12.7 mm)
             and ten 5 in (12.7 cm) rockets
             or 2 000 lbs (907 kg) bomb load
             or long-range fuel tanks

Performance:
Top speed 440 mph (702 km/h)
Range 2 050 miles (3 300 km) with drop tanks
Ceiling 41 900 ft (12 800 m)

A formation of P-51 D Mustangs of 31st Fighter Group over Italy on 12.VI.44. Note the newer „tear-drop" style cockpit canopies providing better 360° vision. (HF)

Bomber crews

The following photographs are intended to give an impression of the battle stations of American bomber aircrew. Typical features that had to be endured during operations were the cold, boredom and tension during the long flights, fear of enemy AA fire and the brief but intense combats with the German Luftwaffe.

Left the ball MG turret of a B-17, on the right, the two waist gunners of a B-24. (HF)

This shot shows a waist machine gunner in a B-24. He is wearing the new AA helmet over his head and shoulders to protect him from AA fragments – photo taken on 12.IV.44. (HF)

These young crewmen wearing their flying jackets, pose in front of their B-24. (HF)

This crew of a B-24 Liberator is fully equipped with high-altitude gear, parachutes and Mae Wests. Their sheepskin jackets, padded trousers, boots and gloves are to protect them from the biting cold at approach level, around -40°C at 24 000 feet (7 500 meters) above sea level, that gnawed at them. Also clearly visible is the front turret with its two 0.5" caliber machine guns – and the sheer size of the aircraft. This scene, taken in Italy on 12.IV.44 is probably a prayer service before an operation. (HF)

The large photo shows the interior of a B-24; upper left the pilot, upper right the co-pilot, upper center the flight engineer / top turret gunner, upper right of the bay the radio operator / nose gunner and below, the bombardier / nose gunner. (HF)

The inset shows the cockpit of a B-17. (HF)

A bombardier in the Plexiglas nose of his B-17; in front of him is the Norden bombsight that was used to steer the aircraft during its bombing run. Also note the ammunition belts of the left and right nose guns. (HF)

Aerial photographer and waist gunner in a B-17. (HF)

Big Week

Immediately on our arrival at 1./805 in St.Valentin-Langenhart, we Amstettners began training on the equipment and guns so that those AA Assistants born in 1926 could be relieved. They organized a number of farewell parties with the troops and the officers, and soon afterwards disappeared from our sight.

Big Week

Within two weeks already, on Tuesday, February 22, 1944, things started to get seriously hot. The Americans had apparently completed preparations at their Italian airbases, obtained enough aerial reconnaissance and now began their air offensive against armaments targets in Greater Germany. These operations were conducted by both the 8th USAAF stationed in England, and the newly established 15th USAAF based in Italy under the code name "Argument". In the history of the war in the air, however, this offensive became far better known by its unofficial name of "Big Week".

One of the first targets of the 15th USAAF were the Steyr works, about 15 km distant – in other words quite close to our position:[28] *„...Today there was a lot of action around Steyr. Powerful emotions when we heard the bombing. A dull rumbling that lasted for 7 minutes..."*

Bombs falling on the Ball and Roller Bearing Works in Steyr, somewhat to the east of the town, on 2.IV.44. The plant lies to the left of the bomb in the center of the photograph. After the ball bearing factory in Schweinfurt was badly damaged in the fall of 1943, the Steyr facility became a major pillar of the German armaments industry and a frequent target of the 15th USAAF. (HF)

---

[28] From a letter dated 20.III.44 written to my cousin Erich, at the time on active service in France. See Appendix, page 254 showing the envelope and an extract from the letter.

Ship „33" shot down

From the entry in my combat diary dated February 22, 1944, it can be seen that 15 salvos or 51 rounds were fired by our battery at the attacking and departing formations. We were unable to observe a hit, but saw one next day on the 23rd when a German fighter, a Focke-Wulf 190, shot down a B-24 Liberator bomber: „*...It came down, gradually breaking up and crashing in St. Valentin. A radio operator parachuted out and landed in the middle of the battery. He was an American, a fine looking figure...*" Willi Reichebner remembers that after the order to cease fire was given, the "Yankee" was invited by Captain Ludwig, our battery captain, to his officers' quarters for a cup of tea and stayed there as a „guest" until he was picked up by a truck with Luftwaffe markings.

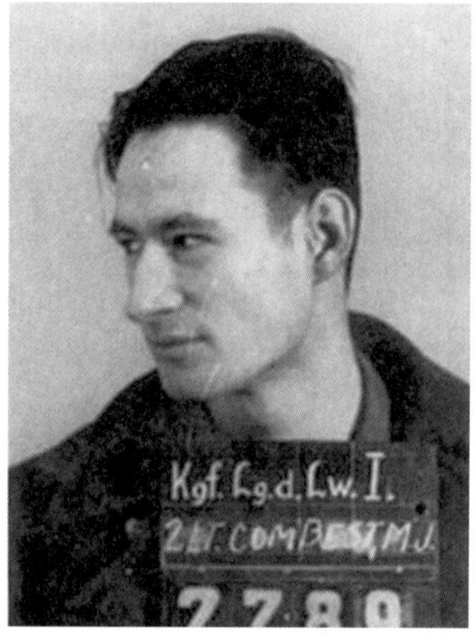

Left; the co-pilot 2nd Lieutenant Merwin J. Combest jumped with his parachute and landed in the middle of our position. Right; the tail gunner Sergeant Martin Yerick, who lost his life in the action. Years after the end of the war, his nephew contacted me.

Such events naturally burn themselves deep into one's memory: alerted by the chattering of a fighter's guns, we boys left our posts at the Malsi, ran out of the bunker into the open and stared at the impressive action taking place over our heads. There was the pursuing fighter, the bomber breaking apart and then the American floating down on his parachute into the middle of our position and subsequently marched to our battery captain[29] by a soldier with his rifle slung over his shoulder. The American looked down amazed at us adolescents, who were then severely chewed out for having abandoned our positions on the fire

---

[29] His name was 2nd Lt. Merwin J. Combest and he was not the radio operator, but the co-pilot of the aircraft. It was his eight mission over enemy territory. After being captured, he was sent to the Luftwaffe prisoner of war camp No. I. (Barth)

control radar, even though we were not at action stations. According to my notes, only five salvos amounting to 25 rounds were fired.

Photos of wreckage from the downed B-24 J Liberator taken by the author and scattered across the position he was serving in. One shot shows the right-hand vertical tail, carrying the tactical number 33 and the series number (4)2100255.

There was a subsequent Missing Air Crew Report dated February 25, 1944[30], an extract of which follows:

Machine and crew were part of the 15th American Air Force, Bomb Group 376, Bomb Squadron 512, stationed at San Pancrazio, Italy / the target was Steyr, Austria, high altitude mission, visibility and weather conditions good. Loss of the aircraft was the result of an enemy fighter attack / aircraft type: B-24 J, AAF series number: 42-100255 / eleven crew members on board of which five were killed, the others were taken prisoner.

Crew of Ship 33: standing rear: flight engineer 2nd Sergeant Olson (not on the fatal mission), waist gunner left Sergeant Perrin, waist gunner right Private Capogreco (†), tail gunner Sergeant Yerick (†), nose gunner 2nd Sergeant Fairley (†), kneeling front; pilot 2nd Lieutenant Chase (†), bombardier 2nd Lieutenant Nesbitt, navigator 2nd Lieutenant Pine (†), co-pilot 2nd Lieutenant Combest. Not shown on the photo are the three auxiliary crewmen: flight engineer Technical Sergeant Agresta, top turret gunner 2nd Sergeant Smith and ball turret gunner Sergeant Phelan: all three survived the incident.

There are also surviving eye-witness accounts from crews of other aircraft about the incident in which five young Americans who were not much older than us, lost their lives. Below, a statement made by the tail gunner of Ship 31 that was flying ahead:[31]

---

[30] See Appendix, pages 260 et seq.
[31] See Appendix, page 259

Big Week

```
»US ›Confidential‹ equals British ›Confidential‹
           512. Bomb Squadron (H)
            376. Bomb Group (H)
         Office of Operations Officer

                                 24 February 1944

The following is a statement of 2nd Lt. Clyde J. Keator, Seri-
al Number 0-683716, on plane number 31. Mission dated: Febru-
ary 23, 1944.

My tail gunner, Sgt. H. R. Hall saw ship 33 which flew direct-
ly behind us fall out of formation to the rear. The plane was
smoking. Three chutes appeared and ship then went into a ver-
tical dive and disappeared.

                               sign. Clyde J. Keator«
```

Raid on the Steyr Ball and Roller Bearing Works. The damaged target is concealed by smoke. (HF)

The following day, Thursday, February 24, 1944, there was another raid on Steyr. This time we fired 72 rounds in 14 salvos: *„… then came a Fortress, apparently damaged by the Steyr flak that put up fierce barrage fire. We let off a salvo* *that burst perfectly and the aircraft banked away on fire towards Mauthausen. You can imagine the yelling from the battery...*"[32]

After these three days, the Americans suspended their attacks on Steyr. They had suffered heavy losses: German fighters and anti-aircraft guns shot down 226 bombers and 28 fighter planes; in all, the Americans lost 2 600 airmen. That meant that we had a temporary rest until the summer. Apart from a few reconnaissance aircraft, Lightnings and Mosquitos, there was no excitement or anything to defend against. Nevertheless, there were repeated calls to action stations, but the American raids were evidently directed against more distant targets.

Mosquito with American markings. Note the special black and white stripes around the wings and fuselage that were applied to all Allied aircraft during the Normandy invasion. (HF)

---

[32] It was the B-17 G piloted by 1st Lieutenant Charles E. Abramson (series number 42-31437) from 352nd Squadron of the 301st Bomb Group. An „aircraft factory" in Steyr was targeted. The aircraft crash-landed to the east of Enns an der Donau at 13:11 hours – all nine crew members were taken prisoner. For an American account of the incident see Appendix, page 267.

A damaged B-17 returns to base after a raid on Steyr. The damage was caused by a rocket fired by a German fighter. (HF)

Routine in the position

Daily life in an AA battery on home soil was strictly regulated by the duty roster:

Morning	Reveille with breakfast and ablutions	07:00 – 08:00 hrs
Morning	Military duties	08:00 – 12:00 hrs
Midday	Lunch and rest for the AA Assistants	12:00 – 14:00 hrs
Afternoon	School lessons, study time, roster duties	14:00 – 18:00 hrs
Evening	Evening meal, leisure time	18:00 – 22:00 hrs
Night	Sleep	22:00 – 07:00 hrs
Sundays	Clean sick bay, inspection of quarters, leisure time	

That was our normality, but what was normal in those days! We were in the military and there was a war on that increasingly affected life in our homeland too. The alarms and orders to take up action stations interrupted the daily roster and confused everything. On an almost daily basis, at any time of day or night, we rushed outside to man the guns or systems, even when isolated enemy aircraft drifted around in our airspace. Staying with the normal state of affairs:

Daily routine

Early morning

Around seven o'clock, when the duty officer burst in, blowing his whistle and shouting his orders loudly „On your feet!" you were woken up, but were not yet wide awake. In my "Amusing Retrospective of the Year" I noted down: „*Everyone is fast asleep – nobody moves, everything is quiet – when the Duty NCO, the idiot, suddenly wants to wake everyone up."* No hope of slumbering on. Depending on his disposition or mood of the day, this unpleasant "alarm clock" stood there for a while checking that everyone was getting up or accompanying the process with encouraging words, or disappeared immediately to wake up the next barrack only to return shortly afterwards and again, depending on his disposition or mood – to get the last dawdlers out of bed with polite or crude words, but invariably loud ones.

Given the lack of proper sanitary installations, the morning wash and brush up was perfunctory at best or dispensed with entirely. There were only a few washbowls and cold water. Luckily, few of us needed to shave yet. Breakfast was eaten cold, but the barrack detail did bring a pail of coffee, the quality of which is beyond description, but at least it was the one warm thing in our stomachs on those generally cold mornings.

Two AAA from Graz peering peevishly into the morning light – a barrack detail trudges off to fetch coffee.

On some days the whistle blew to the order of „Fall in for morning exercises!" that consisted of calisthenics or a two-mile run; the more athletic NCOs in particular were specialists in this aspect. My entry for Sunday, 16.IV.44 notes: „... *Today again we did not get up. Sgt. Siemers came in like a whirlwind and made us do early morning exercises...*" There were a few among us who appreciated this method of being woken up, for example our Max, a district running champion, but most of us avoided the pleasure whenever possible. There was a danger related to shirking though, which was rewarded with square-bashing at midday or in the evening.

Morning

According to the roster duties began at eight. It was pinned to the blackboard in the orderly room and duties were announced together with the previous day's orders. The duty roster alternately covered military affairs and events:

Station or battery exercises were conducted almost daily. Relaying of commands from the tracker crews to the guns was practiced repeatedly; from simulated target acquisition to azimuth, height and range readings input into the Malsi converter or fire-control unit. Their computed outputs for azimuth, elevation and fuze settings were transmitted to the guns. Everything was relayed via throat microphones and headphones. Later, using the fire-control unit, these data were transmitted fully automatically to the optical indicators, aiming and coincidence needles on the guns.

These exercises were also essential because of the frequent changes within the crews as a result of sickness, leave, transfers or newly assigned troopers, AA Assistants, Flak-V soldiers or, from the winter of 1944/45 onwards, female AA Assistants. By now, we „old hands" had honed virtually all these exercises to a fine art. If anything, we found this eternal practicing boring rather than strenuous, but quite the opposite when we were detailed for square-bashing or infantry drill.

The aim of **infantry exercises** was to re-establish a level of discipline in the mob and to refresh our ability to march in formation. This ranged from straightforward lining up in rows of three to „Attention!", „Leeeft turn!", „Company about turn!", „Riiight turn!", „By the left, quick maaarch!", „Left–two-three!–left–two–three!"… „Let's have a song!" … „What, too tired today!? – Down! – On your feet – march! – Down! – On your feet - march!" and so on.

We boys born in 1928: still able to smile after a spell of infantry drilling.

This was definitely not fun and extremely unpopular, especially when the weather was lousy, or worse when the NCOs, otherwise known as drill pigs, were in a bad mood or had a score to settle with us – nobody ever forget such things!

Occasionally, drill was preceded by **roll-calls**. These could take place at any time night or day and were intended to check personal hygiene and cleanliness of items of equipment. There were roll-calls held in fatigues, full uniform, 2nd dress, overcoat, with or without packed rucksack, either all together, or one after another: this we called the "masked ball". For inspection of gas mask with container, boots, canteen including knife and fork, there were „all-present and accounted for" roll-calls, like the one we had already experienced in Wegscheid.

Saturday, 18.XI.44: „...*This morning after reveille we stayed under the blankets for a while because it was extremely cold and we had nothing for heating. When we fell in, the Lieutenant inspected the state of our boots. I, together with a fair number of others, had our names taken. At 10:00, after ground target practice and station exercises, the drill really got going.*
Hounded across the fields – we were in a state! My right hand was covered in mud and I mumbled to Tubert that it would sit nicely in his face – fortunately, being a Prussian, he did not fully understand my Austrian dialect. Then, after 22:00 hrs, action stations. Couldn't they have come a bit earlier? Same as yesterday: approach, fly past. It went on until 01:00 hours."

In the course of 1944, our normal exercises were extended to include **infantry combat training**. This was a result of the heightened response levels of all AA batteries and military installations stemming from the fear of revolts and uprisings by the innumerable foreign workers in the surrounding camps, or by the inmates of the Mauthausen concentration camp that was quite close to us.

Combat training or the **ground defense exercise** consisted of a map exercise with assault and defense scenarios, including night ones, based on a ring of foxholes dug around our position. To make the exercises more realistic and in case of a real emergency, we were issued with Italian-made rifles and blank rounds, plenty of which were expended and much to our satisfaction.

In our case, these combat exercises were particularly frequent in the months of the fall of 1944. Wednesday, 1.XI.44: „...*at 01:30 hours stood down from action stations (attack on Vienna). At 02:30 hours an exercise against the railroad AA took place. We rushed for a full hour to reach the forest via Langenhart and the Nibelungenwerk to confuse the enemy; a total success. We took the position, but half of us were casualties. Everything went smoothly. Sepperl Wallner and I were firing like madmen. There is to be yet another war game next week. ...Drill Sergeant Christiansen is leaving us today. As is our cook whose name is also actually Cook. We can notice the difference in the chow already.*"

As part of the combat exercises, we tracking crew were also being instructed to fire on **terrestrial targets** and getting practical training on the guns themselves. As a result, we were also busy on Sundays that would normally be days off. Sun-

day, 15.X.44: *„Pöppler, that rat, came in a second time after reveille at 07:30 hrs
and said that we should be prepared for a dressing down. I was standing guard
from 09:00 – 11:00 so I did not have to listen to the CO's lectures. No harm done.
Then, short battery exercises until 12:30 hrs.*
*Bast had visitors during the lunch break. His sister and Helmi Senker had come
and were talking about their pending draft for service in the East. I fell asleep
around 13:30 hrs and completely missed the ‚start of duties on Sunday afternoon'.
What a load of crap. No free time for oneself at all. In ground defense I take the role
of gun captain on gun Caesar. Barking out orders. Then we did our study hour and
got ready for the masked ball with packed rucksack at 17:30 hrs. There was supposed to be an all-present roll-call, but it was only half as bad as I expected. Josten gave us a sermon about morale. Am feeling really sluggish and pissed off with
everything. Willi feels exactly the same. It's nearly always like this shortly before
going on leave. Pöppler has been detailed off to Passau for 4 – 5 weeks. Thank God
not transferred. Would be a real pity for us and for him!"*

These ground defense measures also had a name. Wednesday, 27.9.44: *„… suddenly in the evening 'Imminent Danger'. AA Assistants have to stand guard with
their rifles. It's my turn with Köfele from 20:00 – 22:00 hrs. Had a good chat with
him. Wieser got the thin end of the wedge and had to stand guard twice during the
night…"*

From time to time our outdoor activities included **cleaning ammunition and
equipment or fatigue duties** such as shoveling snow. However, we regarded
these chores as R&R rather than work, which invariably infuriated the NCOs in
charge. For the gun crews, however, life could be strenuous as Josef Lammerhuber recalls:

> »…Cleaning the guns one Sunday: I was K2 on gun Emil. The K3,
> Pvt. 1st Class Meisters was supposed to clean the breechblock
> of the 88 mm gun, which meant that the breechblock wedge
> [43 kg] had to be removed. The Pvt. 1st Class said that he had
> to change out of his dress uniform first and went to his bar-
> rack. While he was away I removed the wedge by myself – only
> my hands showed the marks of the effort. This ›deed‹ earned me
> a lot of respect and after that I was rarely picked on during
> the daily roll-calls…«

Not unpleasant in the course of our military duties were the various presenta-
tions and training classes that were part and parcel of our AA operations and
equally essential for doing the job properly.

The included **aircraft recognition**, during which we practiced identifying and
naming all the aircraft that might be operational in our airspace. Not only our

own Messerschmitts, Heinkels, Junkers, Focke-Wulfs and the like, but also the American Liberators, Fortresses, Lightnings and Mustangs, plus those of the Royal Air Force: Halifaxes, Wellingtons, Spitfires, Mosquitos and the Russian Ratas, Yaks etc.

This skill was less important during action stations when many pairs of eyes were focused on our airspace, but all the more so when we alone as aircraft spotters peering into the sky at almost any time of the day or night, using the excellent vision aids. At such times we were part of a tightly woven network of observers across the country, keeping a constant watch on our airspace.

We were connected to each other and to the next higher unit by a telephone loop so that the guns were already alerted when an aircraft was in the vicinity.

For example, Kronstorf, the neighboring battery reported: „One He 111 at low altitude from nine three" which meant that the machine would pass on a west-east axis at any moment. This was very important because of my shortsightedness. Once I picked up the aircraft, I could then pass on a corresponding report.

Operating as an aircraft spotter was not such a bad job. I could get lost in my own thoughts and feel remote from all that military and school stuff. In the winter months we were protected from the cold by a so-called sheepskin greatcoat; felt overboots were supposed to fulfill the same function, but I always feared that my toes were going to drop off from the freezing weather.

A permanent feature throughout the wartime period was protective measures against the possibility of gas attacks. Not only did servicemen have to carry their gas masks, even on leave, but they were regularly indoctrinated in **gas protection training**. On average we underwent such training at least once a month during which an NCO, invariably dubbed by us the "Gas Heini", would appear in our position to instruct us. We were not only informed about the various types of lethal gases – blue cross, yellow cross, etc. – including their effects, how to respond and protect oneself, but there was practical training too. This included the highly unpopular gas chamber test:
One barrack room that was used to store various items would be filled with tear gas and we entered the ghastly place with our gasmasks on. Then, the gymnastics would start to cause a shortage of breath „... Up on the locker, at the double!" ... „Under the beds!" ... „Ten knee-bends!" and similar. By that time we were breathing heavily and then the order would come: „Change filter!" followed by „Remove ... in your left hand ... in the right ... raise your arms ... and to the side..." it was never ending. Of course, you never found the screw cap the first time until you got a good lung full of tear gas after which the „*sniveling and puking*" (says my diary) did not stop for a long time, not even when we were back in our own barrack.

High-power optics for spotting aircraft.

Relieved from aircraft spotting duty, 14.III.44

Aircraft spotting with 2./695 during combat operations (o). Note the bricks suspended from the tripod – a trick still used by photographers to enhance stability. (HR)

This training was all based on experience with gas and gas warfare from the First World War and consequently long out of date. After the Second World War, the former Reich Minister for Armaments Albert Speer wrote in his book „Inside the Third Reich”:

> »...among our ›Wonder Weapons‹ was a poison gas known as Tabun; it penetrated the filters of all the gas masks known at the time and even contact with residues could prove lethal!«

It does not bear thinking about: what if...?

Definitely more interesting and far less strenuous were the instruction sessions related to our actual task and combining our practical training with theory, i.e. **AA ballistics, guns and equipment**; subjects that interested us and were important for when things got nasty. This was particularly true of our training on the Predictor 40 [Kommandogerät 40] fire control unit. Tuesday, 7.XI.44: „*...Afterwards, instruction on the Predictor 40 with Karli Pöppelmann who, as usual, burped during his lecture. He is a very nice guy but is incapable of explaining anything clearly. Then we practiced with the system. Once, I took the position of B4. That went smoothly and not so boring. Around 13:00 it poured with rain, but we maintained action stations until 14:00 hrs. Marburg was bombed heavily...*”

Friday, 24.XI.44: „*Thank heavens the duty orderly did not come until 07:00 hrs. Lousy weather outside, rain, but still warm. Trained on the Predictor again this morning. First, setting up the battery, then the parabolic antenna, and finally the B6 battery switchgear and generator. Rather exciting. Actually, I find it interesting. The NCO is a really nice guy. Those disgusting blood sausages were served up again for lunch...*”

There was always something new to be learned during the **CO's lectures**, first given by Captain Ludwig, and later Lieutenant Göttinger. They included informative and sometime amusing input about special events that were going on around us. These lectures always had a certain intellectual level. That could not always be said about those given by the NCOs, which frequently led to sarcastic comments from our side.

Boring on the other hand was the **political or NS indoctrination** taught by a number of different speakers and which, following the attempt on Hitler's life on July 20, 1944, became increasingly frequent and intense. In addition to our own senior officers, NCO Bleicher was a frequent lecturer. Then there were „National Socialist Guidance Officers” (NSFO) who came to our position and repeatedly sold us the same old line about the outstanding wartime situation and the new wonder weapons that were in the pipeline. Their job was to fire up our fanaticism and will to resist, and promise us the glorious ”Endsieg” [Ultimate Victory]. Saturday,

Daily routine

15.VII.44: *„NS Indoctrination. NCO Bleicher enthusing again. Already forgotten about what…"*

Tuesday, 22.VIII.44: *„Huth had us out on early morning gymnastics. The whole of my chest is hurting from a wasp sting. NS Indoctrination. Bleicher mumbling on about something. I slept well. CO's lecture, Göttinger was moody. Action stations. Attack on Vienna…"*

A formation of B-24 bombers dropping their loads on Vienna. Note the black patches of smoke between the aircraft caused by bursting shells from heavy AA fire – one direct hit could seriously damage an aircraft. (HF)

Equally political, but held in a much edgier and more aggressive tone of voice, were the visits to our positions by **Recruiting Officers from the Waffen-SS** who tried to sign us up as volunteers for the Waffen-SS. None of us were keen, not even those few who still retained a trace of NS idealism. We were glad to have survived the training methods of the Luftwaffe that were harmless compared to those of the Waffen-SS, and did not have the slightest intention of finding out what might await us with that bunch. Their lectures were presented in glowing terms: the comradeship, the latest weapons, the outstanding decorations for bravery, and the glorious future after the ultimate victory and so on… At the end of

Contemporary propaganda poster showing AAA manning a light AA gun, promising fame and honor – note the War Merit Cross with Swords worn by the standing AA Assistant.

each lecture, every single one of us had to answer the question of whether we were volunteering with a yes or a no. It needed a bit of moxie to do the latter. One of my comrades from a neighboring battery talked about the response given by the smallest boy who, when challenged with the leading question:

„Well, are you volunteering for the Waffen-SS?!!"

blinked innocently and replied:

„Naah, my Ma won't let me!"

By the fifth year of the war it was an unwritten law that, as high school students, we reported for duty a reserve officers; this meant that we were classified as **„Reserve Officer Applicants"**. Eventually we would have to join up anyway, so by becoming applicants we had some say in the choice of the branch of the service to serve in and were off the hook with regard to the Waffen-SS. Moreover, to live up to that other old soldier's golden rule of „never get yourself noticed", we volunteered as reserve officer applicants in precisely the same branch we already belonged to, the AA Artillery, and where we stood the least chance of being promptly sent to the front. Our CO took note of this move with satisfaction and we were left in peace by the Waffen-SS recruiting officers, who were skilled and obtrusive in the efforts to influence us. I have to admit though: they somehow impressed us with their dashing uniforms, medals and ribbons awarded for valor and the convincing manner in which they presented their lectures.

Details of what happened when we reported as reserve officer applicants, allowing us to sew the red stripes on the epaulettes of our uniforms, is recorded in my diary with the entry for Monday, 13.XI.44: *„...09:00–11:00 hrs cleaned our quarter. Assaulted the position again from Langenhart and crept around the houses with Pöppler. Mail included order to report to Steyr Defense District Command about volunteering as reserve officer applicants. Willi and Spindi have given up wanting to be jet fighter pilots. Together with Spitzi Senker and the rest of us, they are joining the AA. Instruction this afternoon with Figl, who really knows how to teach..."*

Friday, 17.XI.44: *„Should have been gas chamber exercise this morning, but praise the Lord it was cancelled. The station exercises with the fire-control unit. Action stations at 10:00 hrs. Strong formations from the south. Direct approach. At a range of 30 km they turned away to the east. We already thought that things were about to get noisy again, but there was not a soul to be seen. However, the Vienna batteries would have seen them. The enemy attacked Salzburg again. Load of crap. All over by 13:00 hrs. Then we had to get the train to Steyr as quickly as possible. Saw our class teacher Frau Stefflin and her house that had taken a direct hit from a bomb. Only issued with provisional acceptance slip by District Defense Command office. In town we stuffed ourselves with buns and met quite a lot of AAA girls. At the railroad station we saw Kriegler, our former medic. On the badly overcrowded train we teased a tiny AAA girl. Then walked around St. Valentin for a while because it seemed bad tactics to get back in time for the exercise. Back home we fed Bast and the others a story that we had been to Frau Steffelbauer's place, that she had offered us tea and that we had seen her much prettier sister. Bast's eyes grew a big as a coffee can."*

Postwar shot of the Salzburg shunting yard showing the massive destruction caused by bombing raids. (HF)

At the end of the day, our ruse with volunteering turned out to be pointless: Martin Bormann, Hitler's Personal Secretary and Head of the Party Chancellery, signed a decree covering the relief of the AAA born in 1928 and termination of AAA instruction. Moreover, all AAA were to be transferred en bloc to the Waffen-SS; we were really lucky that events never developed that far:

»Secret   To E III a 2231/44

Memo

Subject: Relief of the Luftwaffe AA and Navy Assistants born in 1928

A meeting on this subject was held on 31.10.1944 in the Party Chancellery, headed by State Secretary Klopfer…

State Secretary Klopfer informed briefly of the intention, in agreement with the Wehrmacht, to relieve the entire 1928 year of Luftwaffe AA and Navy Assistants – a total of around 200 000 men – and to put them at the disposition of the Waffen-⚡⚡ per 31.3.1945…

[Staff Chief Möckel:] It will be difficult to provide replacements for the Luftwaffe AA and Navy Assistants by 31.3. as such replacements would have to be trained as quickly as possible…«

Midday

After more or less strenuous duties in the morning until around 12:00 hrs, the chow detail got ready to collect our midday meal from the cookhouse. As food was dished out into and eaten from our mess tins it meant that everyone frequently went to the cookhouse themselves as, depending on what was being served, only a limited amount of food could be carried in a covered container at any given time.

The cookhouse was located in the living quarters of the gun crew. The way there was just a dirt track across the fields that turned into a mudbath when it rained. As mentioned earlier, with the exception of the Friday blood sausage, the food was both good and plentiful, and consumed in our barrack room.

Lunch break in our barrack room

I cannot remember what was done about washing up – but given the general lack of water and washing facilities, it was likely superficial at best, but good enough for our mess kits to pass muster at the unexpected roll-call inspections.

There were strict orders on a midday nap for all AAA after the noontime meal. To us it seemed totally redundant because as adolescents we did not feel any inclination for it at all. So there we lay around on our beds, some perhaps falling asleep until the duty orderly woke us up at 14:00 hrs for afternoon duties. For many of us that afternoon nap became so ingrained that they still need it to this very day.

Afternoon

As a rule, school lessons or study sessions were ordered for us high school students at 14:00 hrs instead of military duties. Whereas at the beginning of our training in the battery, lessons were sporadic only, a routine gradually emerged and we found ourselves sitting on our benches listening to the teachers on an almost daily basis.

How was it possible that, contrary to all military practices, we high school students were able to pursue such civilian life activities during our tour of duty?

After discussions and objections of the various ministries about auxiliary wartime assignments for the youth of Greater Germany, and following a lecture by the Commander in Chief of the Marine [German Navy] attended by Hitler, the latter issued a Führer Directive on January 7, 1943 wherein he only agreed to the wartime deployment of high school students provided they were given 18 hours of lessons each week. Prescribed for high school students were three hours each of German, history, Latin and mathematics, plus two hours each for geography, physics and chemistry.

Satisfying these requirements was not only difficult for military reasons, but also for the schools themselves, who continued to teach the girls and exempted Hitler Youth Leaders, but were still expected to provide the teachers. Teachers on active service were subsequently exempted so that they could teach the Luftwaffe AA and Navy AA Assistant boys.[33] As a result, classes began sporadically for us from March 1944 onwards, whereby the teaching staff varied somewhat:

Monday, 3.IV.44: *„10:30 – 12:00 hrs battery exercises, followed by an order for boot inspection that did not take place. Afternoon, the uninspiring gas protection lectures. Then, once again, school classes on physics with our CO from 16:00 to 17:45 hrs...”*

Tuesday, 11.IV.44: *„Afternoon again the boring gas protection thing followed by biology classes with a Captain...”*

Friday, 28.IV.44: *„Routine day. Aircraft recognition training, followed by equipment and battery exercises. Afternoon, lessons. German class with head teacher. Then, geography and biology with our new teacher. He knows how to make classes interesting, but otherwise seems to be a master of nonchalance...”*

With the arrival of the new teacher, Dr. Figl, came a new semblance of routine and order in our schooling. From now on, as well as being a Corporal and active

---

[33]   Order of District Air Defense Command XI dated 18.11.1943

AA gunner with another battery in the Linz/Steyr area, he was our class mentor. From talking to him outside of classes we deduced that he was politically indifferent, tending more towards our orientation. Not surprising, considering he was the cousin of our first postwar Federal Chancellor, Leopold Figl, although we only learned that much later. In time we also came to put a lot of confidence in him.

As everywhere else, school classes began with the "Hitler salute", i.e. standing and with the right arm outstretched, and ended in the same manner. One day we agreed to try a variation on Figl. This was not without risk in case he reported us and then things could really get nasty. But we thought we knew him well enough and that this risk no longer existed. Nevertheless, the outcome of the „experiment" was uncertain. One day, the lesson ended thus:
Figl, standing, with his arm raised:
„Heil Hitler!"
We, standing but without raising our arms:
„Auf Wiedersehen!"
His astonishment was considerable. He stared at us for a while and then said with a slight smile:
„Don't do that to me again!"

And that was the end of it. We never did it again, and certainly not with any other teacher. I did not make any notes about the incident in my dairy – with the political background of my family that simply would have been too dangerous. There was enough risk about the whole affair as it was.

In the spring of 1944, classes were held with teachers who rotated frequently or only appeared sporadically. In addition to our Director, Dr. Rieger, mentioned earlier, other teachers put in occasional appearances. From our Amstetten High School these were Frau Dr. Berta Steffelbauer, our class teacher, (German, English), Frau Dr. Schwab (Latin), Frau Dr. Emmerich (Mathematics); other members of the external teaching staff were our Battery Commander, Captain Ludwig, as well as Messrs. Göttsbachner and Bieler.

To this day, our comrade Sepp Lammerhuber can still recall an incident involving Herr Direktor Rieger:

»We were given the task of writing an essay in German by the following week. I had been granted leave at that time precisely, but fortunately remembered that in the 5th grade I had once written an essay on springtime and that our teacher had read it out aloud to the whole class. It must still be around somewhere. Dead right! Took it back with me and handed it in. Then came the thunder and lightning: >A true Germanic boy does not write such things! A Germanic boy is as tough as leather

Daily routine

> and as hard as Krupp steel!‹ My essay from high school had been romantic and based on Uhland's poem: ›The gentle breezes have awakened, they whisper and weave day and night.‹«

In the summer months of 1944, we were taught with a certain regularity every afternoon from Monday to Saturday: Dr. Figl took chemistry, geography and biology, Frau Dr. Schadauer taught German and history, Captain Haas gave lessons in history, Latin and biology, plus a Herr Demmer who taught mathematics and physics. For the life of me I cannot remember the latter, but he gets repeated mentions in my diary.

That routine, however, was frequently disturbed, interrupted or even made impossible by any combination of:

- Action stations, including false alarms,

- Aircraft observation duty and standing guard,

- Lack of sleep after night-time alarms or exercises,

- Celebrations or cinema shows,

- Sickness and leave,

- Quarantine in the barracks because of a case of diphtheria, and

- Live firing exercises in Rust in Burgenland.

It also often occurred that the expected teacher did not, or could not, come. In such cases, the procedure was study hours or „self-teaching" that was checked by the duty orderly or even by the CO himself. Saturday, 4.XI.44: „*...Attack on Linz. Worrying sound of heavy bombing. We could hear the crack of delayed-action fuzes late into the night. Those poor people in Linz. Hackl and Steinbauer are both in Linz today. I wonder when they will get back and what they have to tell. Hopefully, they did not get caught up in it.*
In the afternoon, our Lieutenant caught us reading instead of studying. That meant we had to get out and work. Spindi and I went to the forest to get pine branches; it was a pleasant walk. Unfortunately, we did not bring enough and so we were sent back again.
At around 17:30 hrs all AAA assembled in our barrack room because the Lieutenant had to announce those who had enlisted as pilots. Willi, Spindi and Zeiss had their names taken. They will probably leave at the end of the month already. We also fired today: seven salvos (41 rounds) at a returning formation."

The efforts of our teachers to impart the syllabus of the sixth grade by the end of June 1944 and then that of the seventh grade from July 1944 to February 1945 were both enormous and laudable. Not only did they teach mornings in their schools in Amstetten or Linz, but they then had to make the considerable return

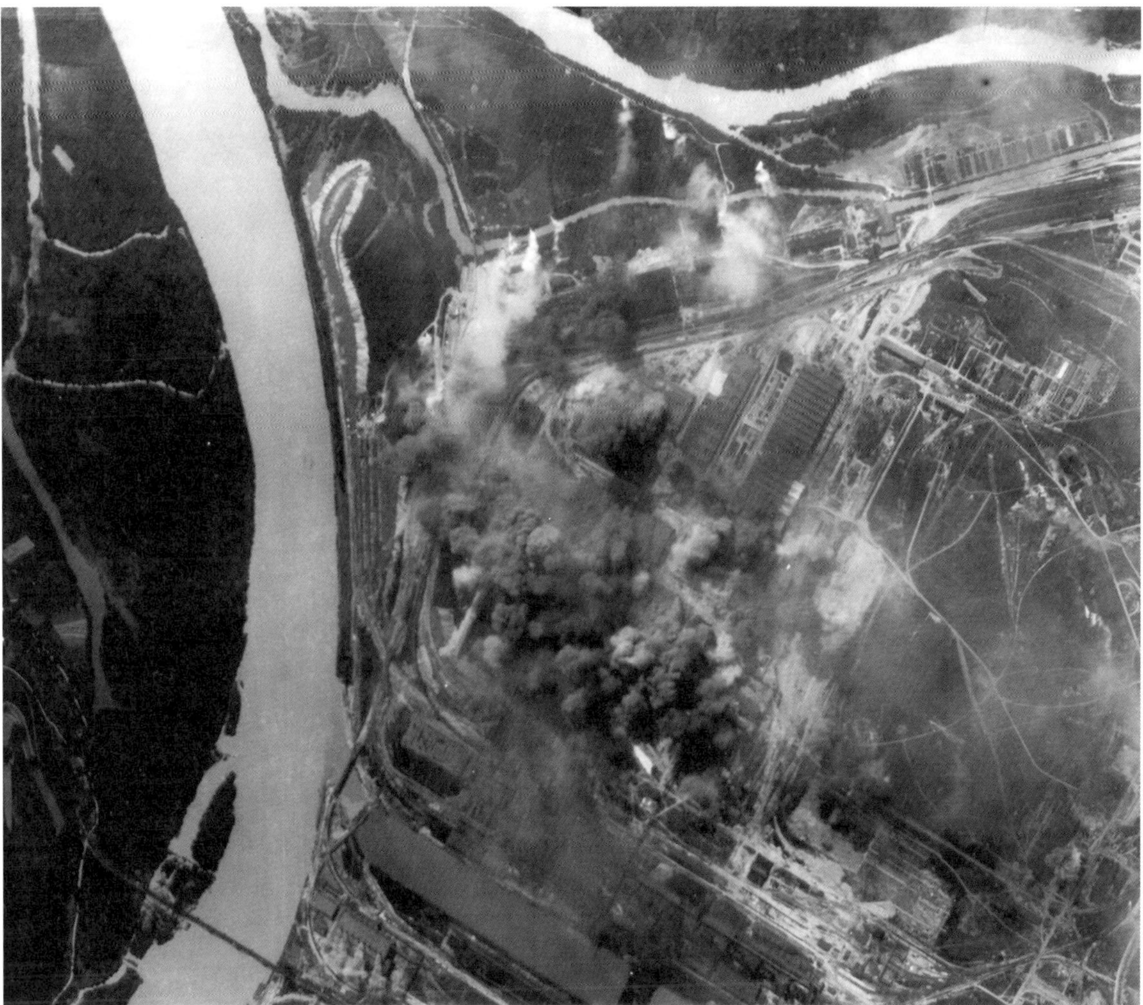

The "Herrmann Göring Steel Works" in Linz were plastered by a hail of bombs. (HF)

trip on foot and by rail to reach us. As the war continued, this undertaking became increasingly dangerous because of low-level strafing, not to mention the inevitable lateness of the trains and other wartime inconveniences.

When schooling did take place, those teachers were faced with a bunch of unenthusiastic adolescents. We were fully aware of our doubtful futures as we sat there slouching and listening with a marked lack of motivation. There were even tests to justify the marks of the AAA of the 6th and 7th grades, but we were far removed from any normal pattern of schooling with regular teaching, homework or disciplinary measures. For example:

Wednesday, 5.IV.44: *„Afternoon should have been a chemistry class with our CO; he did not turn up, but there was a sudden call to action stations..."*

Friday, 5.V.44: *„Classes this afternoon in German, biology and history. We almost fell asleep. Suddenly alarm sirens – but it was just a try-out by the guys from the*

RAD. Aggrieved, we turned back. In the evening there were herrings in sauce and potatoes. Tasted fine, but everything now stinks of fish…"

Saturday, 1.VII.44: *„In the afternoon, Figl informed us that there would be a test on Wednesday. Maybe I can avoid it if I travel to Linz (because of my eyes), but he had better not give me lousy grades!"*

Thursday, 6.VII.44: *„…Then there is a palaver here, or rather in Amstetten. Figl apparently did not mark so strictly. Good grades, also for the guys from Schadau. I should think so too…"*

Friday, 7.VII.44: *„Classes in the afternoon with the CO. Arrived late because I had to report to the CSM beforehand. Had to fetch cider for Siemers at the double and then, because Eggert wasn't around, I filled the glasses. He collared me and dragged me off to the duty sergeant who was taking a nap and said I should come back at 14:00 hrs, then again in the evening – again nothing. Crime apparently forgotten."*

Tuesday, 8.VIII.44: *„…Practically no lunch break, 1.) so many alarms (3x), then 2.) Bertl [Dr. Steffelbauer] arrived early. After barely 15 minutes break, it was time for preparation. We all rushed out when Metzger shouted ‚Action stations!'. Pöppelmann herded us back in again, but we were not keen on getting started again so soon. Therefore, we dawdled back down the track in a long line, with Pöppelmann bringing up the rear, trying to get us to speed up a bit. When he asked yet again: ‚Why are dragging your feet?! Can't you get a move on?' Leischi drawled: ‚No way!' and we plodded on slowly. In the face of this opposition, Karli had to throw in the towel.*
Again in the middle of class. Stefflin is reciting the fascinating Nibelungenlied, or we have to explain parts of it. Then, our mumbling is interrupted when Karli, who is outside, roars: ‚I'm gonna chew their assess when I get hold of them!'
We also note from the pale mark around her ring finger that our flirtatious class teacher has slipped off her engagement ring. Later we see how, with swaying hips, she greets the Lieutenant. After classes we are sent out to collect ears of grain for dumplings…" (See photograph on opposite page)

Monday, 21.VIII.44: *„…Figl taught our class. Took a look at the bomb craters on the edge of the forest. Impressive shrapnel fragments…"*

Tuesday, 26.IX.44: *„…Haas marked me up in history, probably a ‚very good'. Never got such a good grade so easily…"*

Wednesday, 4.X.44: *„Figl turned up again this afternoon. Was supposed to teach. Willi discovered a condensation trail and rushed out to the range finder. Grasping the situation immediately, I shouted ‚Action stations!!' Complete uproar until the false alarm calmed down! Pannhorst inspected our quarters several times this* *evening and threatened to make our lives hell because we had not swept the floors properly. But nothing happened. Only Sachtler turned up who made a note that we had not swept and dusted again...”*

Tuesday, 10.X.44: *„...Then classes with Haas. As expected, most of us had a black mark. Nobody knows a thing.”*

Friday, 3.XI.44: *„This afternoon, Dr. Schadauer thought she could intimidate us. Said that because we had no chance of repeating anything, she would give us all a black mark. In our reports we really did get a 5 (poor). If she ... knew that we don’t give a damn!”*

Friday, 10.XI.44: *„She came again this afternoon ... Frau Schadauer and threatened us again. We couldn’t care less. Who knows where we will be next year?...”*

Tuesday, 14.XI.44: *„Captain Haas was supposed to turn up again this afternoon. Instead, he honored us with his absence. We were not bothered and even did a bit of studying. Suddenly, the Lieutenant burst in and caught some of the class reading novels. Of course, that meant press-ups again for them...”*

Friday, 1.XII.44: *„Frau Dr. Schadauer came again this afternoon and was bitching because nobody had the essay she wanted. We all thought that live firing was scheduled... I managed to avoid it and instead got my gear ready. Disappeared at 18:00 hrs and was home by 20:30 hrs. My leave has started...”*

Our class teacher Dr. Berta Steffelbauer pays her respects to battery captain Lieutenant Göttinger.

One afternoon in the fall, Willi and Spindi decided that they were not keen on attending class. While we sat up front listening to Frau Dr. Schadauer’s explanations, those two were at the back lying on their bunks. At some point it entered Willi's head to do something about his pal's lack of diligence and to wake him up with a fright. They still had their rifles with them from standing guard. He loaded his own with a blank round and fired it! Above and beyond its original intention, there were other effects too: we found it amusing, but Frau Professor not only got the shock of her life, but was unbelievably outraged by this insolence – how could anyone dare to do such a thing! We were grinning all over our faces when she stormed out and complained bitterly to the CO, who promptly came in, investigated the incident and gave the instigators a thorough chewing out. Josef Lammerhuber remembers another incident involving Frau Dr. Schadauer:

> »In Frau Professor's history class, we were hearing all about the Reformation and Martin Luther. I was not satisfied with her explanations and told her so: ›What you are telling us can't be entirely correct!‹. She continued with the class, but said to me: ›Come to me after the lesson!‹
>
> And off we went the two of us, the elegantly dressed Frau Professor and I, the AA trooper in my cotton drill fatigues, pacing up and down the track. And she said to me: ›You are absolutely right, but I have to say these things. I attend Holy Mass in Amstetten every day and deeply believe in God.‹
>
> At that moment, I found Frau Professor much more likeable and later, when I had become a Priest, I met her often.«

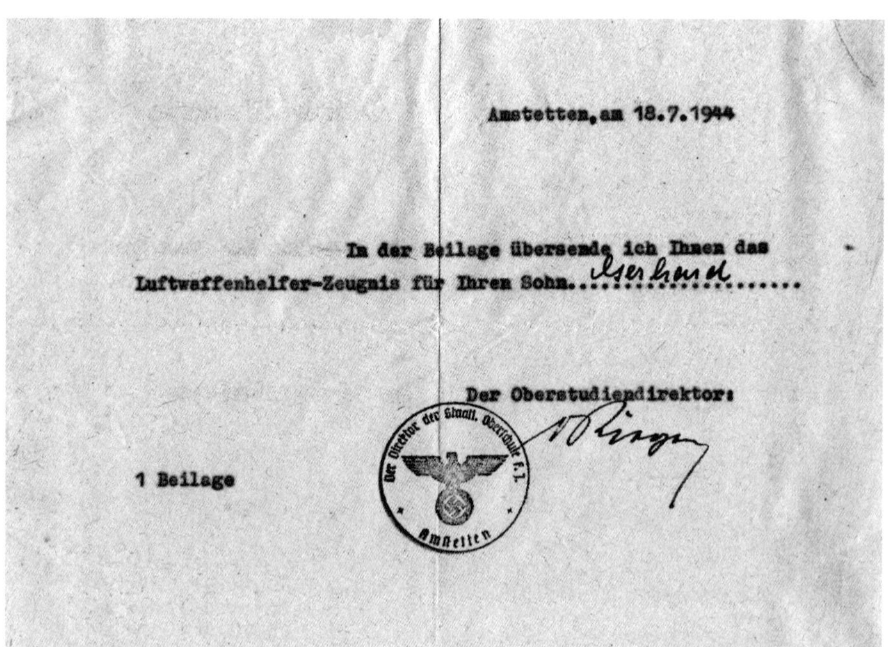

The moment of truth: our school reports were sent to our parents by the Amstetten High School on 18.VII.1944. My report showing the unsurprising barely satisfactory grades are reproduced on the following two pages: befriedigend = satisfactory, gut = good)

STAATSGÜLTIGES ZEUGNIS

Katalog-Nr. _9_   Schuljahr 19_43/44_

Luftwaffenhelfer-Zeugnis

Der Schüler _Oberleitner Gerhard_

geboren am _7. IV._ 19_28_ zu _Ybbs a. D._

im _Gau Niederdonau_, Sohn des _Oberleitner Johann_

in _Ybbs a. D._, zuletzt Schüler der _sechsten_ Klasse

der Oberschule für Jungen $\frac{\text{Naturwiss.- mathem. Zweig}}{\text{Sprachlicher Zweig}}$ ~~des Gymnasiums~~, ist seit _5. 7. 1944_

als Luftwaffenhelfer eingesetzt und hat an dem für Luftwaffenhelfer angeordneten Unterricht mit folgendem Ergebnis teilgenommen:

Leistungen in den Pflichtfächern:	
Deutsch	befriedigend
Geschichte	gut
Erdkunde	befriedigend
Biologie	befriedigend
Chemie	befriedigend
Physik	befriedigend
Rechnen und Mathematik	befriedigend
Latein	befriedigend
Griechisch	

OBERDONAU

Lwh 1. Oberschule für Jungen, Jahreszeugnis. — Q 0171 44 1178

STAATSGÜLTIGES ZEUGNIS

Auf Grund der Leistungen und des Verhaltens im Unterricht und im Einsatz und in Anwendung des Erlasses des Reichsministers für Wissenschaft, Erziehung und Volksbildung vom 22. Januar 1943 — E III a 3360 — wird der Schüler in die Klasse _siebten_ der Oberschule (des Gymnasiums) versetzt.

Feldpost Nr. L 28911
Luftgaupostamt **Wien** am 13. Juli 194**4**

Unterschrift des Betreuungslehrers:

Unterschrift des Einheitenführers:

Hauptmann u. **Batteriechef**

Unterschrift des Leiters der Schule, der der Schüler angehört:

Schulstempel.

Unterschrift des Erziehungsberechtigten:

Leistungsstufen in den Fächern:
Sehr gut (1) — Gut (2) — Befriedigend (3) — Ausreichend (4) — Mangelhaft (5) — Ungenügend (6).

OBERDONAU

Even though we missed most of the curriculum of the sixth and seventh high school grades, and the postwar situation did not allow us to catch up with much of it, all of us eight comrades turned out fine: one of us (the K3 Franzl) became a subject teacher at secondary modern school, and the other seven gained academic qualifications and made their way in life.

I made the last entries in my diary relating to school on Wednesday, 31.I.45: *„...Demmer was going on and on again, the man is a real screwball!"*, and then I left for a long leave until February 20, 1945. That date was the beginning of serious goodbyes into an uncertain future, but more of that later.

Evening

From 18.00 hrs onward, we AA Assistants were off duty and school classes, with the exception of aircraft observation and standing guard, disciplinary measures, action stations and the like. Otherwise, we were pretty much left in peace and we could dedicate our time to self-improvement or contributing to our personal development, something that was extremely important to all of us. So, what did we do in our spare time?

First of all, we ate. Meals were generally cold, consisting of bread, sausage, cheese, margarine and synthetic honey, but there were sometimes warm evening meals and, once a week, a milk soup with noodles.

Leisure time: „cooking over an open fire", the author on the left...

...Fooling around in our positions: AAA „inspecting" the radar system of the battery...

...listening to our battery band "cheery and lighthearted", all members born in 1927...

We wrote letters, played cards, chess or other board games, and lots of reading when we would retire to our beds. I wrote up my diary and in the fall, drafted the "Amusing Retrospective of the Year". On mild evenings in the warmer part of the year, there were long walks with close friends and deep and meaningful conversations. During daytime we played soccer or dodgeball with the troopers once the fields had been harvested.

...reading...

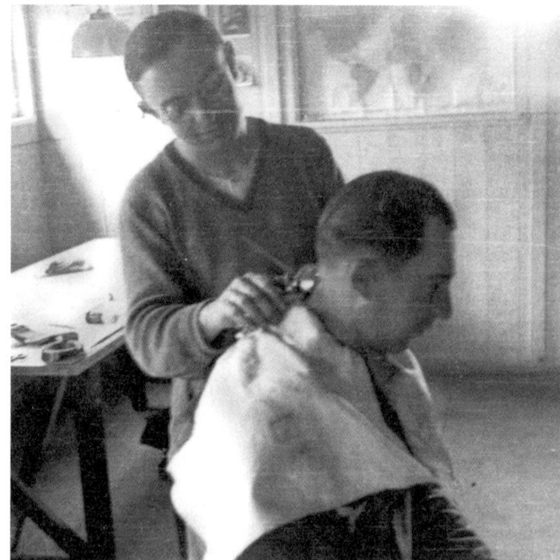

...or short back and sides.

In the cold, dark months of the year, one of our leisure pursuits was organizing fuel for the stove. During the first winter, there had been regular issues of wood and coal, but in the last winter of the war 1944/45 there was no such thing and it was up to each of the barracks to provide their own fuel supplies. Wood was available from the nearby forests, but coal was carried in large goods wagons standing at the railroad station of St. Valentin. Everyone of 1./695, including the troopers and NCOs were involved in the „fuel operations". Going to the forest was harmless, but organizing coal was forbidden and extremely dangerous because it was punishable, being not only the theft of vital wartime supplies, but also counted as sabotage. But what else could we do, maintaining our own defensive capacity was no less vital!

Every evening, groups from the individual barracks set off across the fields covered in snow, pulling simple sleds carrying crates or jute sacks to the railroad freight yard, about 1 km distant. Once there, they would climb on the wagons, throw down chunks of coal that were loaded into the crates or sacks, and then make the return journey. In other words, we were involved in the "Kohlenklau" [coal theft] that the propaganda machine branded as being particular damaging to ultimate victory in adverts and on posters. Don't even ask what would have happened had one of us been caught in the act!

We did it nevertheless, and it was tolerated by our superiors who would not, however, have covered for us if we were caught. Friday, 19.I.45: „...*Went with Willi to the railroad station to requisition coal. Suddenly we had the feeling that someone was following us. We ran off towards the Eisflak, i.e. in the opposite direction to our position. The light was getting closer. We speeded up and worked our way across the fields. We slaved like beasts. The crate fell into the snow. Loaded it on again – keep moving. Arrived back at barracks completely exhausted."*

"Kohlenklau" propaganda aimed directly at those troops „requisitioning" fuel for themselves: „ No matter how well disguised he is, we'll nab him because we are on the alert!"

Tuesday, 30.I.45: „*...footslogged with Sepp to fetch coal. Loaded up, slogged home."*

Naturally, everyone took their turn on these operations. One day, a Flak-V guy who was assigned to our living quarters in the bunker declared that he would not go thieving! Despite insistent reminders and my efforts at enlightening him that „requisitioning" had nothing to do with „stealing", he remained stubborn. As the senior in the barrack, I had no other alternative but to adopt tougher measures; Wednesday, 7.III.45: „*...A minor affair with a Flak-V man. He did not want to fetch coal and when he protested too loudly, my hand slipped and his face twice got in the way of my fist. Franzl, who was backing me up, and I threw him out during which procedure he felt my fist again. He then fetched the CSM who gave him a severe reprimand, but gave me a bit of a dressing-down too. Anyway, it worked and the next day he went out to fetch coal."*

Each time it was vital to get our uniforms and boots into shape for roll-call. Not an easy task considering the innumerable operations and drills across open fields.

Full kit inspection for the AA Assistants around the guns on 12.IV.44, the author is fourth from the left. In the foreground with his back to the photographer is Company Sergeant Major Christiansen, to the right is battery commander Captain Ludwig.

There was also pleasant evening entertainment on the radio, and we lay on the bunks closest to the loudspeaker listening to music or operettas and theater broadcasts. Particularly popular were the musical request programs that were transmitted throughout Europe.

Evening mood in Barrack V: the entire class and three friends.

One such request was the „Lied der Luftwaffenhelfer" [AA Assistants' Song] that we liked a lot, not only because it referred to us, but because of its catchy melody. We tasked Franzl Wieser, who had the best and most legible handwriting, with writing to the Deutsche Rundfunk in Berlin, requesting the words and the music. Shortly afterwards, our request was fulfilled in neatly printed form. About this AAA song that got lost over the years, Nicolaisen writes that he repeatedly tried to track it down and learn more about it. After extensive research, a „...Herr R.O. made contact, complete with text and the melody that he played himself...” Then, a Herr Müller contacted Nicolaisen, but with a slightly different text that read:

>>We youths from school are living
 as troopers with the AA guns.
 Aunt Frieda is totally against it,
 because the war is so inconvenient.
 But that it not so important, and
 it is only right that we are firing back,
 the good old days of Karl May, are long gone,
 the good times are over!
 Alarm, alarm - the enemy identified,
 strange birds are overhead!
 Dollar gangsters are hurling fire.
 The night is black, our anger cold,
 tomorrow a fresh ring adorns our barrel:
 for Jim from Wales and Jack from Canada,
 we boys from the AA are on the scene!
 When the last round is being fought,
 are you, am I part of it?
 Then we'll see Jack and Jim on the ground:
 Achtung, open fire!«

It was certainly not the text that impressed us so much at the time, but rather the slightly jazzed-up melody that, according to Nicolaisen „...was quickly taken off the air by Goebbels...”

Not every evening resulted in uplifting or even useful ideas, there were brainless ones too. Many of those hours were boring and we did not have to organize coal every night. Tuesday, 6.III.45: „...*Spindi, and yesterday Ruhaltinger, put a live round through a locker. Soon we won't have any furniture left...*” Some explanation is needed: for the purpose of standing guard and for field exercises we had been issued with a rifle with both blank and live ammunition. This was part of our equipment and was stored in our living quarters, the bunker. There had been no proper training to speak of, just the basic safety measures. We were instructed never to point the rifle at anyone, how to load and fire it and the like, but that was about it. We never had target practice and thus no concept of what effect a live round could have, so one day we decided to find out.

A chunk of firewood, a large, tough rootstock from the forest, was selected as the victim and placed in a locker. We believed the bullet would remain embedded in the target having already penetrated the wooden locker door.

Having figured this out we stood to one side as Spindi loaded the rifle with a live round, aimed and fired! Our surprise was complete: the bullet not only smashed the rootstock, but penetrated the walls of both lockers, drilled it way through several layers of the heavy greatcoat hanging on the side panel of locker no. 2, and destroyed the gas mask and container that were also hanging there. Now we knew. Shortly afterward we demobilized and Spindi had some explaining to do about the demise of his gas mask when he handed it in to the quartermaster.

As the evening came to a close we settled down to sleep, but not before neatly laying out our uniforms over a stool, ready to grab in the event of a night-time alarm. The two barrack orderlies on the rota cleared and swept up, with one of them reporting to the NCO duty officer who also switched off the lights.

Action stations

The readiness of an AA battery had to be ensured day and night, all other duties or leisure activities were subordinated to that rule. As soon as „Action stations!” was shouted and the manually operated siren at B1, plus the alarm bells in all the barracks sounded, everyone had to stop what he was doing and move to his equipment or gun at the double.

Throat microphones and earphones were put on immediately and communications to the tracking systems and the guns tested by relaying trial data from the detection equipment to the fire control director and onward to the guns. In this way, with the feedback from the tracker and gun captains of the battery, the „technical fire-control officer” could report action stations to the „tactical gun captain” and upwards to the next higher authority, the battalion.

Frequently this „Alarm level I” was preceded by No. II, the so-called ”Foreplay”. This was generally the case when larger enemy bomber formations were detected at long range and were still approaching. Then there was still time to respond, duties continued and manning of the equipment was kept to a minimum. When the bombers had reached a certain proximity, full-scale alarm was sounded and action stations taken up.

The alarm levels were visible on a square wooden board about 30 cm by 30 cm. There were two code configurations: a red background with a black II for the foreplay and a yellow background with a black I for full-scale alarm. If there was no board on the pole this meant: all quiet.

Often, alarm level I was sounded without the foreplay, for example when lone enemy aircraft appeared suddenly without having been detected beforehand. In such cases, fast reactions were of the essence, with only seconds between „Action stations" and „Target acquired" or „Open fire!".

In most cases, however, a period of inactivity followed those first essential preparations and the long wait began.

That was bearable by day. A lot could be seen, for example on clear days, far to the south, a brightly glittering armada of bombers with their condensation trails behind them, would appear to be headed straight for us. As they got closer, however, they almost always flew overhead and onwards to their intended targets. Usually they thundered past at an altitude of around 20 000 ft (6 000 m), which was beyond the effective ceiling of our guns. The sound generated by such a mass of heavily laden, four-engine aircraft was both truly impressive and unforgettable.

A formation of B-17 bombers with their condensation trails behind them. (HF)

By contrast, waiting at night or in foul weather was incredibly boring. We would stand around in groups having a chat or sometimes singing songs like „Sanitätsgefreiten Neumann" [Medical Corpsman Neumann] and other bawdy ballads that we picked up from the troopers, or try to sleep sitting, because there would be no let-up in duties the following day.

Left: the Gun Captain resting and waiting; right: a number of „quarantine cases" separated from the others, passing the time during action stations and reclining on aircraft wreckage (see also page 157 et seq.), the author is reading.

The reports of the AA transmitter created some variation. When alarm level I was sounded, it would operate in place of the civilian broadcasting service, transmitting coded reports on the immediate air threat. For example, a "coffee cup" with the emphasis on the first syllable meant that a single enemy aircraft was stooging around, or a "cake" referred to the city of Linz, while "rain on the cake" told us that bombs were being dropped on Linz. "Bulls" was the name given to the heavy AA batteries and when we heard "All bulls Monica!" this meant they were forbidden to fire, for example, on a coffee cup. "Salamander" on the other hand was the liberating command for everyone to „Open fire". A "buzzard" was a German fighter in our air defense space and if it was "weeping", we knew that it was damaged and flying slowly at low altitude. Finally, when we heard "bedroom – wool" or "bedroom – elderberry" (AA transmitter shutting down) we could get back to our quarters.

Alarms were not yet so frequent in the spring of 1944, but as the Western Allies gained absolute air superiority, they grew steadily as the year progressed. Now, there were almost daily raids on strategic targets in Germany and the occupied territories. And, as the number of enemy escort fighters grew, there were an increasing number of low-level attacks on railroad facilities, trains and the civilian population, even individual farmers working in the fields were targeted.

Thursday, 12.X.44: „*...Today was another day of repeated alarms. We had to get out of our bunks at 02:00 hrs already. But the guys had woken us up because of a German machine. At 06:30 hrs again alarm level I until around 07:45 hrs. Then had to stand guard and crank the siren again about 08:00 hrs, this time until 08:45 hrs. Only individual aircraft. Next, battery exercises. Another alarm during lunch. This was called off by 14:30 hrs. Demmer arrived and we had a maths lesson until 18:00 hrs. Expects us to do a study hour afterwards. What has got into his head!*"

The tracker team at action stations on 12.IV.44: waiting – waiting – waiting…

Friday, 13.X.44: *„…Today will go down in the history of Langenhart as the ‚Day of the 9 alarms'. It started between 09.00 and 10:00 hrs,*

     2.)   *11:30 – 12:30 hrs (2 salvos on a Mosquito, beautifully placed),*
     3.)   *13:30 – 13:45 hrs,*
     4.)   *14:15 – 14:45 hrs (Mosquito over our battery),*
     5.)   *15:00 – 15:10 hrs,*
     6.)   *15:20 – 15:45 hrs (Mosquito),*
     7.)   *16:30 – 16:35 hrs,*
     8.)   *16:50 – 16:55 hrs and*
     9.)   *17:10 – 17:15 hrs.*

The last three were false alarms. Must be some nervous bastard with the battallion who sounded the alarm because of an Me 110 that was flying at high altitude (producing condensation trails) by way of target practice…
Situation in the air was reported this evening: formation in Steiermark, approaching N.D. [Lower Danube]. We were already thinking that the Nibelungenwerk was today's target, which would have been highly inconvenient because ‚Minna of Barnhelm' [classic German comedy by Gotthold Ephraim Lessing] *had just started on the radio."*

Firing bell experience

Of the innumerable action stations situations I recorded one incident that was worth remembering, i.e. Wednesday, 15.XI.44: *„A fine morning, but bitterly cold. Getting dark again. NCO Sachtler instructed us briefly on types of ammunition, fuzes etc. In the second hour, 30 minutes of action stations instead of training on the AA director. In the 3rd hour we were just being assigned to the ground combat troops when alarm level I was sounded around 10:20 hrs. Initially there were individual aircraft over Linz. Tubert picked them up neatly with the radar at 15 – 20 km and tracked them to 30 – 35 km. They were always passing by us until suddenly, formations of 5 – 7 machines or more turned up. I was manning the firing bell. At the end of the first incoming flight, I pressed the firing bell button without having received a command. To this day I don't know why. While I was sounding the bell, I realized that I had my thumb on the button, which gave me a bit of a shock. Considered quickly whether I should keep pressing, or if I should stop. Continued pressing; it sounded as if a goat had crapped on a drumskin.*[34] *It started snowing heavily. All over by around 13:30 hrs…*
Thank heavens Demmer did not turn up. I slept a bit that afternoon, then cooked

---

[34]   Explanation: as I had pressed the firing bell button on the fire-control unit without the corresponding command "Salvo!" from the Technical Fire-Control Officer, the loaders did not know whether they should load and fire. Some did so, but not at the same time which was standard procedure, and the salvo sounded ragged (invariably an excuse for us trackers to bad-mouth them).

myself sausages and took up my position for aircraft observation at 18:00 hrs. My toes froze into blocks of ice..." No entry in my diary, but never to be forgotten is the terrible chewing-out I got next day from our CO.

Military postal service

Because we belonged to a „unit with a field postal number", i.e. an 88 mm heavy AA battery, we AAA also enjoyed the privilege of being able to use the services of the field postal service. This was also laid down in another regulation which stated that we were „separated from the family on operations". Our field postal number was „L 28.211 - LGPA Vienna" – never to be forgotten.

All field mail was free of charge and we could send and receive as many letters, postcards and packages as we wanted. Those letters, of course, were the only means of remaining in touch with our folks back home. There was no telephone line and trips home by rail were not exactly a pleasure and rare anyway, even though we were not that far away from home.

When the field post courier arrived everyone turned out. On 5.V.44, our field post courier, PFC Dunker, celebrated his 10 000th km on his bicycle. Our CSM, 1st Sergeant Christiansen welcomes him, to his left, wearing gloves, is our battery commander, Captain Ludwig.

We generally wrote our letters in our free time in the evenings. It may well have been that some were written surreptitiously during study hours in the afternoon. The duty NCO collected our mail when he did his evening inspection. Everything was marked with the stamp of the unit and the battery courier carried it to the St. Valentin post office next day. There, to maintain secrecy, a so-called camouflage stamp without any location was applied to prevent any connection between the field post number and the position where the sender/recipient was serving. Finally, mail was forwarded to its destination, which was either the home post office of the recipient or, in the case of mail to a field post number, the responsible office of the field postal service.

Mail from home was routed in the opposite direction via the local post office to the field postal service of the Luftwaffe, i.e. through the so-called Luftgaupostämter [Air District Post Offices], located in all major cities of the Reich and the occupied territories. In our case it was the LGPA Wien [Vienna].

The field postal service was a blessing and functioned up to the very last day. During my time as a Luftwaffe AA, I wrote a fair amount of letters and corresponded extensively. Practically none of it survived – a real pity.

What the day may bring

Leave and off-duty hours

Item 24 of the decree of the Reich Minister for Aviation and Commander in Chief of the Luftwaffe dated January 26, 1943 and relating to AA Assistants states:[35]

```
»Leave and off-duty passes.
 AA Assistants are allowed 14 days vacation twice each year.
 Given their youthful age, vacation is to be granted under all
 circumstances…
 As a rule, off-duty passes are limited to 21:00 hours only.
 Accordingly, off-duty time is to be set earlier…«
```

These regulations were observed meticulously in our battery. In 1944, I was given extended leave twice, the first from August 13 to September 7 (albeit fairly late) and again from December 1 to 14. And then once again during my second year as an AA Assistant, from February 1 to 17, 1945.

Once at home, things were logically pretty dull. After a while, sleeping for hours on end and killing time were not the solution either. In summer we could go swimming in the River Ybbs with friends who were younger and therefore not yet called up, but in the colder season, leave was spent in visiting relatives, gossiping, babysitting for neighbors and the like. Just about anything except studying or doing something else useful – we didn't go away on vacation anyway.

There was some travel too. On August 31, I traveled to Vienna to visit relatives. As there were alarms almost every day, and I did not intend to spend my precious hours in an air raid shelter, I moved on to see my childhood friend Gerhard in Ybbs. He was really a high school student in St. Pölten, but now a Luftwaffe AA Assistant on an 88 mm battery in Marchfeld near Rasdorf/Pysdorf, where he was acting as the K3 of the gun platoon.

---

[35] Reich Minister for Aviation and Commander in Chief of the Luftwaffe, Az. 11b Nr. 1/43 (Chef d. Lw./I Wehr 1 III) : Luftwaffenhelfer : 26.I.1943, Pt 24 (reprinted from Nicolaisen, page 262 et seq.)

This battery, the 7./533, was part of the AA belt located in and around Vienna[36] and saw action virtually every day. Early in the summer it was transferred from Wiener Neustadt-Heideäcker, where it had survived severe attacks, to Vienna where there were increasingly heavy air raids to defend against. It had already scored or shared in 33 kills and was decorated with the AA combat medal as a result; we were green with envy. At the close of the war, and after all AAA had been demobilized in March 1945, the 7./533 was involved in ground combat against attacking Russian tanks and suffered severe casualties.

B-17 G and a B-24 H returning home after attacking targets in Vienna on 7.X.44. (HF)

Getting to Gerhard was quite a trip: by streetcar and bus from the Wiener Innenstadt [Vienna Inner City] to Gross-Enzersdorf and then about half an hour on foot along a dead straight road to Rasdorf/Pysdorf in a totally flat field, a rather barren area.

There was the position; it looked just like all the others: tracker and gun crews, barracks as living quarters and wooden shacks known as "Finnish shacks". What struck me were the huge piles of ammunition – sure signs of heavy fighting. The weather was hot as Gerhard showed me the gun Emil that was assigned to.

---

[36] According to Banny this force was made up of 61 heavy batteries mustering 432 guns.

Shortly afterwards when the noon alarm sounded, I was able to help out as an ammunition bearer; coming from a tracker crew I was useless for anything else. Fortunately, the situation did not grow more serious and this time there was no combat.

Left: visiting my pal Gerhard in the position of the heavy AA battery 7./533 in Marchfeld near Vienna. Right: the author on Gerhard's gun, a bit out of place as a tracker crew member.

Ammunition crates carrying 88 mm rounds at the side of the road: a sure sign of heavy firing by the batteries surrounding Vienna.

That afternoon I trundled back down the dead straight road and immediately took the train home. Vienna was no longer that inviting city where one wanted to stay longer.

I repeated the visit to Gerhard on Tuesday, 12.XII.44: *„…at 08:00 I traveled to see Gerhard by the same route as before. Just about everything is smashed in District 21. Vienna East railroad station is burning. In the Wehrmacht Report they originally broadcast that the Burgtheater and Staatsoper were burning, but later corrected that statement. Met Gerhard, chatted about a lot of things and he accompanied me nearly all the way to Enzersdorf. He promised to visit me…"*

The rail trips to Vienna or the immediate vicinity were unauthorized and could have had serious consequences had I been checked because the leave pass was only valid as far as Ybbs and I was traveling in uniform.

Out of sheer boredom I even traveled in civilian clothes to our position in St. Valentin: *„…Next day [23.VIII.] I traveled to Langenhart, as I was bringing photos (total price RM 64.-) and wanted to see if they had brought down any bombers. The alarm was sounded just as I arrived. It is a great feeling to be with the battery in civilian clothes and totally uninvolved. I just went to Körner in the machine assignment bunker. At first he did not recognize me and even presented himself. I did not know what to do until he finally recognized me. Did not learn much. They had only fired two salvos. It seems that Seggau fired quite a lot. At present there are around 500 aircraft stooging around in our airspace at any one time."*

But even extended leave comes to an end sometime – Friday, 8.IX.44: *„My wonderful leave has come to an end; the other diary too. I am only now conscious that I was at home. I arrived yesterday, and instead of sleeping in my feather bed I am stretched out on an excelsior sack covered by itchy blankets rather than my duvet.. Not much has changed. Schmutzi also arrived today. Did not take much part in duties this morning…"*

At home on leave, with parents and relatives

The short furloughs that mostly last two to three days and often include the weekend are mainly to restore body and soul, and to enjoy Mother's cooking. They were never boring because the stays were simply too short.

Drawn by the author in his sketchbook: „An AA Assistant stands on the threshold / with huge suitcases and packages / and when he finally appears in the light / and the others stare at him / he lowers his load to the floor / and sighs: What a delight!!! I'm already back again!!! Load of crap!! It was better back home!"

Occasionally, when the situation in the air permitted and the readiness of the battery was not jeopardized, we were given a pass to visit the market, either to an appointment with the hairdresser or the photographer, or if we needed something specific – but what? Those things cost money; we always had cash in our pockets from our pay, but there was practically nothing to buy. If we did, then it was with our ration books for food, clothing and the like. But there was nothing else that we needed or would have given us a little enjoyment.

Just like the RAD, our service pay was 50 Reichspfennig per day. It was paid out once every ten days and we had to report to the orderly office to collect it. And, because there was virtually nothing to buy, we always had a few spare marks in our pockets.

Compared to nowadays, business was also slow in the St. Valentin market. We found it a pretty boring hicktown with nothing apart from a few bars and one coffee shop near the rail station where we could get something to drink, or eat if we had ration coupons. I do have fond memories of the cider though. Without ration coupons we could order a so-called „house dish" made of vegetables, plus potato cakes.

Short furlough at home: left in February 1944, right Bimbo with his master in October 1944.

We were also allowed to accompany visitors to the rail station. If we had to visit the doctor in the battallion in Rems or do anything else over there, this was under service conditions. In any event, leaving the position depended on the approval of the duty sergeant or the CSM and needed formal and smart signing off and even smarter reporting back for duty.

Our Sepp Lammerhuber, who then already wanted to become a priest, remembers:

> »In the time I was with the AA, I was granted permission to attend a church service twice on request:[37]
> The first time was on December 8, 1943, when I was allowed to attend evening mass in the parish church of St. Valentin. There, I borrowed a New Testament from the Chaplain, which some of my comrades took a look at. The second time was on Easter Sunday 1944:

---

[37] "In matters of the church, the decision lies with the parents, guardians or the juveniles themselves within the framework of the law."
The Reich Minister for Aviation and Commander in Chief of the Luftwaffe, Az. 11b Nr. 1/43 (Chef d. Lw./I Wehr 1 III) : AA Assistants : 26.I.1943, Item 16 (reprinted from Nicolaisen, pages 262 et seq.)

The author as AA Assistant 1st Class, ready for furlough in his „customized" winter uniform: no Hitler Youth armband on the left sleeve, no AAA chevron on the right breast, but wearing a Luftwaffe belt, plus Luftwaffe eagles on his cap and above the right breast pocket. Carrying his camera as always.

> While my comrades were cleaning our quarters and preparing
> everything for an inspection, I was able to celebrate Easter
> Sunday at church. When I came back, I was able to report an
> immaculate Eastertide barrack. Even the stack of our stove had
> been decorated with fresh foliage, the bed sheets served as
> tablecloths and bright spring flowers adorned our toothbrush
> mugs, the washbowls were clean and the lockers tidied...«

I set off one such „official trip" on January 10, 1945. Like everyone else, I had to undergo a medical examination to determine whether I was fit for the Reich Labor Service (RAD) and/or the Wehrmacht. We had already been examined for our aptitude to become AA Assistants, but only superficially.

I was ordered to report to the Pioneer Corps barracks in Melk where I appeared before a medical board and underwent the standard medical inspection procedure. As far as I could see, I was the only one with a normal physique, all the others were narrow-shouldered boys and old men. Wednesday, 10.I.45: *„Woke up by myself at around 05:00 hrs. Freezing cold. I'll never forget the way to the rail station* [there was snow on the street, slippery and bitterly cold]. *In Ybbs* [a short stop at the station on the way to Melk] *I gave my rucksack* [with my underwear] *to my mother to whom I had written beforehand. Naturally, I was declared fit for wartime service – Replacement Reserve I. I'm just pissed off because I've been assigned to the RAD. Back in Ybbs I met Heini and Erich who were on their way to ski camp... I took a bath and cleared off back to camp with fresh gear and provisions. Fell asleep. Woke up in St. Valentin and staggered out half awake* [to our position] *where I flopped onto my bunk and fell asleep again."*

I had been issued my military service book in Melk. When I was demobilized, I had to hand it in at the orderly office where my service record was updated. See page 4 shown opposite with the entry dated 7.IV.1945: „Served as AAA (HJ) from 5.1.44 to 11.3.45". Many years later, I was actually awarded and paid a pension based on that documented evidence.

Movies

At irregular intervals our battery was able to watch movies. A Luftwaffe film troop would arrive at our position with a large projector that was set up in the mess together with the screen.[38] These events were rarely announced much beforehand and could occur at any time of day on any day of the week. They were a welcome diversion from our service duties and sometimes even replaced our school classes and study sessions.

---

[38]   Report of a film crew in Appendix, page 258

Gerhard Oberleitner's service book, issued on 10.1.44., the entries on pages 4 and 30 entitled the author to draw a pension.

The troopers and we AA Assistants sat rather uncomfortably on benches and stools that had been set up. Generally we watched a full program, comprising the main film, the weekly newsreels and occasionally, a cultural documentary.

One aspect that caused a commotion and resulted in protests on our part was the regulation stating that many of the films were not suitable for us greenhorns on „moral grounds" and that we were not to be allowed to watch them. Wednesday, 21.VI.44: *„A new hassle has been announced; we are not allowed to watch films that are not suitable for minors. Pigshit...!"*

Fortunately, our superiors did not take these regulations too seriously. What wasn't unsuitable for minors in those days? According to my diary, between Easter Monday, April 10, 1944 and Sunday, December 30, 1944 we were able to enjoy many of the popular films of the day. These could sometimes be interrupted by alarms to action stations and occasionally included the newsreels; I recall the one on December 30, 1944 showing the swearing-in of the Volkssturm.

Whenever possible we also went to the movies when we were on leave, or in transit, e.g. on May 14 in Bruck a.d. Leitha on the way for live firing in Rust. Wednesday, 28.VI.44: *„Traveled today with Lothar to the youth club in Linz. Really nice. Good food. Watched ‚Jud Süss'* [notorious Nazi anti-Semitic propaganda melodrama] *in the morning,*

Movie shown December 26, 1944: Hypocritical Florian

then visited Hans (my brother recovering in military hospital). *Afternoon in Parkbad until 14:00 hrs. To the movies again: ‚Die vertauschte Braut' with Anny Ondra. Entertaining nonsense. Then supper at the youth club. Traveled back home again at 21:20 hrs. We saw someone wearing the Knight's Cross."*

On leave in Vienna, on Tuesday, 12.XII.44: *„Then went to the movies: ‚Der Meisterdetektiv' ... rubbish!"* and again on Wednesday, 13.XII.44: *„Went to visit Aunt Berta in the morning, ate at her place and went to the Apollo cinema at 14:30 hrs: ‚Standschütze Bruggler'. Excellent..."* And finally, while on leave in Ybbs in February 1945, I saw the „Die Feuerzangenbowle" with Heinz Rühmann, an absolute highlight, but also the last movie I enjoyed during the Third Reich and in wartime.

My modest literary ambitions were not limited to entries in my diary and clumsy poetry summarizing the "Amusing Events of the Year". I also attempted and worked on other literary means of describing our daily routine or special events, even portraying our NCOs and officers as if they were figures from Ovid.

Sicknesses and other ailments

On a perfectly normal day in April, namely on Sunday, 16.IV.1944: „*We did not get up again today. Siemers barged in like a whirlwind and put us through early morning exercises. Won't hurt us. Morning inspection by our Captain. In the afternoon, I lay down in the meadow and slept. Not particularly good weather.*
At 17:00 the acting sanitary officer turned up because Weichinger had high fever and a sore throat. He was sent to the sick-bay with suspected diphtheria. By 18:30 hrs we were all under quarantine. Initially for 14 days. I'm curious to know how long it will last. Great life."

Now we were all in a state of emergency, i.e. the entire crew in barrack V. Initially, that meant being confined to quarters, no duties, no school classes, in other words tediously boring! 17.IV.1944: „*Passed the morning with fooling around and reading. Unfortunately, we only got turnips for lunch. Slept in the afternoon from 13:00 – 15:45. Then went for a stroll ... at 17:00 someone was sent to get our provisions and dumplings ... CSM looked in at 22:00 hrs, I cleared up, everyone was lying in bed, some were still reading at 23:00 hrs because yesterday we got light in the back of our quarters...*"

18.IV.1944: „*The CSM the s.o.b., woke us up at 07:00 hrs already. We lay around in the grass daydreaming. It was incredibly warm ... Pi was sent to Linz for a check-up as he is suspected of having diphtheria, but came back the same evening...*"

19.IV.1944: „*Raining outside so we sat indoors the whole day doing homework, playing cards or writing letters. Quarantine is supposed to be lifted tomorrow. Or has the medic just made fools of us?...*"

20.IV.1944:[39] „*Adi's birthday was a day like any other. At 09:00, Pöppler suddenly burst through the door because we had not been woken up and were still sleeping. It is raining. We stayed in our quarters the whole day ... suddenly, action stations at 15:30 hrs...*"

---

[39] Adolf Hitler's birthday

Sicknesses and other ailments

When action stations were announced we naturally had to fall in, but kept apart from the others while we were waiting for the trial data to be relayed, lounging around, for example, on the wreckage of the Liberator in our position.

As a result of being locked in all day doing nothing, there was often friction between us. For example, I discovered that some of my "friends", who lost that status for a while, had been reading my diary and making sneaky remarks about some of the entries – 22.IV.1944: „...*None of them is a decent comrade, they are all bums with the exception of Lammerhuber, and maybe Lakitsch...*" This crisis of confidence prompted me to tear out a number of pages covering the period September/October 1943, a time when my father was imprisoned in Poland, having been taken into preventive custody by the Gestapo as a "Political", and I had put down my thoughts about it on paper. Impossible to know what other stupidities might have entered the heads of these idiots.

This animosity ebbed away gradually when the quarantine was called off. Then there were other things that called for the collaboration of everyone involved. Wednesday, 26.IV.44: „...*after 08:30, NCO Meissner really woke us up: ,Gas mask test in 10 minutes!' great start to the day. Sergeant Beitz was in fine fettle: 3 filter changes, a total of 80 knee bends in two series. That had us snorting and weeping, but the gas masks remained tight; rounded off the day with some footslogging ...*"

It was five weeks before our patient and initiator of the quarantine rejoined us. Wednesday, 7.VI.44: „...*Toni Weichinger is back. However, the roof of his mouth is paralyzed and when he speaks, it is as though he is chewing a dumpling that wants to get out through his nose.*" No dumpling came out, but any liquid that he tried to drink while eating, did. We kept encouraging him to drink something because it was hilarious when it all spurted out of his nostrils.

Our senior member, Josef Lammerhuber, remembers the quarantine particularly well:

> »...One of the guys in our barrack contracted diphtheria. He was taken to hospital in Linz and our quarters were placed under quarantine.
>
> It was a wonderful time, no duties, just laying in the sunshine or taking it easy in our shack. The Russian prisoners of war toted our food from the cookhouse, the water we needed for washing and a bottle of beer – they were rewarded with a generous ration of hardtack. The time passed quickly when we played cards or other games. No ›alien‹ entered our barrack with the board on it marked:
>
> ›No entry! Danger of death!‹
>
> To which a bug wearing a red-blue bow had been added.

Everything was fine until one day the CSM passed by and took note of our cheery mood. When he entered the barrack he saw how contented we were, but also the dirty water from our morning scrub that was still in the washbowls under our bunks!

He shouted for me because I was the senior in charge and roared:›Report to me in the orderly office at 11:00 with this mob and clean washbowls!‹ We scrubbed everything squeaky clean and fell in…

There were no further consequences, but the quarantine was lifted – and that was a real pity.

However, we decided unanimously that one of us would report a really sore throat next morning. The ›patient‹ was shipped off to Linz the next day for a medical examination but, of course, no sign of an infection could be detected…«

Apart from this one case, I cannot recall any other serious illness as we seemed to be a pretty robust bunch. I am only able to report on my harmless ailments because I had noted them down on 10.V.44: „…*Also I have one hell of an abscess on my neck…*" This carbuncle was extremely unpleasant, particularly during our live firing exercise in Rust between May 15 and 26, because my neck was getting stiffer all the time. And it hurt too.

There were numerous alarms in the Whitsun period from May 28 to 30, 1944, at night too. Raids on Vienna, Linz and Wels. Tuesday, 30.V.44:
„…*Action stations at 09:20 hrs. Incoming flights from the south. 400 aircraft with fighter escorts. Attacks on Linz and Wels. Not in our sector. Lightnings overhead. Hurled 5 salvos at them. They beat it. Tremendous AA fireworks over Linz. Constant explosions over there. 11:15 normal standby.*

The author, nursing the abscess on his neck.

After lunch I sloped off to the medic because of the carbuncle. It is getting bigger all the time. I should go and get it lanced, but it was not possible. Oppressively hot…"

While the author was nursing his abscess, the war continued: attack on the Wels freight terminal. (HF)

Wednesday, 31.V.44: „*This morning went with the medic to the sickbay to have the carbuncle lanced. There was an alarm at 03:00 already, at 05:00 I was on aircraft observation. Abscess was lanced under anesthetic. What a relief not to have that knot in my neck any longer ... acting sanitary officer is a great guy. In blazing heat the medic and I returned to our quarters. This afternoon I overslept and missed classes.*"

Sicknesses and other ailments

Then I was assigned to barracks which meant that for the next few days I was accompanied by the medic to get fresh dressings on the wound. All the while, tension was building up between the AAA and the NCOs. Friday, 2.VI.44: „*Went to the sickbay again this morning. This time Hetl came along as he claims to have had a heart attack. My wound was dressed again. In Valentin, Hetl and I did a bit of shopping.*

In our position in the meantime, there was a gas chamber exercise going on, followed up by a 'masked ball'. After supper, Beitz drilled all the AA Assistants with the exception of me, Lakitsch, who is going on leave, and Schmutz. Beitz is leaving in a week and he is really piling it on for the last time ..." Saturday, 3.VI.44: „*Back to the sickbay this morning while the others are sweating on duty. Serious warfare between us and the tracker crew NCOs, in particular Sgt.Beitz. No leave and curfew. See if we care...*"

And this time, because of a carbuncle on my neck, I missed this phase in the coexistence between the various members of the battery. From the barrack window I shot photos of my comrades as they fell in dressed in their fatigues and with full packs on their backs for another session of square-bashing.

A rather fuzzy shot from the barrack window: "masked ball" – falling in dressed in fatigues...

Monday, 5.VI.44: „*...Unfortunately have to take part in regular activities again. Boot inspection, masked ball in the evening because I got my name taken. First in sports gear, then 2nd dress and finally 1st dress with gas mask. Beitz is an idiot. Enough to drive anyone crazy!*"

Already mentioned several times, the "masked ball" was a mean system used by the NCOs and sergeants to keep us in line. We were repeatedly ordered to change our uniforms and to fall in all for inspection: „at the double – fall in, 2nd dress! ... in fatigues with gas masks! ... in 1st dress!". After falling in we were hounded across the fields with orders of „Down! ... Up – at the double!" And so on, until we were finally dismissed back to our barrack. Disgraceful. This happened all too often when there was tension between us AAA and the NCOs.

Sicknesses and other ailments

On Friday, June 23, I traveled to see the Luftwaffe eye specialist in Linz because of my shortsightedness: „...*Was in Linz today. Had to wait quite a while at the eye specialist's surgery ... Then went to the optician, have to go again next week, hooray...*"

The eye specialist chewed me out for not coming to him earlier, I needed 3.5 diopters correction already! Glasses were prescribed, but I never wore them! They had circular lenses mounted in a nickel frame, plus another pair for wearing under the gas mask; they were even worse, with elastic bands on each side to hold them in place. Nobody can wear such a thing! As a result of not wearing those glasses I always came last in the aircraft recognition competitions – so what!

My health was fine throughout the summer. Then came the much longed for and long overdue extended leave; luckily the weather still held. However, in the fall I started to get unpleasant skin problems:

Sunday, 1.X.44: „...*Horrible itching in the nose. And then a head cold on top of it ...*"

Monday, 2.X.44: „...*have a disgusting abscess on my face, under my nose, my chin and on one hand. If it doesn't improve I'll have to report to the sickbay...*"

Tuesday, 3.X.44: „...*I noticed that the abscess is getting bigger and therefore reported to the doctor together with Stossier. Stossier is suffering from stomach troubles and was given a dose of castor oil. In my case, he diagnosed the problem immediately and dabbed something on that burned like hell... After 4 weeks in the sickbay Spindi is back with our crew again... The thing I have is extremely unpleasant. It's only when you have something like that, that you realize how great it is not to be suffering from anything like it...*"

Wednesday, 4.X.44: „...*Reported to the sickbay with Hackl and Paclik. The medic scraped off my scabs and dabbed the remedy on again. Burned like the devil. Applied a white paste over that, which already disappeared by the evening...*"

Thursday, 5.X.44: „...*Went to the sickbay with Urschitz. He had a carbuncle similar to the one I had lanced. This time the medic did not scrape off my scabs, but simply dabbed the cure-all ‚Precipitatsalbe' on again. We then roamed around Valentin for a while...*"

In this way the eczema, that in itself was unpleasant because the white ointment always made a mess of my uniform, gradually got better, until on Wednesday 11.X.44 I was able to note in my diary: „...*My eczema has healed. Unfortunately, I don't have to report to the doctor any longer. Will go again though to get a slip to have my teeth checked...*"

Parents' evening visit

The decree of the Commander in Chief of the Luftwaffe dated 26.1.1943 also stated:

> »Visits to the quarters of the AA Assistants by family members are to be permitted during off-duty hours«

Our parents and relatives made good use of this privilege even though traveling by rail was becoming increasingly dangerous.

My mother was a particularly frequent visitor and brought me, her youngest, provisions and fresh underwear as often as possible, and looked after my well-being. She was obviously the most diligent of the mothers and I used to get teased by my comrades because of it, but I didn't give a damn.

My brother also visited me from the hospital where he was recovering. As a 19-year old armored engineer he had lost a foot in Russia; my cousin Erich who was on leave from France also came to visit, as did others sporadically.

Visiting the author in his AA position are his wounded brother and the latter's wartime buddy.

Father was only able to come twice because of pressures of work. The first time, he came to Wegscheid, and then to our position in Langenhart in June 1944. The reason for that was a so-called parent's evening that was organized by us AAA, probably at the instigation of our Battery Commander, Captain Ludwig, who was a school teacher in civilian life. We prepared various sketches, while our band "cheery and lighthearted" practiced to provide the musical setting. Sunday, 18.VI.44: *„An important day again. In the morning I played electrician, laying the cables for the loudspeakers that we have now placed in our quarters. Later, the parents' evening, a really big event. Performances included ,The Sentinel' by Stute, Kober and Hetl. Then, The Cranes of Ibicus' with nearly everyone participating and finally, ,The Operation' with Diendorfer, Stute and me. Pazelt was seated under the table. Father and Mother were here, they brought food and underwear. Overall, everything went off smoothly."*

That summer there was another celebration that had a touch of idealism about it. Whereas we wanted nothing to do with the Hitler Youth, this event was organized entirely as a „Homeland Evening" in honor and commemoration of Walter Flex[40], who had been introduced to us as a major role model because of his patriotic wartime poetry and idealistic novels. In German literature classes his novel „The Wanderer Between Two Worlds" was virtually mandatory reading and his lyrics, for example, „Wildgänse rauschen durch die Nacht" [Wild Geese Winging Through the Night]. The writer and poet fell in World War I and consequently, was supposed to be even more of a „role model" for us "Germanic Youths"! The Walter Flex ceremony was held on Thursday, 13.VII.44: *„Dull weather. This morning idiotic gas exercise during which Cpl. Bauschatz gave me the good news that my gas mask had attracted the most attention from the inspection committee. No wonder, have not been cleaning it much… Walter Flex ceremony this evening. Really good. Cpl. Josten in particular did an excellent job of reciting from ,The Wanderer Between Two Worlds'…"* That was all.

Parents' evening and the Walter Flex ceremony were the only events of a slighter higher intellectual level during our existence in the battery. There, we AAA were still a united group where everyone knew everyone else. Later, when the 1927ers were demobilized, apprentices in the same age group took their place as AAA, then the „Flak-V men" of the same year and ultimately the female AA Assistants.

Battery parties

These were decided by the CO on a case to case basis and at his discretion. The entire battery, i.e. the NCOs, the crews and the assistants participated. Music was provided by our band, which got increasingly smaller as time went on, there were a couple of speeches, but above all: a lot to drink! The first party we experienced was at Easter 1944. I made precise notes in my diary – here a few extracts, Saturday, 8.IV.44: *„Today exceeded everything that has happened so far.*

---

[40] Deutschen Schriftsteller, 1887-1917

On duty this morning, bathing and cleaning our quarters this afternoon.
Battery party began at 19:30 hrs. Everyone was wearing his dress uniform. Booze coupons had been distributed beforehand. Things got started with a speech by our Captain; then ‚Heimat Deine Sterne’ [Homeland, Your Stars] was played and the stars were pinned onto the newly promoted Master Sergeants Albert and Schmitz. Hell of a noise.
Then the CSM spoke about memories of the formation of the battery. Cpl. Bleicher made the final speech. Wine was served, with the music playing under the motto of ‚cheery and lighthearted’. The band was led by Cpl. Umland and was made up of: PFC Skoda, the AAAs Strohbach (Struppi), Pazelt and Endres. They played well. AA Assistant Hetl acted as an amusing Master of Ceremonies. The musical excursion started in the North Sea and ended in the south of Europe. We shunkled until the benches groaned. Ours collapsed. Cpls. Bauschatz and Habermann were sitting next to me. We continued shunkling on the floor. A lot of wine was drunk and the noise kept getting louder. Cpl. Delart sang great songs, one of which was auctioned off.

Our band ”cheery and lighthearted” in the mess

We started to feel tipsy. After the second break, everyone was well under way. I stood in a corner with PFC Bauschatz who put a paternal arm around my shoulders and gave me the benefit of his wisdom. After a while I had to step out and jostled to get through the door. I happened to turn my head, only to see Finder with bulging cheeks. I tried to dodge, but received a gush all over my best uniform jacket; today it stinks horribly.

Battery parties

The CSM was still handing out coupons, and the noise was getting even louder. Little Hisi was already seriously canned and under the weather. All the AAAs, the PFCs and the NCOs were addressing each other in the familiar ‚Du' form. Hetl had negotiated this liberty with our Captain.
Struppi performed an excellent solo to roars of ‚encore' until he played again. Our medic also gave did a good job.
Cpl. Bauschatz toasted us AAA guys enthusiastically and claimed that we were fine fellows.
After 1 ½ liters I was getting dizzy, but was still able to follow what was going on. A song made a welcome change.
The kitchen crew and NCO Habermann were the subject of a number of speeches. Cpl. Elfert was a lot more talkative this time around.
Sgt. Siemers also made a speech, but I cannot remember what about.
Suddenly realized that Struppi was missing. Then he came back in and announced that he had just puked. He looked like it too.
Then it was time to get back to our barrack. Outside there were a number of prostrate bodies..."

Then follows a description of various levels of intoxication of our different superiors, and what happened in our quarters afterwards. All respect for our officers and their authority had gone to the dogs, there was total disorder and one hell of a mess. Finally, towards the morning: *„...Lammerhuber did his best to get everyone into their bunks, but in the case of Pi, nothing helped. Every now and then, he would stand to attention, but gabbled without stop. In the end, our suffering Senior dropped into bed, but Pi continued chattering for another half an hour before even he fell asleep."*

The morning after the night before.

Sunday, 9.IV.44: *„In the morning immediate clean-up of uniforms. Wieser had fallen in the mud. Czadek, Willi, everyone was cleaning. I was no exception.*
First half of the day spent with general fooling around. Alarm from 09:30 to 10:15.

Battery parties

Then, at 11:30, the CO ordered a full roll call that I took a photograph of afterward. That afternoon we went for a stroll, really nice..."

I guess that for most of us, this battery party was the first major bender of their lives. More were to follow during our time in the military, but never as heavy as this one. They became more frequent, particularly towards the end of hostilities, almost certainly a sign that everything was „going down the tubes".

Rough times

Allied reconnaissance in 1944

The following activity report of a photo reconnaissance wing dated 10 May 1944 shows that Allied aerial observation was a permanent feature in the spring of 1944. They always had us „in their sights":

<pre>
»Mediterranean Allied Photo   Secret
  Reconnaissance Wing   10 May 1944

              Activity Report NO.H.I.215
              Activity at the A.F.V. Factory
                           of
    Reichswerke A.G. ›Hermann Goering‹ (Nibelungen Werke)
                           in
                  St. Valentin (Austria)

         [Geographic information omitted]

                  Date: 24.4.44
</pre>

1. Report H.95 was issued in December 1943 describing this works as an A.F.V. Assembly Plant; subsequent information has identified the works as the A.F.V. Factory of Reichswerke A.G. ›Hermann Goering‹ (Nibelungen Werke)

2. The following signs of activity can be seen in 24 April. (the Arabic numerals in brackets refer to the illustration & key on Report H.95).

   (i)   At least 8 armored cars in the yard immediately N.W. of (16). The presence of an overhead traveling gantry crane over the yard and railway sidings suggests that this is a loading bay.

   (ii)   Approximately 22 railway flats near the loading bay.

   (iii) 6 medium tanks parked at the N. corner of (15).

   (iv)   6 probable light tanks on the works road N.W. of (15).

   (v)   Other unidentified vehicles in the works area. (some in motion)

(vi)   Railway wagons on works sidings.

(vii) Stock of coal and building materials.

(viii) Personnel in motion near the workshops.

(ix)   Many vehicles or A.F.V. track marks on the roads and tracks to the N.W. of the works.

3. Constructional activity since 12 December 1943 (Sortie E.359.) is as:

(i)   Building (17) is now externally complete and appears to be a dispatch or stores building.

(ii)   Building (12) is still in course of construction.

(iii) N. of building (8) and in a clearing of the wood, three small concrete structures have been constructed; they are partially buried and may be for fuel storage.

4. Little progress has been made on the possible testing track (18) which was under construction on 12 October 1943; however, a road enclosing a triangular area of the forest adjacent to the works shows definite track marks on its surface, and it seems likely that this is used for the initial testing of armored cars and probably tanks.«

Lockheed F-5 Lightning reconnaissance aircraft of 90th Photo Reconnaissance Wing in Italy. (HF)

The long approach to the short bombing run

Whereas we air defense personnel were going about our duties down here, or passing our off-duty hours as pleasantly as possible, the reality up there in the air was completely different, although we were oblivious to it at the time. It was

Above: Equally as important as the reconnaissance flights themselves was the subsequent evaluation of the information gathered; both together were the key element of operations planning. Below: Major General Nathan F. Twining, Commander 15th USAAF, studies aerial photo intelligence. (HF)

only after postwar literature provided a considerable amount of valuable insight into the „other side" that we learned about what our opponents were experiencing in the air on their long flights toward the target, i.e. toward us.

Thousands of men on the bases of the 15th US Air Force were permanently occupied with keeping an enormous number of B-24 Liberator and B-17 Fortress bombers armed and operational for attacks on German Reich territory.

Difficult meteorological conditions on 31.I.45 at an airfield in Italy. (HF)

The planners in the headquarters, operations officers, technicians and maintenance personnel were all busy drawing up flight plans, fuelling and arming the aircraft with bomb loads and ammunition to ensure that take-off, outbound and return flights were a smooth as possible. For the aircraft crews of the individual bomber groups, mission orders were normally issued late in the afternoon of the day before the attack was planned to take place.

Before dawn on the mission morning, aircrews were woken by runners. After a generous breakfast they would hurry to the briefing room. Standing in front of large-scale maps, with a red thread indicating the route from Italy to the target, operations officers would explain as carefully and accurately as possible the details of the long flight to target, expected fighter and AA defenses, as well as the weather conditions. Many indications of potential heavy resistance by, for example, massive AA fire, were greeted with groaning, whistling and joking. The briefings ended with the mandatory synchronizing of watches; and there may have been some additional specific details for the navigators and pilots.

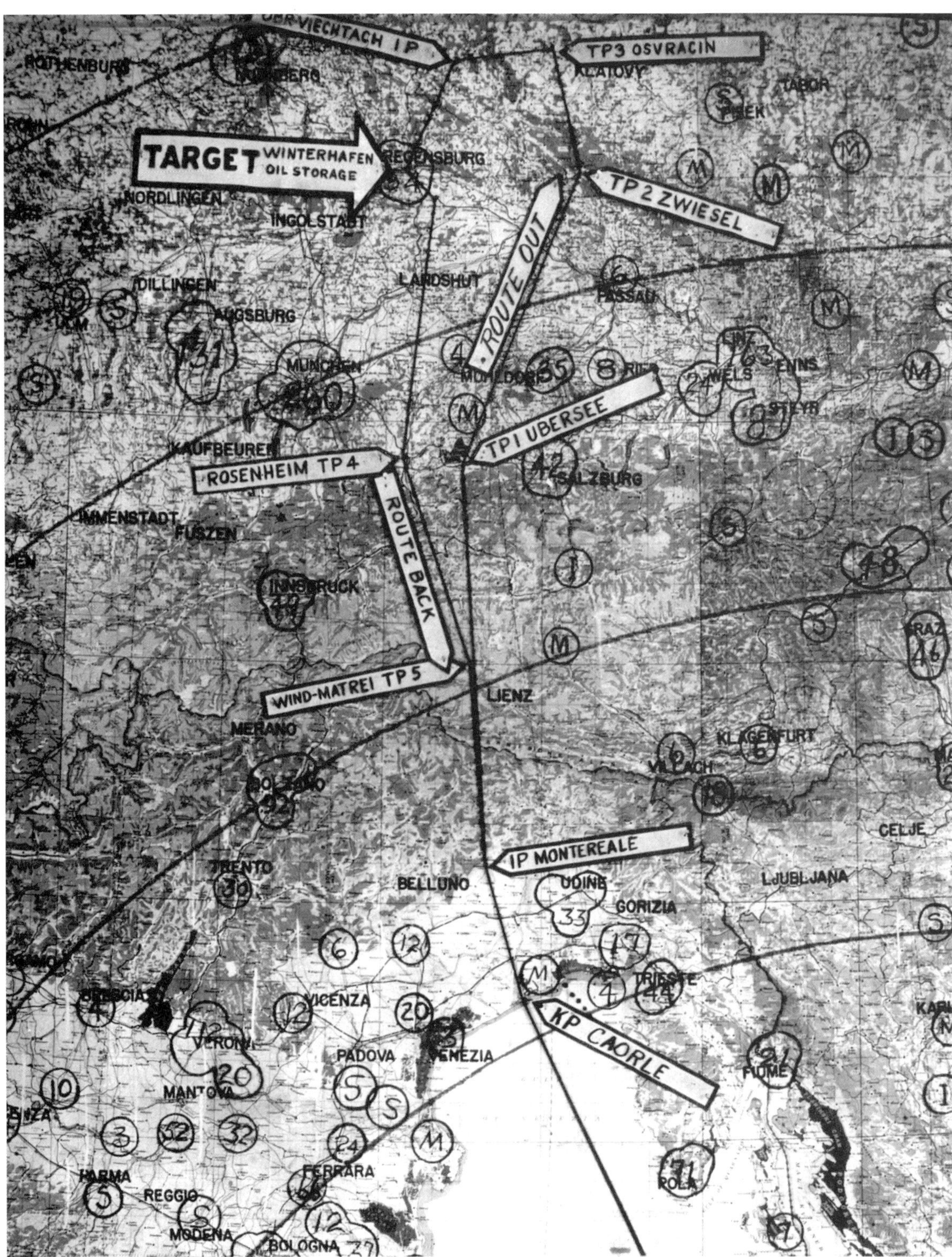

Copy of an operations chart prepared for an attack on Regensburg. Circles containing numbers or letters indicate AA positions and effective ranges. Note on the right of TP 1 Ubersee (Turning point 1) the effective range of 163, the AA battalion to which the author belonged.

Once each ten-man crew had boarded their aircraft, the hatches had been closed and the pilots had run through their checklists, the bombers taxied to their start positions from where, with their engines roaring, they would lumber into the air at thirty-second intervals. Slowly gaining height they would gradually reach their allocated position within the formation of several hundred four-engine bombers. At an altitude of around 20 000 feet (6 000 m) that mighty armada, thrusting ahead of the impressive condensation trails of its innumerable thundering engines, and glittering in the brilliant winter sunshine, would turn towards its distant target.

Operational briefing of 414th Night Fighter Squadron in Italy. (HF)

In the closing wartime months of 1944/45, this was an almost daily spectacle stared at in amazement by those people living in areas that had nothing to fear. On clear days, others including us, all worrying about whether it was their turn to take a pasting, could see the streams of bombers at a great distance coming towards them from the south.

For the men in those machines, however, every single operation was extremely unpleasant, exhausting and arduous. They sat for hours in cramped positions, wearing baggy, heavily padded flying gear to protect them from the extreme cold, ballistic vests against AA shell fragments and voluminous parachute packs. Their faces were covered by uncomfortable oxygen masks and even the slightest physi-

Allied reconnaissance in 1944

High in the skies over Austria, these B-24 fly towards their target. (HF)

P-51 D Mustangs dominated the airspace over Austria; here, aircraft of the 31st Fighter Group. (HF)

cal effort meant a struggle. Adding to these physical discomforts was the grinding monotony, particularly for those crew members who had nothing to keep them occupied. These were the five air gunners who sat inactive in their turrets. Only the navigators, the radio operators and of course the pilots were occupied from time to time to break the boredom. The others stared out into the endless sky, many took along reading material or were simply lost in their own thoughts.

In the vicinity of the target area, German fighters, the Messerschmitts and Focke-Wulfs broke the monotony; then there was not only plenty to observe, but plenty to do too. Given the firepower of the seven heavy 0.5" (12.5 mm) machine guns on each bomber and pointing in every direction, the number of bombers shot down by German fighter pilot was surprisingly high. However, their own losses were also severe and, towards the end of the hostilities, this resulted in total Allied domination of the skies.

American humor in a contemporary newspaper.

In the midst of exploding AA shells, the bomber formations turned towards the target area. The leading machine would be switched to autopilot, that was linked to the Norden bombsight with which the bombardier steered the aircraft during the attack run-in. After opening the doors of the bomb bay, he could still correct to port and starboard or for trim, and release the bomb load at the best possible moment. With that first visible bomb, the bombardiers of the other aircraft in the formation also released their loads.

For every one of the airmen in their Liberators and Fortresses these minutes over the targets were periods of extreme tension. In a maelstrom of exploding AA shells, the sight of neighboring aircraft in flames, hits and damage to their own machines and injured crewmen, their fear, but also respect, for the sinister and invisible opponent, against which they could not defend themselves, grew.

Only when they were outside the effective range of the heavy AA and on the return flight to their bases in Italy did the tension gradually ease. The mood among the crew would improve steadily the closer they got to home base. Everyone was relieved at having survived another operation, bringing them closer to the total number that would ultimately earn them the right to return home to the USA.

Days of major combat

It was surely a coincidence that particularly heavy attacks were launched on our area by the Americans immediately after the assassination attempt on Hitler on July 20, 1944. Friday, 21.VII.44: *„Night 23:15 hrs foreplay, promptly followed by action stations. We trotted outside and already: ‚Radar. Target acquired', and data: salvo fire-group. Rrrrrr. Bang – bang bang. Totally irregular! In time, other laggards turned up, particularly Pi, who was woken by the firing. After that, all the salvos were coordinated. Total of 47. Later, we fired on another formation, total of 368 rounds. Meisters was slightly injured by a shell fragment.*
At 02:30 we crawled into our bunks after a good gossip. A lot of stuff had been blown off my locker. Our quarters were in a pretty disorderly state.”
Saturday, 22.VII.44: *„The day began at 07:30 already with reports of sightings. Ghastly...”*

The next few days were quieter. There was a bad weather period with rain and the usual, routine duties. Sunday, 23.VII.44: *„As always, morning spent cleaning our quarters and inspection by the CSM. This afternoon, surprise visit from Mother. Went for a walk in the rain. Then to the movies. They were showing ‚Heimkehr' [Homecoming] and ‚Wenn die Sonne wieder scheint' [When the sun starts shining again]. First was a propaganda film, the latter was great with Paul Wegener, Paul Klinger and Bruni Löbl.*
Performance ended at 10:30 hrs. Max came back from the district athletics day, he is the double district champion, winning both the 800 m and 1 500 m events.”

Max, back from a successful athletics competition.

Aircraft reporting duty on service with Battery 2./695 (o). (HR)

Nothing particular happened on the following Monday, but Tuesday, 25.VII.44 was a different story: „*Alarm was sounded at 05:30 hrs. 2 Lightnings. Could have fired, but no azimuth readings from either side. Hell of a fuss in the Madhouse* (our name for our bunker).

Expected more alarms, but instead National-Socialist indoctrination. Subject Enemy Propaganda! Lecturer NCO Josten. Action stations again at 10:00. Seems as if the enemy wanted to attack Vienna, took us on instead. Lots of firing, but not as much as during the night. The reason: Metzger. He always want to fire accurately, but doesn't grasp that the more salvos we fire the better our chances. Nevertheless, battalion scored 7 kills. The Eis-Flak [Railroad AA] shot particularly well. One direct hit. The machine was blasted into smithereens. Things back to normal at 01:00 hrs. Linz was attacked."

B-24s of the 451st Bomb Group hammering the "Herrmann Göring Steel Works" in Linz; smoke from the target area can be seen in the background. (HF)

No classes that afternoon. Several alarms were sounded, an FW 189 mistakenly identified as a Spitfire, later the Railroad AA fired at an unidentified aircraft, but we could not see anything. Günter Wiesinger wrote about this attack on Linz:[41]

---

[41]   Wiesinger Günther : Bombs on the Ostmark : Journal "öfh nachrichten" 2/93

>Of the some 165 days during which sorties were flown against
Austria (by the 15th USAAF), one can be singled out – July 25,
1944. The first raid on Linz took place that day…
The Americans assembled around 450 B-17 Flying Fortresses and
B-24 Liberators for this attack. Fighter escort was provided
by an estimated 200 P-51 Mustangs and P-38 Lightnings. The
payloads consisted almost entirely of 1 000 pound (454 kg)
bombs. The attack was flown at an altitude of between 6 000 –
7 000 meters. Logically, this armada did not go undetected by
German radar.«

The first German fighters of II./Jg 27 took off from the Fels airfield at Wagram at
09:59, soon to be joined by machines of II./Jg 302 from Götzendorf. Together
with the Messerschmitts of I./Jg 300 from Wörishofen and the Focke-Wulfs of
II./Jg 300 flying from Holzkirchen, around 80 aircraft attacked the bomber force,
engaging in a fierce aerial battle with the escorting Mustangs and Lightnings.
According to Italian reports, another 18 Italian Messerschmitts under the command of JG 53 in Tulln attacked a number of the departing bombers in the early
afternoon. Wiesinger continues:

>American losses on this day were relatively high. There are
strong indications that the AA also scored exceptionally well.«

AA Assistants with 2./695 (o): the K 3 is loading the 88 mm gun with a shell. (HR)

The American 461st Bomb Group in particular was hard hit. In the Upper Donau area, its Liberators came crashing down in Hofkirchen, Luftenberg, Zell bei Zellhof, Rechberg, Steyr, Hargelsberg, Schwertberg and Molln, but also in the neighboring districts. Many of the crew members succeeded in baling out of their damaged and stricken aircraft by parachute, but many did not.

Navigator and bomb aimer Milton Radovsky baled out over Molln and was taken prisoner. He described the experience in a letter to a friend in April 1946:[42]

»That certainly was a hot time that last day. Everything was quiet and peaceful all the way up to the target. I had borrowed a book… and was enjoying the trip. But all of a sudden – planes – and they weren't P-38s either. I was down in the nose alone. I had opened up the bomb bay doors on the B-24 plane and was calmly (heh, heh) waiting the opportunity to scream, ›Bombs away! Let's get the hell out of here!‹ While this was going on, all hell was breaking loose. The Germans were making all their attacks from the tail. The first indication I had that things weren't exactly hunky dory was when I saw Pappy Boyer's plane catch fire, blazing like a son-of-a-gun, and veer off to the left out of the formation.

Then our troubles started. The tail turret, and with it the gunner, were blasted. Over the interphone I heard: ›Plane at 6 o'clock. Low, coming in, get him Willy, get him!‹ ›I can't. I can't.‹ Duffy Drew, bombardier in one of the ships behind us, said he saw our tail turret shot to bits and Williams (Willy), the gunner, slumped over.

We finally got to the target and dropped our little kisses with the flak something like you could bake a cake on. I happened to be sitting down on that step when we started the turn wondering what the hell I was doing there when there came a loud burst with the smell of gunpowder or something in the oxygen mask. My hands suddenly went numb and I could see that my gloves were torn with blood oozing out. Ahhh! My blood! I looked down and there was a hole in the floor about an eighth of an inch from my boot…

There was flak still coming up. Everywhere we turned, more flak. The fighters were still buzzing around and were starting to make their attacks from the nose. By this time we were by

---

[42] Published in the Denver Post in December 1981

ourselves as most of the planes in our flight had been shot down or had joined other flights which we couldn't do because old 66 was a little hard to handle (tail shot up, two engines out, etc.) She was dying but still had a little life left in her. One German started down at us from 12 o'clock high. By this time Pilot Kane was somewhat p.o.'d and pulled up to meet the attack. The German came on but started to pull up. Kane pulled up again. The German, fearing that the crazy American meant to crash him, turned off. This action by Kane without a doubt saved those of us, who hadn't already been killed.

About this time a lot of smoke and fire began billowing in the nose. I stuck my head up into the astrodome and saw Kane and Kistimeir making preparations apparently to abandon ship. The electrical system had been out for some time so I figured it was time for me to exit. I banged the nose gunner on the back (it didn't take him long to catch on), made the usual preparations, and then I lowered myself through the escape hatch. But the bag of my parachute got caught! The nose gunner finally had to push me through with his foot. I opened the chute almost immediately and my crotch and legs hurt for two weeks after the shock. Just then I saw a plane, a German, passing close to one of our chutes and he flipped one wing over and appeared to be about to come my way when something changed his mind and he dived down towards some clouds. A second or two later I heard a whirring and a flight of six P-38s zoomed past me after the German. I had a suspicion that the latter had missed making mince meat of me by a hair's breath because Kane later found our ball gunner hanging by his chute from a tree with his body full of bullet holes.

…I hit the ground hard on my back in somebody's front yard in the hills. It was so quiet and peaceful that I could hardly believe what was happened. I didn't fall in with a bunch of angry civilians, which happened to a lot of fellows who were clubbed, pitchforked, knifed or burned, yes – burned to death…

I began struggling out of the chute harness when a woman appeared and motioned me towards the house. They washed and bandaged my fingers and gave me some water. I thought I was with the underground. Silly boy! They led me down a path and after a bit, an angry little old guy with a rifle appeared and took me in tow. I finally arrived at a large house on the veranda of which I was surprised to see Korstinen nursing his wounded leg. They finally tied us together, told us that if we tried to escape we would be shot without warning, and a little blond SS guy marched us down the road. We were later overtaken by a large open truck with Kane sitting in the cab with the driver, and the body of Roberts, the ball turret gunner, in the back along with Rogan dying in pain.

We climbed in the back and tried to make Rogan comfortable but without much success. He was still alive when we left the truck at a little town where we were questioned...«

In the spring of 1984 the writer of this letter, accompanied by his wife, returned to the place where he was taken prisoner. There, he learned that the air gunner Sgt. Rogan had been refused medical assistance by the local responsible physician Dr. Grisl, and that he had died the same evening he had been taken prisoner.[43]

What did official German military reports have to say about that eventful July 25, 1944? The report of Luftgaukommando XVII [Air District Command XVII] follows:[44]

»*Luftgaukommando XVII   Location,*   25.7.1944
Gruppe I c

Re.: Evening Report for 25.7.1944

Medium-heavy attack on Linz Industrial Works

1. Enemy activity:

    a) Following reconnaissance flights in area of Linz between 05:08 - 06:17 hrs by 2 Lightnings, intrusion of approx. 400 combat aircraft with fighter escort from 10:19 - 10:39 hrs in 5 formations between Gurkfeld and Pettau, heading north. Proceeded between Graz and Fürstenfeld towards St. Pölten. From there on westerly bearing towards Linz to attack Linz Industrial Works.
    Fighters: combat formations with fighter escort and fighter screening eastwards until in the direction towards the west of Vienna.
    10:50 arrival of a covering formation near Pettau, that

---

[43] When US forces reached the area around one year later, they heard rumors of ill-treatment of Allied bomber crews who had baled out. In Molln, a CIC Investigation Committee heard from the population that Dr. Alois Grisl was the main suspect. Grisl was tried before a court in Salzburg and found guilty. (Dachau Trial US004, began on 26.VI.1946: On July 26, 1944, the defendant, a medical doctor and also the local health officer, gave an American shot down near Molln an injection in order to conduct a medical experiment on him. The victim died the same day as a result of the injection.) The defendant received a life sentence of hard labor and was handed over to the local authorities. After an appeal, the sentence was reduced to 15 years imprisonment.

[44] In fact, 16 four-engine bombers and three fighters were shot down; subsequently, 46 bodies were recovered and 57 aircrew taken prisoner.

picked up the returning formations at 11:35 hrs in the area of Steyr. In total approx. 100 – 150 fighters.

Altitude: Combat formations   5000 – 7000 m
              Fighters   3000 – 7000 m
Speed: Combat formations   360 – 400 kmh
              Fighters: 400 – 500 kmh

Aircraft: Fortresses, Liberators, Lightnings, Mustangs. Returning flights from Linz area 11:29 hrs, course south, massing over Judenburg-Klagenfurt outbound east of Laibach from 11:54 hrs. A smaller formation flew over Villach, dropping bomb load on Main Railroad Station around 11:56 hrs.

Last outbound flight: 12:35 hrs east of Laibach.

Attack: from 11:15 – 11:45 hrs on Linz Industrial Works and St. Georgen (SS construction site). On return flight, bombs dropped on Main Railroad Station Villach.

Alarms: Vienna   10:41 – 11:39 hrs
            St. Pölten   10:39 – 12:04 hrs
            Linz   10:55 – 12:20 hrs
            Steyr   10:50 – 12:05 hrs
            Villach   11:55 – 12:30 hrs

Air district clear of enemy: 12:35 hrs

b) Post-attack reconnaissance by an enemy aircraft intruding around 14:00 south of Gurkfeld heading north along the air district border to Steinamanger 14:22 hrs where it was lost sight of.

Altitude 3000 m

Speed: 450 kmh.

14:10 hrs a Lightning was sighted near Millstatt (ICH 7) heading south without any identifiable target, exited near Laibach at 14:19.

2. *Own operations:*

a) Heavy AA fire from Linz and attacks on returning aircraft in the area of Bruck, Marsburg. Individual reports not yet received.

b) Fighters: 8.Jagddivision: take-off at 09:49 hrs
                64 Me 109
                22 Me 410

c) Kills: not yet reported.

3. *Air-raid protection:*

a) Smoke screens: Linz and Steyr 10:50 – 12:20 hrs, effective
                  Wr.Neudorf   10:35 - 11:35 hrs effective
                  Moosbierbaum   10:38 - 11:33 hrs, effective.

b) Air Defense Battalion (mot) 17 deployed in Linz.

c) Deployment of decoy and signal rocket system:
   Defense system Südmeer and major fire equipment Wieder-
   see deployed, but without success.

4. *Weather:*
   Approach area and Kärnten, Steiermark 3-5/10 increasing cumulus cloud at 1500 – 2000 m, ceiling 2500 m rising.
   Above that 3-4/10 flat layer of cloud at 3000 m, highest
   peak in the clouds.
   Upper and Lower Danube initially 1-3/10, later 3-4/10 stra-
   tocumulus at 1500 m, ceiling 2000 m.
   Generally hazy, ground visibility 5-10 km, gradually im-
   proving.
   Flight visibility 30 km, wind: virtually still at ground
   level, at 5000 m west-northwest 60 kmh.

5. *Effects of attack:*
   A) Linz Industrial Works

      a) Iron Works:
         power generation plant, coking plant and blast fur-
         nace heavily damaged. Administration blocks 1 and 2
         and main stores lightly damaged. 106 dead, 30 se-
         riously injured, 50 lightly injured, numerous trapped
         under the rubble.

      b) Upper Steel Works:
         6 carpets of bombs laid across the plant site. All
         workshops hit. Major fires at the plant.
         Heat treatment shop and main stores burning. To date,
         20 dead, 100 injured.

      c) Nitrogen plant:
         one workshop under construction badly damaged. Pro-
         duction facilities not hit. No casualties.
   B) Shunting yard and railroad sidings between Herrmann Gö-
      ring Works and Linz partially heavily damaged.
   C) St. Georgen a.d. Gusen (SS construction site) not hit.
   D) St. Valentin: no bombs dropped on Nibelungenwerke.

6. *Casualties:*
   According to the District Administration in the Linz area,

around 1000 dead, incl. foreigners. More precise details
lacking.

7. *Specific remarks:*
According to Luftwaffenkdo. Southeast, the enemy formations
were heard to be using the word Innsbruck either as deception
or as a code name for their target.

> Air District Command XVII
> Group I c
> Br.B.Nr. 24057/44 geh.
> sign. Major«

There was not only plenty to keep us AA Assistants busy, but there was also the suspense of the aerial combats. As the numbers of German fighters declined, those of the American and British Mustang, Thunderbolt and Lightning long-range escort fighters grew accordingly. As soon as they reached the target area with its AA defenses they turned away, leaving the field to the bombers, only to dive on ground targets – preferably railroad trains.

Night attack

Whereas hitherto we had only to deal with American bombers and reconnaissance aircraft, the RAF honored us with their presence one warm summer night, fortunately without much success. Sunday, 20.VIII.44: *„Cleaning out our quarters was interrupted twice by two action stations alarms. However, it was only single aircraft. After lunch we were lying on our bunks listening to fairy tales. Then Mother arrived. She had a word with Pöppler who, of course, was sweet-talking her. This morning we also had yet another argument with Pöppelmann. Every AAA was on my side. Issue: why doesn't Bähr turn out for action stations, but is assigned as the CO's orderly? He was shouting, we were grinning.*
At 22:00 the situation in the air was reported: ‚Intrusions towards Kärnten and Steiermark'. They came closer and closer. And then we fired. Strangely, azimuth and range were stationary. Düppel![45] *Then came the blast. Terrific gust of air through the bunker. Dust crumbled off the walls. Red glow on the horizon. They had dropped their bomb loads on Thurnsdorf. The plant was virtually undamaged. We turned in at 01:00 hrs. No light. Towards the end all the searchlights locked onto a Liberator. Every battery fired on that target. It came down in flames."*

---

[45] Foil: strips of paper 15x247 mm, coated on one side with aluminum foil, known to the Allies as "Window". Innumerable bundles of this foil were dropped by the bombers to form clouds that confused the German radar systems as they drifted to the ground. We used them to decorate our Christmas tree in 1944. I still have one strip as a souvenir.

Night attack

While we were squatting in the Malsi bunker and could only hear the explosions of the bomb loads and other unpleasant sounds, Fritz Senker was „on the spot". He was outside acting as aircraft observer and standing beside the battery commander. Not only did he hear everything that was going on, but had a grandstand view too. He recalls:

»Around 21:00 the radio reported: ›Fast-moving combat formation over Kärnten/Steiermark.‹ Shortly afterwards: ›Formation is over Wels!‹
Suddenly and without any warning, the loud roar of aircraft engines above the battery, which is why the observer used the manual siren to sound the highest alarm level ›Action stations!‹. We rushed to the tracking instruments and guns to take up our positions. The sound of engines grew steadily louder.

Suddenly, enemy Pathfinder aircraft were dropping ›Christmas Trees‹ and innumerable flares hanging from small parachutes. All at once, the light was so bright that you could have read by it. Some of the older, more experienced AA troopers said to us: ›Now we are in the middle of the target area!‹ and then the explosions started already. The first bomb load exploded close to the gun squad, the next stick of bombs fell in the woods toward Ennsfluss.

They missed the Nibelungenwerk!

All guns in the battery fired aimed salvos, but suddenly, the cable connecting the tracker and gun teams was severed by a dropped long-range fuel tank. As a result, no further data reached the guns and they had to deploy box barrage fire. One of the aircraft that was coned by the searchlights was fired on by all the neighboring batteries and was shot down in flames in the area of Strengberg.«

Monday, 21.VIII.44: „*Should have shown a film this morning, but cancelled as no light. Spent morning cleaning guns and equipment. Did practically nothing else. Hans visited this afternoon... Figl taught classes. Inspected bomb craters at the edge of the forest. Impressive shrapnel fragments.*
Still no light this evening. Got stung by a wasp this afternoon. Now my whole body is itching. Pi came back from leave. Huth inspected our quarters. Furious that the barrack detail had not swept up because there was no light. Hounded us out of bed. What an idiot."

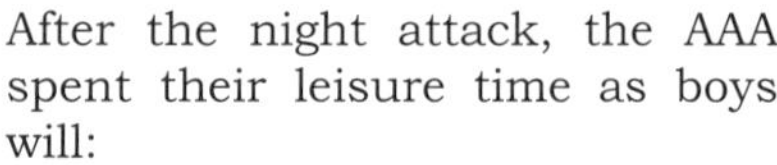

After the night attack, the AAA spent their leisure time as boys will:

Left: Spitzi and Schmutzi standing on the edge of a bomb crater.

Upper right: a group on the Panzerstrasse looking for bomb craters. (RP)

Lower right: collecting bomb fragments in a crater. (RP)

American air reconnaissance after that night-time operation reported the following outcome:

>*Confidential*

Extract

Interpretation Report No. D.B. 188, dated 22. Aug. 1944

Austria

682 Squadron Sortie SM/439 dated 22. Aug. 1944

Linz/St. Valentin (1245 hours)

Nibelungen Tank Works

    Attacked on 20/21st August 1944 by 205 Group.
No previous damage report by M.A.P.R.W.
(Numbers refer to E.O.U. Aiming Point Report I.H.1.)

    Very few craters are seen in the vicinity of the works.
The roof of a Component Shop (Primary Objective No. 3) has been

slightly damaged by fire, while a direct hit has caused considerable damage to the central part of the adjoining unidentified building.

A considerable number of fresh craters as seen in open
country to the North, where there is also some damage to housing at scattered points. The main road and the R/R line to Enns
both been slightly damaged but traffic on both is little im-
peded.«

On the German side, our battery commander wrote his report, following a standard format:

»*Flakabt. 695 (o)*   In Position, Sept. 2, 1944

Report of downed aircraft

1.) Time(day, hour minute) of the   20. August 1944 23:18 hrs
    crash: *Lehen* near Mitterkirchen OD
    Precise name of the crash lo-   Standard form No.   443
    cation, including map sheet   Standard sheet No. 4753
    number and coordinates: Enns and Steyr
                                         r: 5 479 900
                                         h: 5 339 700
    Altitude: 3400 – 2500 m

2.) Which unit achieved the kill: 1./sFlakabt. 695 (o)

3.) Type of downed aircraft: Seri-
    al number or markings: Liberator
                                         DE-ICER   Model B 24, DOR
                                               B 24 E

4.) Nationality of the enemy: Great Britain

5.) Type of destruction and the   a) Flame with light plume
    impact: b) Fell apart
                                         c) Not applicable
                                         d) Initially at a shallow angle,
                                            last 500 m vertical
                                         e) This side of the front line

6.) Fate of the crew: 4 men definitely dead. Excess
                                         number of body parts indicate a
                                         5th and 6th casualty. 1 man cap-
                                         tured in Arcing. According to
                                         him the crew was made up of 7
                                         men.

```
7.) Why was the type of impact
    and/or fate of the crew not ob-
    served?                             Not applicable

8.) Which witnesses                     1. Fritz Guggenberger
       a) clearly observed the impact?  2. Rud. Edelbauer
                                        3. Obgefr. Alfr. Wagner
                                              all from St. Valentin
                                        5. Oblt. Oestreicher, Flakschw.
                                                               Abt. 529
       b) have established the point     Flakuntergruppe St.Valentin Wm
       of impact?                        Rahlfs 3./439 (E)

    Detailed combat report of the battery commander is attached,
    as are 4 witness statements.

                                            I.V. sign. Göttinger
                                                      Lieutenant«
```

Attack of October 16, 1944

Willi Reichebner remembers this air raid:

```
»I will never forget that queasy feeling in my stomach when, as
the elevation tracker on the model 40 fire control director, I
picked up the lead aircraft in the cross hairs and watched how
its bomb doors opened and the bomb load was released. A stroke
of luck that our battery did not take any hits!«
```

My diary entry of Monday, 16.X.44 reports on the long-awaited, massive attack on the Nibelungenwerk: *„Today was again a pretty significant one. After practice in firing at ground targets and instruction on how to use the Panzerschreck[46] sudden action stations. The weather was lousy, fog and low cloud darkening the area. But I felt that they would come. And I was not mistaken.*
At 11:30 we opened fire. The radar was giving atrocious data. I was G1 on the group table!! Bomb load on the Nibelungenwerk, but we heard practically nothing. As the weather cleared again, we fired visually, but beautifully!! 41 salvos.
At 13:30, i.e. after 3 ½ hours, it was over. Action stations again at 14:00. Four Mustangs overhead. Schellschmidt was able to get off 7 salvos at them. Accurate

---

[46] Panzerschreck: simple, tubular anti-tank weapon, not unlike the American bazooka.

too. One machine tipped over immediately. We were also said to have shared in a kill.
Every single workshop, with the exception of one, is reported as having taken hits. We had two more alarms, but nothing turned up...
Spitzi Senker returned from a team leaders' course. He says that AAAs are to be sent to a pre-military training camp[47] for three weeks and that, as a result, our second extended leave is to be cancelled. A load of pigshit if it turns out to be true."

The Americans also reported on this raid:

```
»336 P.R.Wing                              Confidential
 3rd Photo Group RCN., 3 P.T.S.            26. October 1944
 5th Photo Group RCN., 4.P.T.S.

          Interpretation Report No.D.B.248

Localities covered for damage: Linz, Salzburg, St.Valentin
              + denotes prints distributed.
            Numbers refer to annotations of prints.

683. Squadron Sortie 683/724 dated 26 October 1944 (S/L Tur-
ton)


                      Austria

Linz/St.Valentin (1243 hours)

   Nibelungen Tank Works

          Last attacked on 16 October 1944 by 15th A.F.
          Last Report D.B.118 of 22 August 1944

     On photographs of good scale and quality but incom-
plete stereographic cover it is seen that severe damage has
been inflicted on the 2 large assembly shops and on 3 of
the 6 machine shops. Hits have also been scored on R.R.
sidings and stores in the area. Much pedestrian and some
M/T activity is apparent, particularly in the N.E. part of
the works where a large building under construction is seen
to be nearly completed.

1.      This large assembly shop (non-stereo) has been se-
        riously damaged by many direct hits. Large areas of
        roofing have been stripped by blasts and it is
        probable that heavy internal damage has been in-
        flicted. Large piles of debris flanking the R.R.
```

---

[47]   Wehrertüchtigungslager = pre-military training camp

siding servicing the W. side of this building would indicate severe damage to the tracks and road bed, now repaired.

2. Machine Shop: Direct hits and several near misses stripped ¼ of the roof from the building and caused some structural and internal damage.

3. An unidentified building previously damaged has not been repaired.

4. Machine Shop: previously damaged and since repaired has received slight additional damage. Near misses have fallen into piled stores and damaged a probable overhead conveyer structure.

5. Machine Shop: Several hits at the S. end of this building have stripped ¼ of its roof and inflicted severe structural and internal damage. An R.R. siding servicing the S. end has been obstructed by debris.

6. The second large assembly shop has received very serious structural and internal damage, particularly in the N.W. half of the building. Other hits have damaged the N. side. Some new roof sheeting has been applied, probably indicating repair activity has begun.

Prints: 4258-4260+
Comparative: SM/439, 4007-
4009

Memorable events

Live firing exercises at Rust am Neusiedlersee

From time to time, the effective performance levels of the static AA batteries had to be verified. Despite the increasing threat from the air, every battery in our AA regiment was deployed to a firing range where it was rotated through these week-long live firing exercises.

In our case, firing took place at Rust am Neusiedlersee, where we practised „mirror image firing". The idea was that an aircraft flying across the ground would be accessed by the radar, but the ballistic data were displaced by 180 degrees so that the guns fired mirror-image towards the lake. Aircraft and points of detonation were recorded by theodolite type instruments; with images and tracking data being evaluated afterwards.

It was our turn in May 1944. I made detailed notes in my diary. Sunday, 14.V.44: *„Sudden announcement yesterday that we are traveling to Rust today. Order to pack immediately. I was at the sickbay just having my carbuncle lanced when I heard. Packed without further delay... Reveille early at 04:00. Got everything ready to move out at 06:00, departed 07:30 after lengthy shunting by goods train.*
Trip went smoothly. Short stop 08:30-09:00 in Amstetten, the next one in Neulengbach. Arrival in Vienna at midday was great. Our band was playing, the locals were staring in surprise and waving. When questioned about our destination, we answered that we were off to ‚Rustland' [teasing them into thinking we were off to Russland = Russia in German]. *The Viennese were on their best behavior, everyone appreciated our humor and were amazed at our band 'cheery and lighthearted'.*
In Bruck a/Leitha we learned that the trip would continue next morning at 03:30 hrs. We were off-duty, went to the movies, great weekly newsreel and the main film itself ‚Big City Melody' was well made.
That night we tried to sleep in the railcars. Everywhere we turned was darned hard, but I managed, with Struppi and me both sleeping on the floor. The train left on time and we noticed the motion as we dozed. Long wait in Neusiedl, in other hick towns too. We finally arrived in Schützen at 09:00 on Monday, 15.V.44. There, we were picked up by a truck and immediately transferred to the firing range be-

Live firing exercises at Rust am Neusiedlersee

cause we were assigned as the alarm battery. The team before us had shot down four four-engine aircraft during the raid on Wiener Neustadt. Sounds promising. Our quarters are rather nice, but big. Leave is also on the program, so things appear more or less bearable."

Rust am Neusiedlersee in the 1930s (Photo: Allmann)

The barracks above the Neusiedlersee. Buildings were in a better state than in St. Valentin.

Live firing exercises at Rust am Neusiedlersee

The firing range at Rust, directly on the shore of the Neusiedlersee.

Tuesday, 16.V.44: *„Bad start to the day. In the morning we spent two hours cleaning a limber. Since then action stations. We Malsi converter guys were on the guns as the fire control unit 40 was being used. Beizt was drilling the others because we had refused to fetch water for the NCOs.*
I did not have to take part as I had a large bandanna wrapped around my neck because of the carbuncle. Food was quite good. At lunchtime we went to the local tavern to buy beer.
Afternoon with action stations, exercising and, to cap everything: infantry drill. Pretty tough – crap! Fell in at 20:00 hrs to practice on the earlier model mechanical converter. We made ourselves scarce. Tomorrow reveille at 05:30 and firing practice. Can't wait. Turned in at 20:30 already."

Wednesday, 17.V.44: *„Today we fired for the first time. Quite loud... We were not bad at all, not a shot outside the permissible target area... Off-duty: Rust is a boring hick town. But pretty. The camp is only 30 minutes from the main square. Wine is important here. Particularly delightful are the storks, and the town crier with his drum is interesting, but that is about all.*
Firing is scheduled for this evening, too..."

Thursday, 18.V.44: *„There was live firing yesterday evening. We did not get to fire but turned in at 18:00 already. Other batteries were firing throughout the night until 01:00, but we were fast asleep.*
This morning live firing using the Malsi converter. At lunch we were relieved as the alarm battery. By truck to camp where they were showing a movie: ‚The Wife' with Jenny Jugo, very nice. We could have gone into town, but I had a wash and wrote letters. We have to be up early again tomorrow."

Live firing exercises at Rust am Neusiedlersee

The other batteries night firing

Friday, 19.V.44: „*Reveille at 06:00, march-off to firing range 07:00 hrs. Dreadful singing. Firing with the fire-control unit in the morning, lousy results, at the double back to barracks. Rest after eating and then swimming. Then singing and review of the visual trials with the fire-control director, evening meal, tasteless milk soup, much better in the battery.*
More singing supervised by the CSM. Minor clash with Bast, who thought he could wind me up. Our band played a little on the hill above the camp. Then writing letters."

Saturday, 20.V.44: „*Reveille at 07:00, march-off to the firing range at 09:00 hrs. Firing was cancelled because of poor visibility. On the way back only we AAAs provided the musical accompaniment. We whistled, sang and marched at our own pace. The troopers could not keep up with us. Unfortunately, Siemers was in a bad mood and we had to march all over again. We snappy AAAs could turn more quickly because we really are sharper, but we certainly did work up a sweat.*
Roll call at 15:00 in no. 1 dress. Idiotic. ¾ of us got our names taken. Not surprising. Sports with 'Lofty' in the afternoon. Then hanging around doing nothing, swimming, writing letters, updating diaries, jawing until last post. Have also discovered something interesting: nowadays, I can sleep well and soundly during the day. Moreover, I have developed one hell of an appetite even though I have not squatted on the latrine for days."

Sunday, 21.V.44: „*Singing in the morning. Then, leisure time. This afternoon it was unclear whether we would be firing this evening or not. Off-duty until 19:00 hrs. Waited with Bast for an extension. When nothing was announced we went to St. Margarethen. Lucky to hitch a lift in a car.*
The movie started at 17:30. Wallner and I were on the way back to barracks when we bumped into Sgt. Bohne, who informed us about the extension. Whizzed back into town which is why I watched the movie ‚The Bathtub on the Barnhouse Floor'. Most enjoyable.
Eight of us marched in line back to barracks. Behind us the CSM. Suddenly ‚left

turn, march!'– we execute the order and stand pissing at the edge of the road...
Then at the double back home. At 22:00, P..., Lewi and Weilharter turn up drunk
as skunks. Fine affair. Siemers shouting, the CSM roaring...
I am writing these lines with the last of the ink in my fountain pen + H_2O. I am out
of ammunition."

Monday, 22.V.44: *„Reveille at 05:30, march-off to firing range at 06:30. Firing with*
the Malsi converter. March back to barracks, leisure time until lunch. Afternoon rest
and then review of firing results. Invariably good at the beginning, then they dete-
riorate. After that, evening meal and off-duty time. I stay in our quarters. Find eve-
ryone childish and dumb."

Marching to the firing range – *„dreadful singing"*

Tuesday, 23.V.44: *„reveille at 07:00. Marched once again to the firing range but*
did not fire because the target drone disappeared once the first battery had fired
its salvos. Action stations from 10:30 to 11:00. Nothing turned up though. Bitterly
cold though, and the wind is blowing hard. Marched back to barracks at the
double. Thank heavens we did not get into a sweat.
Yesterday I forgot my mug in another barrack. Can't be found today, I guess that
Lothar has confiscated it. Got a card from my Mother sent from Maria Zell. They are
doing well. Have to stop now. Still have lots on my mind, but have run out of ink."

Wednesday, 24.V.44: „*Reveille at 06:00, march-off to the firing range at 07:00 hrs. Fired from 08:30 to 10:00 and then suddenly action stations. Rushed back to camp. Sighted masses of Americans on the way. Alarm battery fired everything, including 10.5 cm. Well placed shots. Shells were bursting directly ahead of the Yankees' noses. Right above us too. Got into cover. Continued our march. By then the Americans had already scooted again..*
Magnificent aerial combats while we were marching. Siemers was off his head again. Two Americans (fighters) were chasing an Me 109, but it side-slipped them elegantly and escaped. Sound of firing in the air. Endless new waves. And the rumbling in the Wiener Neustadt is formidable.

We leave at 14:00 by truck. Still no train by 14:30. Waited until 18:30 and things got hot.
Hetl and Pazelt earned 4 points each because the served as aircraft trackers with the alarm battery that scored two kills. They should have such luck.
At 20:00 we arrive in Bruck. Standing around the whole night. Struppi and I elect to sleep on the floor again."

Back to the railroad station by truck...

Thursday, 25.V.44: „*About yesterday: before we turned in, an airman told us about his experiences. Highly exciting.*
The abscess prevented me from sleeping well. Still in Bruck. There is supposed to have been a stick of bombs that destroyed the railroad track bed and a locomotive ran straight into it. Great. Scuttlebutt says that we will be diverted via Vienna. We will see.
At 10:30, we march the 2 ½ km to Bruck to eat. In the evening, our band plays in the open air. Complete success. The troops, who traded postage stamps for ciga-rettes, were thrilled. At 21:30 we settled down to sleep again. At midnight we final-ly moved off."

Live firing exercises at Rust am Neusiedlersee

... and onwards with the Reichsbahn until the journey is interrupted. The author is the second serviceman in the passenger car.

The damaged railroad track and the derailed goods train locomotive in the background.

No lack of entertainment.

The derailed wartime Class 52 locomotive

Friday, 26.V.44: *„Daybreak found us in Grammat Neusiedl. Still not even in Vienna. After an hour, journey continued to Himberg. After yet another hour, we moved off again, and rolled past the destroyed location.*
Numerous bomb craters (150). A toppled war locomotive. Traveled to Vienna without a break. Just stood for a while at Unter-Purkersdorf. Then, straight through to Amstetten. Had an hour on my hands. I phoned home, but unfortunately, Mother had gone to St. Valentin! We reached that hick town at 21:00 hrs."

Saturday, 27.V.44: *„It is amazing how quickly you settle back into life in the position. This morning was spent cleaning our barrack and kit..."*

Normandy Invasion

My diary contains little about the tragic events of the war. We were too preoccupied with ourselves and registered what was happening in the immediate vicinity, and there was a fair amount going on. We were regularly informed about events by the relentless propaganda machine via newspapers and the radio, but we were aware that what we were being fed had little to do with the reality of things. A great deal was concealed from us, too.

For example, we heard nothing about the Moscow Declaration that was made public on November 1, 1943. In it, the Allies declared their intention to re-establish Austria, the first country to fall victim to Hitlerite aggression, as a free nation after the war. For us Austrians that would have been a really interesting piece of information.

We also learned a lot from Allied broadcasts when we were home on leave, even though tuning into them was strictly prohibited. Passing on such news was severely punished. Again and again we read of death sentences being pronounced for listening to enemy transmitters. But people still did it. Mother in particular drew hope from those sources, and so did I.

The Allied landings in Normandy, however, were also reported by our side. Tuesday, 6.VI.44: *„Invasion!!! Terrific battle being fought. British have landed in the Seine Estuary. Hope the outcome will be decisive. Rome fell yesterday. In the morning Company Commander's lecture with 1st Lt. Lanz. Very nice guy. Wish he were our battery captain. None of us are going on leave. CSM is being pig-headed. The troops are all confined to barracks. Then why can't they let us go? Senker has not had any leave for 11 weeks already...*
Classes again this afternoon. There was quite an invasion in our barrack this evening. Senker and Wieser are slugging it out. Things flying around from both sides..."

Wednesday, 7.VII.44: *„Battle against the invasion force is continuing with relentless ferocity. They are hard at it in Italy as well. Confined to barracks..."*

I did make some notes about other wartime events, but only brief ones. Saturday, 17.VI.44: *„Company Commander's lecture this morning. Retribution has begun. Secret weapons! ..."*

Sunday, 18.VI.44: *„...Retaliation continues. In the German Championship, Dresden won 4:0 against LSV Hamburg. Brainless gas mask exercise this morning..."*

Friday, 8.IX.44: *„...After lunch we slept until 15:00 hrs. Then Karli woke us up, he wanted to let off steam, but Willi defiantly declared: ,Herr Unteroffizier, you only just got up yourself.' Karli sloped off...*

Situation: both sides of Lüttich under enemy pressure moving east. Tactical withdrawal from Ypres to the north. Fighting on the Italian-French front. Pressure on the Adriatic coast. Soviets in southeast Siebenbürgen. Bulgaria has changed sides. Strong demands from Romania."

Saturday, 9.IX.44: „*...In the evening, the 1927s went on a bender in civilian clothes. Situation: fighting around Brest, St. Nazaire, Boulogne and Dunkirk; Metz, Verdun. Battles..."*

Assassination attempt on Hitler

Thursday, 20.VII.44: „*Big day today. Visual training with fire-control unit, again in the afternoon. At 18:28 hrs there was a report that there had been an assassination attempt on the Führer. He, however, came out unscathed. Imminent danger of rebellion by foreign laborers."*

As far as I can remember, we were already off-duty and were enjoying our leisure time playing table tennis outside the barrack. It was a beautiful summer evening when someone inside shouted through the window:
„Attempt on the life of the Führer!"
And I, without thinking, asked:
„Has he been done in?"
Then someone said to me:
„You're nuts!?"

Of course, nothing about that exchange is mentioned in my diary. However, on Friday, 21.VII.44: „*Battalion order: all men are to be woken up because of a speech to be made by the Führer. At 12:45 hrs. He simply said that anyone issuing illegal orders against the N.S. government would be shot. Then we went back to sleep. Well barricaded.*
In the morning, action stations from 10:00 – 13:00 hrs. Most of the Yankees persisted in avoiding our area. Then, 3 Mustangs flew overhead, but Pöppler screwed up and we were unable to fire. One hell of a commotion..."

Wednesday, 26.VII.44: „*...In the evening, a small function in the battery to celebrate the failure of the assassination attempt on the Führer. Then we listened to a speech by Dr. Goebbels. He described the events of the attempt and drew his conclusions from it. We also learned that Field Marshall von Witzleben had been part of the plot."*

The affair with the rifle

In the late summer of 1944, following the plot against Hitler, we AAAs were equipped with Italian rifles. We were not given any particular instruction on how to handle them because they were intended for a new arrangement in our duties, i.e. standing guard, previously a job for the troops only. The reason for the increased level of vigilance was the considerable number of foreign labor camps in the surrounding industrial area, and the potential risk of uprisings. Moreover, the Mauthausen concentration camp was close by.

Consequence of the attempt on Hitler's life: AAA were equipped with rifles, stood guard and drilled in the muddy fields for good measure.

Now, in addition to our aircraft tracking duties, we had to stand guard, patrolling up and down the Thurnsdorferstrasse with our rifles shouldered, chatting to each other and trying not to forget the password that was changed every day. We were instructed what to do if any suspicious individuals approached, but fortunately that never occurred. But on Thursday, 28.IX.44: „*The old NCO woke us up at 07:30 and told us we had to get up. We confirmed that we had understood, at which he disappeared evidently satisfied. Unfortunately, I was due to stand guard again at 08:00 and had to crawl out of my bunk. Gamperl and I were on duty. We noticed a man who was up to something in the field near the foxholes and loaded. I also loaded Gamperl's rifle and wanted to put it on safe when a shot went off. Quite a shock. Explained the situation to the Lieutenant who had immediately come rushing out and everything was OK again. As a result, Umland finally taught us to load and secure properly... New arrangement in the battery: temporarily subordinated for guard duties. Seems strange to me...*"

Apart from our superiors realizing that we were somewhat lacking in the military training sector - for example, we never practiced live rifle fire – this incident did

not have any further consequences. One day, however, almost two months later, on Wednesday, 22.XI.44: „*...After 10 minutes break, action stations again at 13:10 hrs. Burgart and I were just about to walk to the mess when we heard the siren of the Railroad AA. As we turned, our alarm sounded too. 3 Mustangs acquired at their turning point. Did not fire. Unfortunately. Demmer was here again.*
Then the armorer NCO turned up and said that I should go to battalion and explain to a captain why the screws on the bolt could turn down (which is how the round discharged from the rifle). *I grabbed the carbine and slouched off down there with mixed feelings. Explained the situation to the Captain, was chewed out a bit by a Master Sergeant about not becoming an officer, that he would write to the Ministry for Youth, etc.* [Back at camp again] *I tell the Lieutenant, who says, ‚he can kiss our ...'! I explain that I had thought exactly the same, to which he replied: ‚Correct, dead right. That was the best thing you could do!'*"

Barracks of the battalion in Rems: headquarters of the command post to which we reported, the field medical officer and other administrative offices.

But, coming back to that specific, quite feasible situation: what would have happened if the suspect in the field had really come closer, had not given the password, and we would have been forced to shoot? It does not bear thinking about!

Promoted to Luftwaffe Assistant First Class

Item 11 of the decree of the Reich Minister for Aviation and Commander in Chief of the Luftwaffe dated January 26, 1943 states:[48]

---

[48]   The Reich Minister for Aviation and Commander in Chief of the Luftwaffe, Az. 11b Nr. 1/43 (Chef d. Lw./I Wehr 1 III) : Luftwaffe Assistants : 26.I.1943, Pt 11 (reproduced from Nicolaisen page 262 et seq.)

Promoted to Luftwaffe Assistant First Class

```
»Ranks and promotions.
 The ranks of the AAA are ›Luftwaffe Assistant‹ (Lw.-Helfer)
 and ›Luftwaffe Assistant 1st Class‹(Lw.-Ob.-Helfer).
 Promotion to AAA 1st Class is possible after 9 months of good
 conduct and performance…«
```

Our predecessors, the boys born in 1927, who had already joined up on September 10, 1943 had been promoted to AAA 1st Class on June 20, 1944. Now it was our turn. Thursday, 5.X.44: *„… Today it is 9 months since we joined the club. When the CSM called us into the mess, we thought we were going to be promoted to ΛAA 1st Class. But he had only a load of rubbish for us. Handed out sector triangles. Then explained that if there were to be fighting, we AAA would be issued the AAA triangles. Load of crap! All of a sudden we're supposed to be soldiers. But we are not even allowed to go to some movies...”*

Saturday, 21.X.44: *„…Arrived back at 12:00 hrs* (from short leave). *Nothing much has changed really. Only that we have become AAA 1st Class. Therefore, did not wear the ribbon on leave for nothing...”*

Warm-up to the party – left: still with the NCO, right: evidently at a very late hour

Now it was time to throw a real party! Tuesday, 24.X.44: *„Quite an eventful day. Not during the 2 hours guard duty, but later on. Battery exercises as usual, lunch break as usual. Capt. Haas took a class in Latin. Still reading Livius. Great. It is about to start:*
In the break we are standing in front of the barrack, chewing bread and margarine and deep in profound discussion, when suddenly, three girls come waltzing up the road. They are heavily laden with parcels. There is a shout: ,Bast, you are about to get a visit!' He burst outside and demands to know: ,Damn, what am I supposed to do with the wenches?' They are his sister, Berti Steiner (strapping) and the Bast family girls. They declared that they have come to visit all of us. Captain Haas wandered around with us and we made a lot of row in Barrack 3. At 17:00 the mystery was solved: Frau Bast had heard about the promotion of us four and, armed with empty bottles, had phoned all the parents who produced the goodies.

Now, the fruit and cookies piled up, as did the cider and schnapps (contributed by us). A number of congratulatory letters arrived. That was all great. We really enjoyed ourselves and wound up Tubert, who promised us an unforgiving barrack room inspection. We accompanied the girls as far as the Panzerstrasse and then had to return to take part in the exercise. It did not last long, however, as everything went smoothly and we were able to continue eating. Any leftovers were carefully stashed. We then squatted around our booze and the day was over.

Tubert, by the way, did not carry out his inspection because we gave him some of our cake..."

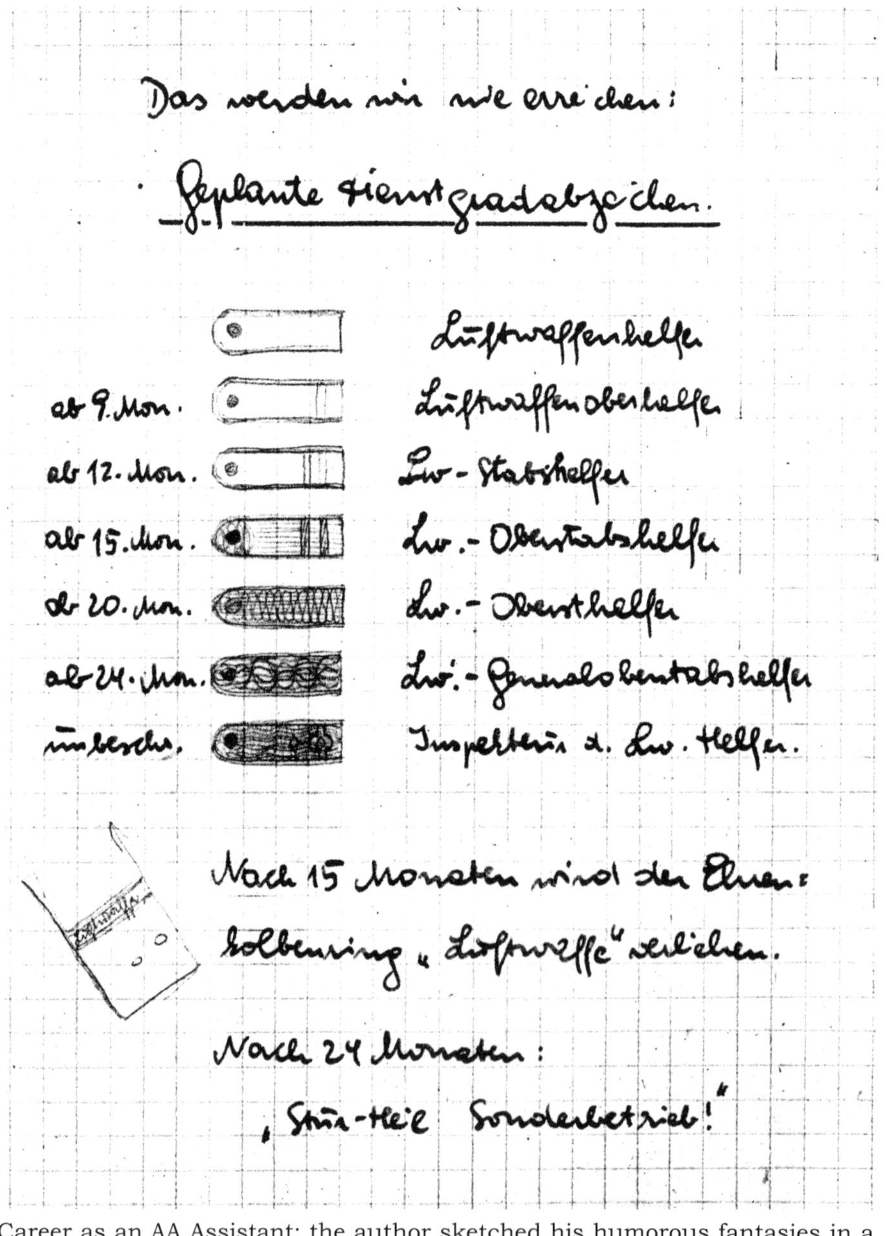

Career as an AA Assistant: the author sketched his humorous fantasies in a notebook – particularly amusing is the „Piston Ring of Honor" (cuff ribbon) awarded to the AAAs by the Luftwaffe.

The sisters of the promoted AAAs set the table: essential preparation for the main celebration.

The entire class together, the author up front. Note the photo of the fighter ace Mölders on the wall behind.

The AAA 1st Class in the other batteries also celebrated: 2./695. (HR)

Official assignment

One Saturday in November 1944, Wallner, Sepperl and I were detailed off for a special assignment: we were to transport, in other words act as pack mules, to carry some technical gear to an anti-aircraft position near the Nibelungenwerk where it was to be tried, tested or put to some other use. It was a miserable, dull day, raining lightly out of low-lying cloud.

Saturday, 11.XI.44:[49] *„At around 08:30 Tubert sent us (Wallner, Sepperl and me) with a jamming transmitter to 24/17[50]. We set off at the double and arrived there around 09:30. A sergeant wanted set the equipment up at the top of the hill, so Sepperl and I had to manhandle the junk up there with the batteries. It was bitterly cold, the wind was blowing and we were ordered to wait up there. But we did stand near the fire that the concentration camp inmates had lit there, talked to their Kapo and, at 10:30, we were allowed to push off again with the equipment...”*

---

[49]   Extract from the original of the author's diary, see Appendix, page 252
[50]   24/17: Tactical number of a Homeland AA Battery

These concentration camp inmates had to dig deep trenches on the windy, freezing cold ridge, probably to protect the factory workers from bombing raids. Their only clothing was a lightweight, pajama-type, striped work overall and they were suffering terribly from the cold. Now and then one would try to warm himself by the fire, only to be driven off each time by the brutal looking Kapo [overseer prisoner trusted by the SS] who was armed with a club, himself almost certainly a „criminal class" prisoner. The group was guarded by soldiers with shouldered rifles. From their armbands we identified as a Ukrainian SS unit.

We wanted to persuade the Kapo to let the inmates warm themselves briefly by the fire, but did not dare to do so. We were in uniform ourselves and that could easily have led to nasty consequences for us.

„...Shortly beforehand, action stations had been signaled and, just as we were leaving, we heard the formation. No alternative but to run uphill to the 3.7 cm. There we ran into an NCO: ,Great – I can use you guys!' he shouted: ,You – over here!' pointing at Sepp. ,Sit on this seat and turn here as soon as you have the aircraft in your sights. And you (meaning me) hold down this lever and shout ,ready' – I'll see to the rest!'" We did not have a clue about how to operate a light AA gun, but our AAA uniforms had promoted us to the status of professionals.

2 cm AA 38 on the ridge above the Nibelungenwerk.

„In the meantime, we heard the bark of our own guns and the explosions of the shells. Below us we could see people streaming out of the plant.
Once the formation had passed overhead, the AA soldiers arrived, the mob. Sepp

and I made ourselves scarce.
At Herzograd we heard shooting. Thought that there was street-fighting already,
but it was two SS men firing at targets with their pistols.
We finally made it back to our battery. There had been a gigantic screw-up there:
transmission on the fire control unit had been switched off and the guns had fired
with cease fire data![51] 3 salvos, 8 rounds..."

And, because during our absence there had been a number of other incidents,
there was pack drill for the entire battery; we were not spared either.

Turn of the year 1944/45

While the war raged on every front and was nearing its terrible end, with the Soviets and the Western Allies poised on Germany's borders, we were trying to defend ourselves against the total air supremacy of the Americans, and to adapt
our modest AAA existence to the prevailing conditions and possibilities. A few
pages from my diary at the turn of the final war year record the situation as we
experienced it.

Sunday, 24.XII.44: *"Got up at 07:00, on duty as aircraft observer again. As usual*
my toes were freezing cold. Did everything I could to combat the problem: tried
sprinting first, next kicking the boards of the emplacement, then marching repeat-
edly around the fire control unit. Nothing helped. I was at the end of my tether by
the time I was relieved. Of course, repeated action stations at midday...
At 18:00 the battery celebrated Christmas Eve. I gave Lt. Göttinger a photograph of
himself as a Christmas present. During the next action stations, he confessed to
having been personally touched. Later, he brought along Senior Ensign Karlheinz
Pfeiffer to join us. We had one hell of a good time..."

Monday, 25.XII.44, first day of the Christmas festival: *"Aircraft observer this*
morning. Then action stations from 09:30 hrs. One formation flew directly past our
effective range. Later, we fired on three machines and so well that we received a
compliment from our CO who claimed that it had been his best Christmas present
ever. We also locked on well to our second target. Finally, we hammered away at a
Fortress that was quietly drifting past, but did not bring it down. ... Wels took a
beating again today..."

Tuesday, 26.XII.44, second day of Christmas: *"Slept until 08:30. Battery exercises*
and alarms between 11:00 and 14:00 hrs. All because of a few isolated aircraft ...
In the evening, the stack of our stove came adrift and smoked the place out again.

---

[51]   Between firefights, i.e. in the cease fire periods, the guns would all be pointed north at an elevation of 80
       degrees – alternately, in close-range positions, they were aimed in all directions with low elevation settings.

That made the stove play up all the more. We were squatting around the stove when the drill sergeant came in. First he chewed out Hackl and Neuhold because they had been in the girls' quarters. Then he declared that General Wagner was coming to inspect us tomorrow. We were to clean up our room. Instead we turned in."

Wednesday, 27.XII.44: „*Again at midday 3 hours at action stations. Linz hit heavily, but we did not fire because the swine always flew around us. Did not leave us in peace until 16:00 hrs. The General did not turn up either. Much ado about nothing."*

Thursday, 28.XII.44: „*Action stations again at 06:30. But only briefly. Short nap during aircraft recognition class... Then 3 hours of alarms. Fired 3 salvos at fighters. Sascha* (a Russian volunteer) *always fired too late. Mother visited in the evening. Her train was so late..."*

Focus of our permanent aggravation: the stove.

Friday, 29.XII.44: „*Infantry training. Barely recovered from the rigors of the Christmas Day, this stupid type of ‚church service' already again. Pfeiffer stormed across the snow covered fields with us... This meant that I was soaking wet on duty as aircraft observer... Then, the usual action stations, snow flurries, allowed to open our top buttons while bombs are being dropped on Wels, with low-level attacks on Passau... Schadauer and Figl called in... They read aloud the Christmas Tale by Walter Flex, rather good. Night exercises. I lay in the snow on the foundation of the fire control unit and pressed the fire bell. In my hand I had the earphones from which I could hear Pöppler and the gun captain shouting. Problems again with communication, fuze setters were not getting their data. By the time I got back to our quarters I was frozen stiff..."*

Saturday, 30.XII.44: „*The year is coming to an end. It was good at times and crap at others. I hope some of next year is the same and that it brings peace... A miracle, no action stations... There had been a hare hunt across the open fields. The bag: 100 hares and 1 fox. We bought one of the hares. It will be delivered to Frau Swoboda tomorrow and she will make us a great stew..."*

Sunday, 31.XII.44: „*Went out taking photographs with Franzi Wieser. Battery exercises in the morning; CO hopping mad about the gun squad, otherwise no heavy duties. Orders issued at midday, during which the CSM announced that each man would receive a ¼ l ration of schnapps. Schnapps? Eckert made it very clear that we were not getting any. As a result, there was no music in the mess. Apart from Russman, Kaiser and Seidenspinner, not a soul came to visit us because we didn't have a drop. We put thumb tacks in the girls' beds. But Christl had hidden in her*

locker (the others were in the mess) *and when we entered we were using less than the choicest of words. Despite repeated demands, the band did not turn up at the mess. This infuriated the CO who ordered lights out at 22:00 hrs... We continued jawing away contentedly in our bunks. Most of us had fallen asleep, but when Kaiser turned up with a jigger, nearly everyone was wide awake. Kaiser had wanted to bring a full bottle, but had been stopped by Elfert. They let the corks pop, but without us. Full of expectation we counted off the twelve strokes of the clock and then it was New Year.*
There was a speech by the Führer, but that must have been when I fell asleep."

Monday, 1.I.45: *„No reveille so did not get up until 09:30. Just cleaned a bit of kit. New Year's wishes all around. Ate our hare stew for lunch, it was very good, nothing else all day..."*

Tuesday, 2.I.45: *„Had the back luck, or rather the good luck to stand guard from 07:00 to 08:00. Was able to watch some action... The Yankees are getting stroppy again. They always come with single aircraft; this naturally means standing-to more often. Requisitioned coal again tonight. Took us quite a while before we found decent fuel for heating. The exercise was cancelled but we still had to fall in. Göttinger was furious because the gun squad was slow in turning out. They got a drilling from Pfeiffer..."*

Wednesday, 3.I.45: *„Pannhorst instructed us on how to combat tanks. 5 times action stations. Morning and afternoon, theoretical maneuvers. I arrived late and got drilled for half an hour together with Franzl, Hackl, Manoch and Schmutzi."*

Thursday, 4.I.45: *„... Not much going on..."*

Friday, 5.I.45: *„One year with this club. Precisely 12 months ago, we lost our freedom. Action stations a few times. That same evening we transferred to barrack ‚Dora, Emil, Frieda'. Crap. 22 men in one room. On top of it all, housekeeping! Had a good chat with Tubert during inspection. My bunk is on the 3rd level."*

Saturday, 6.I.45: *„Slept soundly in my new bunk. Rearranged my books in the morning... We are expecting to quite a few Flak-V lads. Then we will mosey off. In the evening to battalion headquarters for an X-ray."*

Sunday, 7.I.45: *„Snowfall..."*

Climax

January 8, 1945

In his book „The War in Austria" Manfried Rauchensteiner describes, in addition to wartime events on the ground, the operations of the American 15th Air Force, in particular against targets in the Ostmark. In the chapter „The January Raids" he writes:

> »The Western air forces had set themselves ambitious objectives for the January of 1945. They wanted to relieve the pressure on the Soviets on their western front, to finally subdue the German fuel and armaments industries, and then to attack the last of the potential targets in their sights…
>
> It began on January 8 when 121 B-17 bombers, escorted by 105 fighters, attacked the central railroad station of Linz around noon, and the 5 bomber formations dropped a total of 1304 500 lb bombs…
>
> That was only the first wave. At the end of their combined approach, 328 B-24 bombers from five other groups, accompanied by 178 fighter aircraft, split up. One formation of 85 bombers also attacked targets in the area of Linz, while the others, finding their visibility impaired by a thick layer of cloud, bombed as alternative targets the railroad stations of Graz, Klagenfurt and Villach…
>
> There was no German fighter screen whatsoever. In those attacks, the 15th Air Force did lose six bombers to anti-aircraft fire, a seventh though a crash-landing, plus one escort fighter. From a total of 520 bombers and 283 fighters participating in those operations, these losses were minimal…«

According to my diary, Monday January 8, 1945 was an absolutely routine day. Snow had fallen the day before and, despite it being a Sunday morning rest period, we had to dig out the cable pit; in the afternoon NCO Bleicher persecuted us with political indoctrination. Otherwise, *„we were writing and making time."* Compared to the other weekdays with their routine duties, it appeared a quiet one: *„Aircraft identification in our barrack. Sat on the 3rd level* [of the bunks] *with Altmann. Bähr*

January 8, 1945

Bombs falling on the alternative targets of Klagenfurt, above, and Graz. (HF)

and Russmann opposite, eating Spitzi's apples. Below sat August who was throw-ing chunks of ice that he broke off an icicle. Then I reported for aircraft observation duties. Hell of a fog... 11:00 hrs stand to. Fired at formations that were flying back from Linz. Totally frustrated with the FuMG radar that initially, was always track-ing with the parabolic antenna at 15 degrees, although the aircraft were flying at 7000 m. Figl turned up in the afternoon. In the evening the lights went out, so we sat there in the candlelight. Did math with Biehler, studied philosophy while I wrote up my diary. Finally, we fell into the arms of Morpheus."

At the same time, the 376th Bomb Group of the 15th USAAF flew northward from Italy to bomb the railroad facilities of Linz in Austria. My diary entry and the American reports indicate that one of our eight salvos, numbering a total of 48 rounds and mentioned in the battle order[52], might have scored a hit that led to the downing of an aircraft. Did „we down here" have an influence in determin-ing the fate of „them up there"?

The following is quoted from statements made by 2nd Lieutenant Philip R. Scott, the pilot of a B-24 Liberator. His report covers damage to his Liberator "Red Ryd-er" shortly after dropping his bomb load on the target in Linz, the evolution of the return flight of the stricken aircraft along two-thirds of the route until it hit the sea off the coast of Dalmatia, and his rescue by a British-Canadian patrol boat:[53]

> »On January 8, 1945 the 376th Bomb Group headed North to bomb the marshalling yards at Linz, Austria. Our 512th squadron encountered clouds that put a strain on formation flying and also forced us to fly at higher altitudes than planned. Our windows were well frosted by the time we reached the target area. Scraping off this ice to create viewing ports kept many of us busy.
>
> Over Linz flak bursts would be observed at many altitudes and it looked heavy and dangerous to all of us. This was on-ly our second mission to be flying as a complete crew. For this trip we had a new bombardier assigned to us, as well as a cameraman to record bomb hits as we passed over the tar-get. This was not to be their lucky day, nor was it ours.
>
> Our bombs were released toward the target, photographs were taken, and the crew kept busy checking oxygen equipment, looking for enemy fighters and fighting the awful feelings

---

[52] See Appendix, page 251
[53] See also Missing Air Crew Report 42-95285, 8.I.1945 in Appendix, pages 278 et seq.

of anxiety caused by the flak that was bursting all around us.

I saw one B-24, off of my left wing, diving straight down into some clouds. Then, all of a sudden, we suffered a near miss burst that shook up our plane and the number one engine was knocked out. I feathered the prop but soon afterwards I noticed that the number two engine was losing power.

By that time, I could see only two other B-24s and one was a pathfinder radar plane. I followed them for as long as I could but we gradually fell back and eventually were forced to descend into the heavy clouds below. Our navigator did a fine job of guiding on a course that would bring us into the island of Vis, near Yugoslavia, for an emergency landing. There seemed to be no reasonable options due to the solid clouds over the mainland and the coast of Italy was further away.

Then the crew reported that a fuel leak was suspected because the fuel levels in our gages were dropping excessively. We knew that we were in a desperate situation but at least we had the ›good luck‹ of not catching fire.

We made frantic efforts to contact Air-Sea Rescue Units and any friendly air base to report our position and emergency. But, before any response was known to me, our fuel supply ran out. So, I guided our powerless plane down towards the rough seas with all men stationed in ditching positions. Everyone that is except Dick Dumm, our navigator, who was busy on the radio. He finally got a response from Air-Sea Rescue…

I was also amazed to learn Air-Sea Rescue simply said to Dick, ›good luck‹, because they told him that there were 9 or 10 other reported ditching that were ahead of us. There was no chance that they could search for us anytime soon. ›Good luck‹ indeed! With time running, I finally succeeded in calling Dick back to the flight deck when we hit the Adriatic seas in a controlled crash that ruptured the fuselage and the tail section sank quickly… Up forward the top turret came crashing down on impact and water poured into the flight deck compartment. One man disappeared, a second man did not survive his head wounds, and our navigator suffered severe fractures to his forehead and one hand.

January 8, 1945

The crew of the B-24 Liberator "Red Ryder", an aircraft of the 512th Bomb Squadron, 376th Bomb Group, that was hit during the attack on the "Hermann Göring Works" Linz on 8.I.1945; front row: Pilot 2nd Lieutenant Philipp R. Scott , Co-Pilot 2nd Lieutenant Kenneth F. Martin, Bombardier 2nd Lieutenant Knie, who was not on this fateful flight, Navigator 2nd Lieutenant Richard C. Dumm; back row: Air Gunner 2nd Sergeant Gerald L. Harden (†), Air Gunner 2nd Sergeant Colby G. Walker, Air Gunner 2nd Sergeant John H. McDermott (†), Flight Engineer Tech. Sergeant Oscar Snipes, Radio Operator Tech. Sergeant Jack D. Holt (†), Air Gunner 2nd Sergeant Gerald Messing (†). Not shown on the photo are the Bombardier 2nd Lieutenant Robert C. Walker, and the Photographer 2nd Sergeant Löwenthal, who were specifically assigned for the flight described.

Within a few minutes there was nothing left of our big, beautiful Liberator except bits and pieces floating around us. I recall seeing plywood chips, several oxygen bottles and a dark colored blob of canvas bobbing in the waves. This package turned out to be a spare raft that had been stored inside in the compartment above the wing structure. That raft was our ›good luck‹ because we spent 42 hours and two cold nights floating on the rough seas.

On our third day, Dick Dumm got very lucky! He spotted a PT patrol boat just cruising by; he fired his 45 caliber Colt at it while someone else fired our last two red flares. Well, as luck would have it, Dick hit their windshield and that lucky hit led to our rescue but not before one tense moment when the PT came alongside our rafts with their crew pointing machine guns directly at us. It took some talking to convince them that we were American airmen. Dick explained that he was the one who fired those shots to get their attention.

There is a lot more to this story but I've told enough to demonstrate that there is such a thing as ›good luck‹ and then there is also ›bad luck‹ to some of us. No one can explain it or understand it. Things happen, that's it. We took our chances in those days flying our B-24s into battle. We take chances even today, nearly every day. So, I say ›good luck‹ to all of you.«

Scott's report is underpinned by a letter dated November 24, 2004 from 2nd Sergeant Colby Walker, one of the machine gunners of this aircraft, to his friend Richard G. Yerick, who made that letter available to me. In it, the former 2nd Sergeant Colby Walker describes the dramatic events in more detail, including the rescue and the fate of his comrades:

»Dear Rick,
Thanks for the card notifying me that you did receive the copy of Phil Scott's ›Good Luck‹ story. As I mentioned before, this letter contains more detail of events which occurred during the time between ditching (3:30 p.m. Jan. 8, 1945) and the rescue (about 9:30 a.m. on Jan. 10)…

The B-24 broke in two upon impact aft of the bomb bay. Tail section went to the bottom immediately, but I managed to swim away from it despite being several feet underwater. After inflating my Mae West I paddled towards the front section of the plane where others were freeing one life raft from under the wing. The other raft could not be freed, but luckily a spare raft was seen floating nearby (This 2nd raft had a puncture in one compartment and held only 2 men). There were 6 in the other raft, 3 men were lost in the ditching incident directly.

The clouds soon covered us at nightfall. We were at least 5 miles north of Vis, the tiny island off the Dalmatian Coast of Yugoslavia (some 40 miles from the mainland). Vis was guarded by British commandos who maintained the short landing strip… A storm struck with wind, rain, and even sleet at times during the night. Several of us were injured in the crash and the pilot Scott was ill from taking in too much sea water. The assistant engineer, Gerold Messing was incoherent. Tragically he passed away during the night. Waves were 8-10 feet high by morning, and we decided to tie the 2 rafts together for safety.

Next morning we mutually agreed to bury S/Sgt. G. Messing at sea in order that the rest of us would have a better chance of survival. We all repeated the Lord's Prayer in unison as the burial occurred.

The only rations in the rafts were 2 small packs of hard candy Charms and 2 half-pint containers of water. Apparently, some ground crewmen had eaten the chocolate bars prior to our mission. A small distiller was in one raft but the sun never shone, so no water from this solar device was available. We were able to collect a small amount of water in our hands. The storm continued all day Jan. 9 and into the evening as well. Not much conversation occurred as all were miserable and extremely cold. Some snow actually fell for a time.

The rain had stopped by early morning of Jan. 10, but clouds were solid. Waves had lessened considerably and we were hopeful of rescue. Around 9:30 a.m. a ship was seen on the horizon. The co-pilot fired the flare gun and soon the ship was turning in our direction. It approached rapidly and turned out to be a British patrol boat mounted by Canadians. Navigator Lt. Dumm fired his .45 pistol in the boat's direction, and hit the windshield of the craft. Boat came closer with guns tracked on us, thinking we were Germans. We soon were on board, given warm drinks and covered with blankets on the ride to Vis. We were tended by 2nd British Field Hospital.

That evening a British doctor sewed my wounds. Two others were injured but less severely. On Jan. 11 we were flown back to Bari, Italy (15th AF Headquarters). I was placed in the large 26th General Hospital (American Unit in Italian Building)…

Those of us who survived the life craft ordeal gave our .45 Colt pistols to the crewmen on the patrol boat. Apparently, that crew had no such weapons and they were most appreciative. We had to report to 15th AF that the pistols were >lost at sea in the ditching incident<…

The other members of my crew returned to fly more missions after short stays in the hospital until the 376th Bomb Group returned to the USA in late April, 1945.

In 1950… I applied for and was given a direct commission as
a 2nd Lt. In the Air Force Reserve… Ultimately, I retired as
a Major in 1975.«

Attacks in February and March 1945

According to Rauchensteiner, the 15th US Air Force attacked targets in Austria
during February and March 1945 on 21 different days, 16 of which were virtually
consecutive:

»There was hardly anywhere in Austria that could claim it had
not noticed the bombing campaign, even if it was simply to
have seen the gray colored or silvery aircraft flying at high
altitude, to have heard the droning of engines that was characteristic of the bomber formations, or to have noticed the
condensation trails that followed them. If the bombers came
within range of the German anti-aircraft defenses, their guns
opened fire, but not on individual machines as that would
simply have been a pure waste of ammunition…«

Condensation trails in the sky: a daily sight in 1945. (HF)

And then the AA transmitter would broadcast: "All bulls Monika!", i.e. firing forbidden for all heavy batteries, much to our disappointment and frustration.

How did we experience that February of 1945? From February 1–18, 1945 I was enjoying an extended leave at home and my diary entries cover events at home. For example, that on February 5, eight Lightnings attacked a passenger train near Hubertendorf, causing numerous civilian deaths, or that on February 17, a carpet of bombs fell close to the Ybbs Electricity Works, and in the vicinity of our own home, where some of the craters are still visible today. It was a dull day and that typical droning of a larger bomber formation could be heard from above the unbroken layer of cloud. Then suddenly an eerie whistling and a tremendous crashing as around 20 to 30 detonations were heard and felt in the vicinity of my parents' house. Almost simultaneously, the ground shuddered, making the shutters on the windows of the office where I was sitting shake and rattle heavily. Luckily, the electricity generation plant was not hit and the bomb load only caused crop damage in the surrounding fields and lowland forest. The American radar was evidently not as accurate as they claimed.

I learned later that there had been an air raid on the Nibelungenwerk that same day. But there is no entry of it in my diary as it was evidently not impressive enough for any of my comrades to have mentioned it. My combat unit only recorded one salvo of five rounds of ammunition fired on that day. Only American reports and Rauchensteiner's book report any bombing on February 17, primarily alternative targets and apparently with little success, as „No fresh damage is seen to the works" was logged.

However, barely had I returned from leave on February 18, and just settling back into battery life, when things started to warm up again. Monday, 19.II.45: „...*Low-level attack on the battery. 2 Mustangs...*" This brief diary entry reveals a store of memories:

It was a cold, clear winter day with the usual calls to action stations. The guns were deployed for close range firing in all directions, the tracker team was manning the equipment – Spindi, Willi, the others and I on the fire control unit with our steel helmets on. The AA radio station was reporting any number of enemy aircraft, "coffee cups" in code.

From the vicinity of the railroad station there was a sudden chattering of machine guns – and them we saw them: two Mustangs, flying parallel to the railroad tracks and then turning towards our position. „Low-flying aircraft direction three!" – already to be met by a number of our shells detonating with the shortest possible fuze settings. The blasts were really loud because of the proximity of the detonations, but there were no hits, the whole affair was over in a flash. We could clearly see the camouflage of the aircraft and their pilots in the cockpit. A wonder that they did not wave to us! But they were under the guns in an instant, Caesar traversed and gave them a parting shot - Old Bleicher had already barked!

We guys in the tracker team watched the show from behind the safety of the earthworks. Spindi and Willi, the E2 and E3 on the fire control-control director, did not want to miss a trick and so they stayed glued to the eyepieces of the 4 m stereoscope, seeing the aircraft and the pilots sharply focused and as large as life. As the fighters roared over the guns, they shifted their system into high-speed rotation.

After the day's excitement, my diary goes on to report: „*... Action stations again today and then shoveling snow. Low-flying aircraft almost got Franzl Wieser. Greger's trousers also collected a bullet hole when his train was attacked near Melk...*"

Our opponents, the 15th USAAF continued their attacks in March 1945, but with increased intensity. Together with Britain's Royal Air Force, they brought the climax of the air war not only to us, but to the entire territory of the Reich.

American postwar shot showing the destruction of the Linz rail freight terminal. (HF)

For us, this meant actions stations on a daily basis, usually around midday, but mostly without any active intervention on our part. By now, the streams of bombers had pinpointed our position and the aircraft on the extreme edge of any formation or group flew close to the effective range of our battery and that of the neighboring batteries. They clearly had a lot of respect for us; by now we were the only danger they still had to face.

On March 2, they once again had the railroad yards around Linz in their sights where, according to Rauchensteiner, some 386 aircraft dropped another 866 tons of bombs on this primary target. We got in 8 salvos of fire against a homeward bound formation.

It's all over

Comrades who came and went

5th Grade of Amstetten High School

At the same time as we 6th grade boys from the Amstetten high school were mobilized on January 5, 1944, those 5th graders born in 1928 were also called up. Like us, they were initially sent to Linz-Wegscheid for basic training and one month later joined the 1./805 in St. Valentin-Langenhart.

They also received their training on the weapons systems and equipment there, but on April 14, 1944 we went our separate ways: *„…I entered our barrack just as the 5th grade was saying goodbye. Took a few photos. Very few men now for each piece of equipment. Things are not looking good for passes and leave…"*

AAA of the 5th grade of Amstetten High school on 14.IV.44

They have fallen in and the CSM is requesting permission to dismiss from Lieutenant Höfer.

Whereas we eight from the sixth grade had the good luck of being assigned to just one battery during our entire service as AAA, i.e. with the exception of Gunter Bast, the fifth began a vagrant life from one battery to another. First, they were assigned to our neighboring 88 mm battery in Kronstorf, where they met our instructor from Wegscheid, PFC Sinn. Then, interestingly, they turned up with a 12.5 cm railroad AA battery near Linz, reallocated at the docks there to an 88 again, and from there to Saxony. Near Leipzig they again served with an 88 and quartered in a memorable castle. Finally, they ended up in Lochau in the area of Merseburg/Halle, where they experienced the heavy raids against the Leuna-Werke.

Willy Garschall was awarded the War Merit Cross with Swords 2nd Class. During a heavy attack he managed to get his gun operational again.

Because of the frequent reassignments, there were no ongoing school classes for them. After the war, that turned out to be a major disadvantage. Nevertheless, all of them had successful careers.

Grazer

When we arrived at the 1./805 on February 7, 1944, we were welcomed to the barrack where we were to stay by five comrades from Graz. They were great guys, giving us practical advice and helping us through the difficulties of the induction and familiarization phase. *„...We joined the following AAA from Graz who, unfortunately, have been reassigned to Steg: Ofner, Bauer, Nauer, Wurst and Kern...“*

We were only together with them for a month. One very snowy winter day at the beginning of March 1944, they packed their gear, took their leave of us and the officers, and marched off. Like so many other comrades who became friends and accompanied us along our way, we never saw them again.

Taking their leave in a flurry of snow: the Graz guys move on, 7.II.1944.

Year of 1926

It was much the same story with our comrades born in 1926; they were the first wave to be called up in the middle of February 1943, straight from the classroom to the AA guns. They were a cheery bunch, mainly Viennese. We were only together for a few days and first got to know them during their extensive farewell parties.

The youths born in 1926, and relieved by us, take their leave of the NCOs and celebrate their departure with one their comrades dressed up as a girl.

Year of 1927

We were together much longer with the youngsters born in 1927 who were re-cruited from any number of high schools and were drafted for training around September 1943 already. Possibly for educational reasons the majority of them were detached from other Linz batteries and reassigned to us. We welcomed our former classmates from Amstetten: Toni Weichinger, Erich Payer ("Pi"), Gerhard Czadek, Alois Diendorfer (Leischi) and Lothar Halbartschlager; and from Waidho-fen an der Ybbs (as mentioned earlier) the 1927s Sepp Lammerhuber, Ferdinand Strohbach (Struppi) and Max Lakitsch. All of them also „lodged" in our barrack, and we elected Sepp Lammerhuber as our Senior. His quiet and even-tempered manner was ideal for most of us who were hotheads. He was even respected by our superiors.

The 1927s in front of their quarters

I can even remember some of the older boys from the seventh grade by name:

From Waidhofen:	Fred Gerl (Squad Leader) and Hugo Weilharter
From Amstetten:	Richard Pazelt, Stute, Kober
From Vienna:	Fritz Endres, Hetl (with the gift of the gab)
From Melk:	Hans Karlinger and Fred Weigl
From the Burgenland:	Zambo and Stuparits

The 1927s also celebrated their departure in the fall of 1944 and left group by group after we had experienced the events of 1944 hitherto together with them. Wednesday, 13.IX.44: „*... The majority of the 1927s is leaving today. Seemed as if they would have to stay because they had been called up by the RAD to report to Posen on 28.IX. Fritz Endres received a telegram: ,Business badly damaged, apartment too. Coming soon'. Seems that Vienna must have taken a hammering...*"

Monday, 18.IX.44: „*... Toni has left. Leischi returned from Melk, where he got quite a chewing-out, carrying a draft notice for Pi. So he will also leave us tomorrow. He and Toni are being sent to Lehmgraben (south of Königsberg). Really close to the Russian lines...*"

Both of them, Erich Payer and Toni Weichinger, have been missing since the closing days of the war, and probably lost their lives during the fighting in East Prussia.

Klagenfurt boys

They were a wild mob those Klagenfurter. They turned up one day without warning and occupied the bunks of the 1927s who had been transferred already.

It transpired that their situation was just like that of our own 5th graders. They were shifted around from battery to battery, and as the last ones to arrive, were always the first to be moved straight on or transferred before they could acclimatize. They were a very lively bunch. Wednesday, 20.IX.44: „*...This evening, the new guys told us about their experiences. It is great when AAAs get together and talk about what goes through their minds during air raids. One of them even has the same initials as me: G.O. (Gernot Oberlercher).*"

Friday, 22.IX.44: „*...The new guys do not seem to have a very positive attitude...*"

We soon found out that these customers were cut from the same cloth as we harmless lads, Saturday, 23.IX.44: „*Yesterday at 22:30 hrs Stossier came back somewhat under the weather. The others gave him a hard time, put rocks in his bed...*"

They carried on like this, sometimes to the point where it got beyond a joke. Sunday, 24.IX.44: „*...In the evening, Kuni decided to get canned. He drank 2 liters of cider, but spilled half of it. Then started behaving stupidly, really growing into the spirit of things. Also started mouthing off disgusting stuff.*
Stossier was in a bad mood and poured a mess tin of water over Kuni's head, but he would not stop. Next, Stossier grabbed a washbowl full of water and anointed the offender. Kuni just stood there, wringing out his shirt. Our quarters were

awash. But he still would not knock it off. Once again he got a can of water over his thick skull, but continued talking bullshit and put on his last dry shirt. After last post, Stossier tried to strangle him, but he kept on blabbing. He was now bombarded with boots and slippers. Finally, everyone ignored his claptrap. When he fell asleep, they took their revenge, putting paper between his toes and setting light to it..."

Suddenly, there was a glimmer of hope and they were rumored to be moving on (26.IX.), but no such luck, and the nonsense persisted. Saturday, 7.X.44: *„... At 19:00 hrs we wanted to celebrate our 9 months, but it turned out to be a reunion party with the Klagenfurter. Urschi, Coony and Stossi were tipsy, even though the cider was disgusting. Stossi whacked Coony so hard that he disappeared behind the table. That put the fear of God into him... every time he caught sight of Stossi, he was behind the bunks like greased lightning. ‚Keep Stossi off me!' he kept whimpering..."*

The Klagenfurter rovers on 30.IX.1944: from the left: Urschütz, Stossier, Oberlechner, Czernin, Kotzmann, Lapan.

Even though they were a rough bunch, we liked them. I had befriended Urschitz and we were truly sorry when they had to move on. Tuesday, 10.X.44: *„...The news that the Klagenfurter are having to leave us again struck like a lightning bolt. They are being transferred to Wels to a homeland AA battery. Damned shame as I won't be able to go on any more forays with Urschi. But he did promise to write.*

Also leaving with him are: Stossier (Stossi), Oberlercher (Coony), Kotzmann (also a great guy), Lapan and Czernin (the Count)..."

Wednesday, 11.X.44: „*...The Klagenfurter still had to pack and they are supposed to leave at 19:30 hrs. Yesterday evening, Stossier got canned with the Lieutenant ... then I accompanied them to the railroad station because I had to report to the sickbay afterwards. We marched in singing; their packs were being trucked in. Then said goodbye to each one. They were actually a good bunch of guys..."*

Apprentices

In summer 1944, a troop of adolescent civilians, roughly our age, turned up in our positions. Previously drilled by the Hitler Youth, they lined up in front of the Captain. From his brief speech we gathered that it was a group of apprentices who were supposed to be trained as AAA.

Freshly recruited apprentices of our year, now in uniform.

They were housed in a different barrack to us and then passed around until they reappeared in identical uniforms to ours. Apart from duties on the guns and equipment, we had little contact with them. As vocational college students they also received some schooling for which Dr. Figl was made responsible. From time to time, he assigned some of us to teach them(!). And, when we saw the results of the class work we had given them, it was an opportunity for us presumptuous high school students to be amused. Monday, 23.X.44: „*...Figl wrote on the black-board some of the precious classics the apprentices had written in their exercise books, e.g. capital cities: Moscrow, Butterpest, Buderpest, Parees, Geneever and Burn!!! Even though we high school kids were pretty low on academic skills, we did seem to be a little more savvy than our comrades.*"

This lot, too, with whom we had absolutely nothing in common, moved on shortly afterwards.

Flak-V soldiers

Replacing the apprentices in the late fall of 1944 were the Flak-V soldiers. These boys were the same age as us and had been designated soldiers without the de-tour of first becoming „Assistants". They had also been immediately declared as „Flak-verwendungsfähig" [suitable for AA deployment] – a kind of intermediate rank between soldier and militiaman. They came from every imaginable trade, school and area of the Ostmark [Nazi designation for Austria]. They did not need any teachers because no schooling was planned for them; they were simply sol-diers, suitable for service with the air defense.

As with the apprentices, we had very little personal contact with them. I did get friendly, however, with Oskar Greiner who hailed from the area of Wiener Neu-stadt. By now a veteran, I was able to help him come to terms with the pitfalls of military life, and we spent a number of our leisure hours together.

My buddy Oskar Greiner.

He was trained as a range finder on the fire control unit because he had pro-nounced aptitude for spatial vision. And that was almost to be his undoing. He was sent on a training course to Kolberg on the Baltic Sea where he was caught up in the chaos of the final Soviet offensive. With incredible luck he returned home safe and sound by devious routes.

Otherwise, the V-soldiers were trained on the same equipment and guns that we were. Their quarters and provisions were identical to ours, with the exception that they did not get a ration of milk soup in the evenings.

Freistädter

Great guys from Freistadt who shared our AA life during the last months on the guns. They were transferred to us from our neighboring Seggau battery, the 2./695, on September 9, 1944. For some strange reason, they were only a part of their school class, with the remainder being assigned to Ranshofen.

The Freistädter also celebrated their promotion as AAA 1st class.

Together with the Klagenfurt guys, they replaced the 1927s and we got on well with them. We had a lot in common, had been mobilized at the same time and undergone the same basic training in Wegscheid, which was not the case with the 1927s. We celebrated our promotion at the same time, while some of them were quartered in our damp bunker. That sort of experience creates bonds. They were no innocents either; Preslmayr and Neuhold got three days in the brig for being caught by the CO personally in the off-bounds barrack of the female AAAs. Sunday, 28.I.45: „...*Neuhold and also Preslmayr were caught this evening with the skirts, and it was the Old Man personally...*"

The cause of that visit to the ladies was almost certainly Christl for whom many of the guys had the hots. I took a shot of the punishment ceremony headed by Fähnrich [Ensign] Pfeiffer at long range.

Sentence read out before the entire crew: 3 days in the brig.

Our Upper Austrian friends were demobilized from the AA around the same time as we were and had a lot to endure during the last months of hostilities. They, too, also made successful careers after the war.

Female AA Assistants

The last troop to relieve us on anti-aircraft service was the female AA Assistants. These girls, somewhat older than we, took over the barrack in which we had lived for almost a year since January 1944. We had to move, first into another hut and then in that dreadful concrete bunker.

They were also an amusing bunch and, in terms of discipline, under the direct orders of the CO. The NCOs on the other hand were not responsible for them – that was the job of a number of women leaders – only for training on the equipment, but not on the guns. We also had the pleasure of having to teach them. Saturday, 13.I.45: „...*Action stations several times during the day. Willi and I were supposed to instruct a number of skirts as U4 and U6 on the Malsi converter. No way are they going to figure it out. Not our problem."*

The girls wore blue uniforms, specifically tailored for them, that were similar to our own. An effort was made to maintain a certain distance to the male battery crewmen. Not difficult to understand why. It was strictly prohibited to enter their quarters, except on duty. Thursday, 21.XII.44: *„…at 08:00 'coffee cup' hassle. Had to fetch the telephone from the female quarters. It looks like a laundry inside! …"*

Naturally, I had to report on the state of the inside of their barrack to my close friends. We were massively disappointed because we believed that everything in their quarters would be so much cleaner and orderly than in ours. No way. Of course, we had no „lingerie" to take care of!

Minor escapades also led to contacts. Wednesday, 17.I.45: *„…That evening, we hung a dead mouse, found in Sepperl Wallner's school bag, on the door of the girls, who are such a cross we have to bear on the equipment…"*

Despite all good intentions and efforts to keep us separate, it was unavoidable that in time there would be incidents that led to disciplinary measures. It was also unavoidable that there would be associations that formed and developed between the sexes. Wednesday, 7.I.45: *„…A number of pairs have formed: Strolch with Manoch, Spindi is going out with the chattering Fritzi, Ruhaltinger has angled Anni vom Riesen and Bruno paired up long ago with Gerti. Only Franzl and I stay on in the evenings. Combat is rare. But alarms in plenty…"*

After our demobilization in the middle of March 1945, this collection of male and female Assistants „held the fort" so to speak, but not for much longer!

Others

And finally, there were other AAA who did not belong to any fixed unit like us or those mentioned beforehand, but somehow came and went. My diary mentions them in one context or another and now they come to mind again: Edgar Adam (from Zistersdorf), Hans Altmann (Hohenau an der March), Josef Bichler (Pitten), Adalbert Burkert (Lundenburg), Wilfried Erasin (Lundenburg), Erwin Greger (Nikolsburg) and Hans Redl (Gföhl).

We take leave of the battery

Events on the ground were somehow more important than the daily action stations and endless waiting. Most of the time, nothing happened anyway. Hence, for us AAA 1st class living in the bunker, our final weeks with the battery were pretty easy ones. One by one we were demobilized, most of us already with a draft notice in our pockets, to report for duty to the Reich Labor Service (RAD) or the Wehrmacht.

We AAA were demobilized from the guns before the Soviet and Allied fronts came so close that the AA batteries would have to intervene in the ground fighting as was the case later. According to the rules of war, we were not classed as „combatants" but rather as party members wearing swastika armbands, and hence, considered as „partisans". Neither side was particularly fussy about how they treated the latter!

Our replacements were no longer Flakhelfer (the common term for AAA), but rather the Flak-V men and the female AA Assistants. Pity the poor battery captains! My diary contains quite a bit about our final days there. Monday, 26.II.45: „...*It is now 21:30 hrs, just back from requisitioning coal with Franzl Wieser and in the right mood for noting down my recollections of the past week. We did not fire a shot. We are not on duty any more, just standing guard and turning out for action stations. Otherwise just squatting in the cold concrete bunker wasting time... Lots of parties... Willi is out of luck and has to report to the RAD on Tuesday. Hackl, Fürst, Helletsgruber, Gamperl, Preslmayr, Redl and Schmutzi have all left... Linz took a heavy beating yesterday. But those swine of formations keep flying around us out of range."*

Tuesday, 27.II.45: „*In the morning, the telephone was again ringing like crazy. Naturally, nobody could be bothered to get up and answer it. Schellschmidt arrived just in time: ‚Herr Unteroffizier, answer that phone so that the racket finally stops!' rasped a sleepy Ruhaltinger. The NCO sent to wake us up actually leapt to answer the phone and to announce it was morning ...*"

Final furlough

As already mentioned in my diary, trips home and back to camp by rail were becoming increasingly adventurous and dangerous in the final months of the war: American fighters were everywhere and attacked every train they could spot. At such moments, you needed a lot of luck to survive. As a result, people tended to travel in the evenings, with the disadvantage that the trains were tightly packed with passengers. Wednesday, 7.III.45: „*...Was at home from Thursday to Saturday (1.III.-3.III.45) to collect my civilian gear. Adam, Burkert and Greger left with me, but we lost each other at the railroad station because the train was so full. I* *ended up on the coal tender and that is how I traveled. Arrived home by 24:00 hrs. No idea what happened to the others."*

The trip on the coal tender left a strong impression on me. I sat at the far end of the tender, with my feet up on the following railcar. It was bitterly cold and already dark. The locomotive spat steam and glowing particles of coal dust into the air and all over me. It was actually an impressive show, but for what purpose?

Half-frozen, covered in soot and grime I arrived at Kemmelbach station shortly before midnight, and from there marched the 4 km to our village on foot. But I was home, and thanks to Mother's unfailing care, I was in good shape.

The author during his last short home leave.

Demobilization

Back at the battery, Wednesday, 7.III.45: *„Frequent and sustained partying... Little to eat. There is a shortage of bread in particular, and supplies are not arriving. Mostly watery soup for lunch. In the afternoon either Leyrer or Demmer turn up*

to take classes. Otherwise we keep ourselves occupied by playing chess, which has become the game of choice in our quarters.
As always, the stove is a curse. The darn thing is smoking us out – it's a disgrace. Demobilization is not looking good. Many of our number have been sent to Rust on infantry combat courses, or to Steyr to learn to use anti-tank weapons. Now we have to wait until they return..."

Lieutenant Göttinger in his peaked cap in the center with „his" AAA 1st Class.

Sunday, 11.III. 45: *„The farewell evening was fine. On 10.III. Sepp Wallner returned from his ,short leave', that lasted 3 weeks and brought provisions with him. Also cigarettes and other delights. There was dancing in the mess, while the CO and NCOs celebrated with the AA girls in the NCO's mess. Neuhold and I suddenly re-membered our persistent appetites and set off for the stalactite cave where we ate nearly everything that Sepperl Wallner had shared with us. Then we fired the re-maining blank rounds from our rifles. Kehl burst in and demanded to know who had fired. The CO is off his head and thinks that it was the guard. And, we should get ourselves back to the mess.*
Outside we had to fall in and the CO held a petulant farewell speech. His last words were: ,My AAA 1st Class are departing with a bang and I want to give them a crushing dismissal!' We nearly fell over laughing and shook his hand as hard as we could. Then there was dancing until around 02:00 hrs."

As specialists on the fire control unit and as K3s on the guns, Walter Spindel-berger, Franzl Wieser and I, plus three boys from Freistadt, were the last of our group to be demobilized, and still without draft papers – Sunday, 11.III. 45: *„Next*

We take leave of the battery

Gültig für freie Urlaubsreisen auf kleinen Wehrmachtfahrschein

Kriegsurlaubsschein

Der **Lw.-Oberhelfer Gerhard Oberleitner**
(Dienstgrad, Vor- und Zuname)

von **L 28211 Lg.Pa. Wien**
(Truppenteil bzw. Feldpostnummer)

ist vom **12. März** 194**5** bis einschl. **·/·** 194 Uhr beurlaubt

nach **Ybbs /Donau** nächster Bahnhof **Ybbs/ Kemmelbach**

nach nächster Bahnhof

Er reist auf kleinen Wehrmachtfahrschein. Es darf nur der verkehrsübliche Reiseweg benutzt werden. Fahrten über größere Umwege sowie Zickzack- und Rundreisen sind verboten. Die Inanspruchnahme von Wehrmachtfahrkarten oder Fahrkarten des öffentlichen Verkehrs für die im Wehrmachtfahrschein bezeichnete Strecke ist verboten.
Über die umstehenden Befehle ist er belehrt worden.

Ausgefertigt am **11. März** 194**5**

L 28211 Lg.Pa. Wien
(Truppenteil bzw. Feldpostnummer)

(Unterschrift, Dienstgrad, Dienststellung)

Leutnant und Batterieführer

(Dienststempel)

F. 852. Verlag Hermann Buchholz & Co., Hamburg 11, Vorsetzen 35. (12)   E/0830

We were demobilized by issuing us with an open-ended „Wartime Leave Slip".

Gültig nur für die auf der Rückseite Ziff. 1 angegebenen Züge

Kleiner Wehrmachtfahrschein, Teil 2

(Gilt als Fahrausweis und ist bei Beendigung der Reise auf dem Zielbahnhof abzugeben)

für ...... in Buchstaben ...... Personen in der 2. Klasse

für ...... in Buchstaben ...... Personen in der 3. Klasse

für **1** in Buchstaben **eine** Diensthunde

für am Gepäckschalter aufzugebendes Reisegepäck (nicht Handgepäck)
von ...... in Buchstaben ...... Personen
zur einmaligen Fahrt auf der Eisenbahn

von Bahnhof **St. Valentin**

nach Bahnhof **Ybbs/Kemmelbach**

über

Das Fahrgeld ist zu stunden.

Ausgefertigt am **11. März** 194**5**

L 28211 Lg.Pa. Wien
(Truppenteil bzw. Feldpostnummer)

(Unterschrift, Dienstgrad, Dienststellung)

Leutnant und Batterieführer

(Dienststempel)

Lager Nr. 1507 a Hofi, Braunschweig-München-Berlin 00 43

The „Small Wehrmacht Travel Certificate" was our ticket home.

day we handed back our uniforms and took our leave of the battery... A fascinating, but also pointless, phase in my life had come to an end. We looked back just once as we trudged down the Panzerstrasse – a whole year, the final one of the war, lay behind us."

The Panzerstrasse in the Thurnsdorf Forest, dusty or muddy, ran between our position and the battalion to which we reported. We often had to cross it on foot.

Between demobilization and the end of the war

As if the Americans had sensed that „The Best", i.e. the 1./695 (o) had vacated their position, they launched the long-awaited mass attack on St. Valentin and the Nibelungenwerk on March 23, 1945. Both the town and the plant were badly damaged: on a surface area covering 1 000 x 750 m, no less than 609 high-explosive hits were registered. Our battery, however, remained unscathed.

On the 10th anniversary of that terrible day, the March 1955 issue of the works newspaper „Der Ni-Werks Arbeiter" [The Ni-Works Labor Force] described the effects of this raid. After the war, the heavily damaged plant had been partially rebuilt, confiscated by the Soviet occupation forces as „German Reich Property", and operated as a so-called „USIA facility". Instead of tanks, the now totally Austrian workforce produced agricultural machinery and other essential equipment needed for reconstruction. The workers were influenced by Communist propaganda that also explains the unusual formulation and terminology used in the text. After concluding the Austrian State Treaty of 1955, the plant was returned to Austrian ownership.

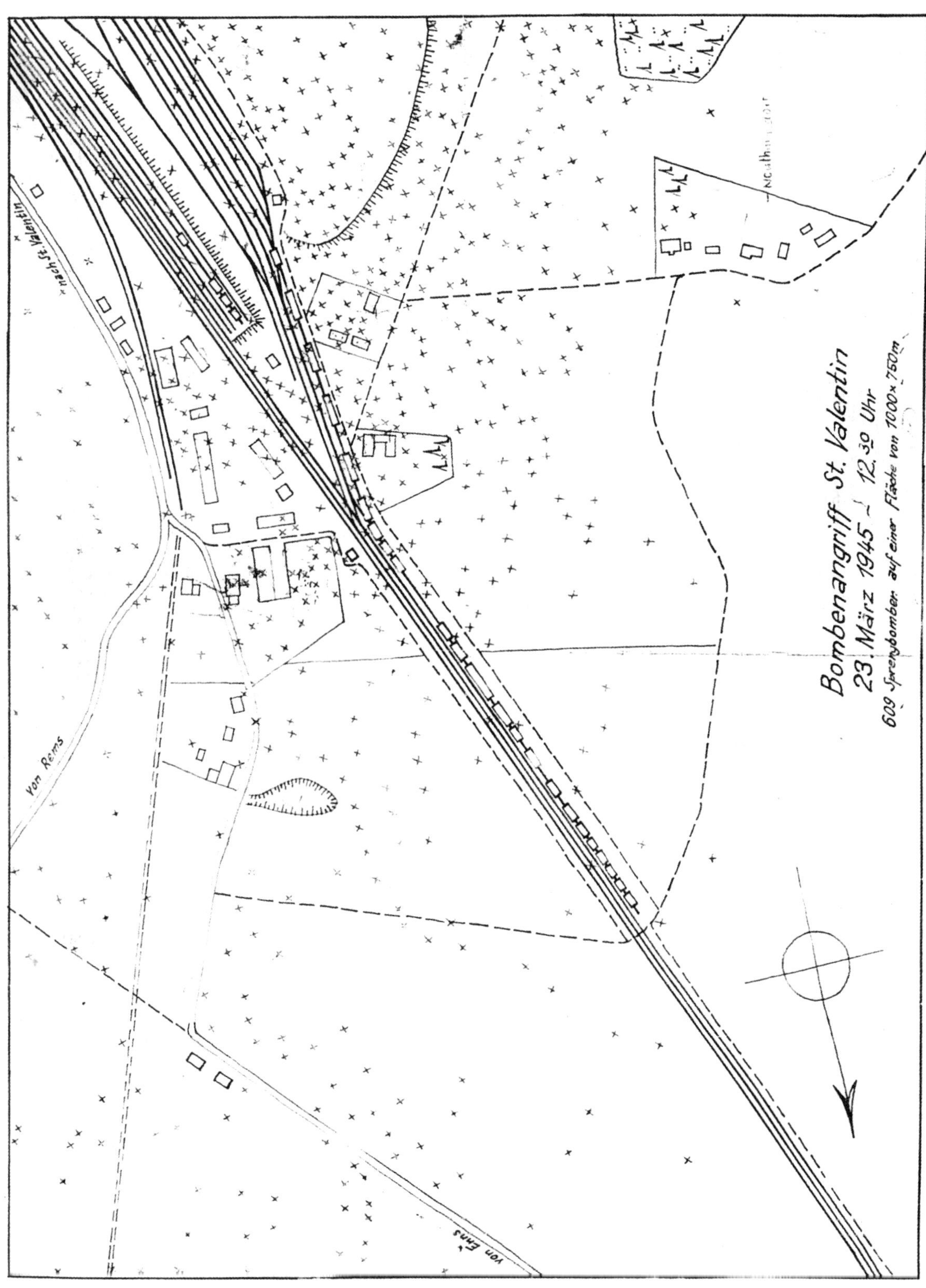

Drawing of the north section of St. Valentin marked with the bomb impacts, published in the March 1955 issue of the newspaper „Der Ni-Werks Arbeiter" [The Ni-Works Labor Force]. Note the position of the Railroad AA guns at the junction to the freight terminal.

American air reconnaissance photo of the Nibelungenwerk taken on 9.IV.45, documenting the severe damaged to the plant (lower right). Also note the approach roads in the forest to the north and southwest of the factory. The photo is framed on the left by the River Enns. In center-left is the village of Rubring, north of it Thurnsdorf; St. Valentin-Langenhart is seen on the upper right. Parts of the AA position 1./695 (o) are visible along the road to Thurnsdorf (see the arrow). (HF)

Between demobilization and the end of the war

As a railroad junction, Amstetten, the town where we went to school, did not escape the American attacks. The first bomb load hit the town, the railroad station and the neighboring villages on November 19, 1944. More were to follow, the heaviest being those raids of February 25, March 16 and 20, 1945. Not only was the railroad yard damaged, but also the Heart of Jesus Church and several residential buildings. There were numerous dead and injured among the population, despite the air-raid shelters that had been built. The last American bombs fell on Amstetten on April 16, with the last Russian ones hitting the main square on the last day of the war, May 8, – at the very moment that American and Soviet ground troops were joining up. The town was bombed a total of eleven times.

In addition to the strategic long-range bombers, fighter-bombers also joined the action: here, the aerial photo evaluation of a low-flying attack by P-51 Mustangs on the Amstetten rail line on 19.II.1945. (HF)

What was to become of us eight „seasoned warriors"?

Most of us were demobilized and sent home in February/March 1945, awaiting our call-up to the RAD or directly to the Wehrmacht. The fronts were creeping closer; the Russians had entered Hungary and were about to take Vienna, and the Western Allies were already standing on German Reich territory. The majority received their draft papers, but not everyone: in the case of the Amstetten boys Fritz Senker, Sepperl Wallner, Walter Schmutz and Gunter Bast, the Reich draft machinery was no longer functioning smoothly. They never received that order and were able to await the end of war at home. They kept a low profile to avoid falling into the hands of a "Heldenklau" ["Hero Snatchers": officers who picked up and shot deserters or sent stragglers back into line]. However, they did experience first-hand those concentrated attacks on Amstetten, with their homes suffering heavy damage.

Only Sepp Wallner moved to Bubendorf bei Wolfsbach where he worked in his uncle's sawmill.

Willi Reichebner joined the RAD in February already, underwent brief training in the Waldviertel region of Lower Austria, reaching Linz with his unit after extensive marches, where they were supposed to face the Americans. However, he and some of his comrades made themselves scarce and, after further long marches, reached home in time to witness the invasion of the Red Army.

Franzl Wieser experienced much the same as Willi. He was also assigned to the RAD, but only in April. Then he was in action against the Americans before also deciding to march home early.

Walter Spindelberger had the toughest time of all: he was taken prisoner by the Americans and then released that fall. He turned up at school for the start of the 8th grade as a slender figure of a boy with a shaved head.

Staatl. Oberschule f. Jungen
in Amstetten

Amstetten, 5.4.1945

An Herrn
Oberleitner,
Ybbs/D.

Ich übersende Ihnen beiliegend Ihr LWH-Zeugnis Abschlußzeugnis .Im Falle der Einberufung zum RAD oder Wehrmacht haben Sie sich mit diesem Einberufungs= befehl sofort bei der Schulleitung zu melden,damit Sie die Ihnen zustehende Reife bezw.Vorsemesterbescheinigung ausgestellt erhalten.
Eventuelle Bescheinigung über Freiwillige Meldung zum Militärdienst ist zur Einsichtnahme mitzubringen.

Der Oberstudiendirektor:

Our school reports were sent to us at home (see next two pages); mine at least was slightly better than the earlier one.

Staatl. Oberschule f. Jungen in Amstetten

STAATSGÜLTIGES ZEUGNIS

Katalog-Nr. 8   Schuljahr 19 44/45

Luftwaffenhelfer-Zeugnis

Der Schüler *Oberleitner Gerhard*

geboren am *7. April* 19 28 zu *Ybbs a. D.*

im *Nieder Donau*, Sohn des *Oberleitner Johann*

in *Ybbs a. D.*, zuletzt Schüler der *siebenten* Klasse

der Oberschule für Jungen ~~Naturwiss.- mathem. Zweig~~ / ~~Sprachlicher Zweig~~ des Gymnasiums, ist seit *5. I. 1944*

als Luftwaffenhelfer eingesetzt und hat an dem für Luftwaffenhelfer angeordneten Unterricht mit folgendem Ergebnis teilgenommen:

Leistungen in den Pflichtfächern:	
Deutsch	sehr gut
Geschichte	sehr gut
Erdkunde	befriedigend
Biologie	gut
Chemie	befriedigend
Physik	befriedigend
Rechnen und Mathematik	befriedigend
Latein	befriedigend
Griechisch	

OBERDONAU

Lwh 1. Oberschule für Jungen, Jahreszeugnis. — Q 0171 44 1178

STAATSGÜLTIGES ZEUGNIS

Auf Grund der Leistungen und des Verhaltens im Unterricht und im Einsatz und in Anwendung des Erlasses des Reichsministers für Wissenschaft, Erziehung und Volksbildung vom 22. Januar 1943 — E III a 3360 — wird der Schüler in die Klasse .... der Oberschule (des Gymnasiums) .... versetzt.

Feldpost Nr. L 28211

Luftnachrichtenamt .... Wien ..... am ..... 11. März 1945

Unterschrift des Betreuungslehrers:

Unterschrift des Einheitenführers:

Unterschrift des Leiters der Schule,
der der Schüler angehört:

Schulstempel.

Unterschrift des Erziehungsberechtigten:

Leistungsstufen in den Fächern:
Sehr gut (1) — Gut (2) — Befriedigend (3) — Ausreichend (4) — Mangelhaft (5) — Ungenügend (6).

OBERDONAU

As a specialist on the fire control unit, I was one of the last on March 11 to be sent home, where I worked in my father's carpentry business until the last day of the war. I had still not been called up, but in the middle of April, my mother came out to the sawmill where I was working at the time and said: „You have to hide now. Someone phoned up and said that you should report for duty, but I answered: ‚Why? Gerhard is with the AA!'"

So now I spent the final weeks and days of the war in the loft of our house. I only dared go out in the forest in the evening to get some exercise. I was bored stiff, no movies, just reading, reading and more reading. Then, at night, the strictly forbidden listening to enemy radio broadcasts that carried the death penalty, but were the only way to really find out what was going on – and finally, the war came to an end.

The war is over: these B-17s have done their duty and are now mothballed in the desert in the USA. (HF)

The postwar period

We know very little about the fate of our battery, the 1./695 (o). It is said to have been engaged in ground fighting near Enns against the Americans who were advancing towards the east and then been captured by them. In the following years we neither heard nor saw anything from our commander, Lieutenant Göttinger, the NCOs and troopers, the female assistants or the Flak-V soldiers, or virtually any of the AAA who shared our fate.

Only we AAA from Amstetten and Waidhofen stayed in loose contact and now, at an advanced age, we have come together again.

A meeting of the Amstetten and Waidhofen AAA in August 2007: from left to right: Josef Wallner, Fritz Senker, Josef Lammerhuber, our guest from America: Richard G. Yerick, Wilhelm Reichebner, Gunter Bast, Gerhard Oberleitner.

Resumes of the 8 high school students

Perhaps readers will find it interesting to learn about how life treated those Amstetten high school students over the past six decades. Here is a summary that reflects on that piece of poetry at the beginning of this book:

Bast ("Social Worker and Recycling Enthusiast")
Matriculation in Amstetten 1947, studied law at the University of Vienna, Dr.iur., Attorney in Amstetten.

Oberleitner ("Sports and Oratory Genius")
Matriculation in Waidhofen an der Ybbs 1946, studied civil engineering and architecture at the Technical University of Vienna, MSc Eng., freelance architect and building surveyor in Reutte/Tyrol.

Reichebner ("Latin Expert/Seeker")
Matriculation in Amstetten 1947, studied law at the University of Vienna, Dr.iur., City Counselor, Head of Internal Revenue Scheibbs.

Schmutz ("Mister Smuts")
Matriculation in Amstetten 1947, studied at the University of Natural Resources and Life Sciences in Vienna, specializing in agriculture, Dipl.-Ing., Managing Director of the Agricultural College of the Cloister St. Georgen am Längsee.

Senker ("English Speaker")
Studied medicine at the University of Vienna, Dr.med.univ., Medical Counselor, State Counselor, Consultant in Gynecology, Senior Consultant of the Gynecological Obstretics Ward at the Amstetten Hospital, Director and Medical Head of the Amstetten Medical Center

Spindelberger ("Doctoral Specimen")
Matriculation in Amstetten 1946, studied mathematics and IT at the University of Vienna, Dr.phil., Management Executive IBM

Wallner ("Nordic Slender"),
Matriculation in Steyr 1947, studied at the University of Natural Resources and Life Sciences in Vienna, specializing in forestry, Dipl.-Ing., Head of District Forestry Inspectorate Amstetten, Counselor

Wieser ("Vilifier of Caesar")
Matriculation in Amstetten 1947, studied at the Academy of Pedagogy (Teacher Training Institute) St. Pölten, Subject Teacher at Ybbs General School / passed away 1981

Amstetten High School

Following the interruptions caused by the war and the postwar period, our German Reich Upper School for Boys started very limited classes again as an Austrian State High School on July 16, 1945. Space was a severe problem as the Soviet Occupation Forces had immediately confiscated our school building in May 1945, which served as a Red Army Military Hospital for the next 10 years. Consequently, classes were held alternately in the mornings or afternoons at the General School for Boys.

Not until 1966 was it possible to occupy a new, generously equipped school building that now splendidly serves around 700 students and 60 teaching staff.

Appendix

Documentation

The author's combat journal

During his service from 22.II.1944 to 3.III.1945, the author kept a tabulated journal on the combat record of his AA battery, the 1/695 (o), in St. Valentin-Langenhart; part of the first page is reproduced here.

Date	Attack	Salvos	Rounds fired	Targets
22. II.	(Steyr)	15	81	Verband!
23. II.	(Steyr)	5	25	Liberator
24. II.	(Steyr)	14	72	Fortress
30. V		5	28	einz. Jäger Lightnings
29. VI.		5	27	Unbekannte M.
21. VII	(Linz)	66	368	Verbände
25. VII.		58	338	Verbände
20. VIII.		40	162	Verbände
24. VIII.		2	11	Mustangs X
23. IX	14.9.	12	70	Lightnings
16. X.		41		Verbände
16. X		7	270	4 Mustangs
19. IX.		4	23	1 Mosquito

The author's diary

Extract from the author's diary. Quoted on page 221.

The author's photography logbook

The author made a note of all the lens and shutter settings and relevant data for every photo he made. After receiving the prints, he evaluated the quality of each one (see legend lower right). This is a reprint of the first of many double pages in his logbook.

The author's "Amusing Retrospective of the Year"

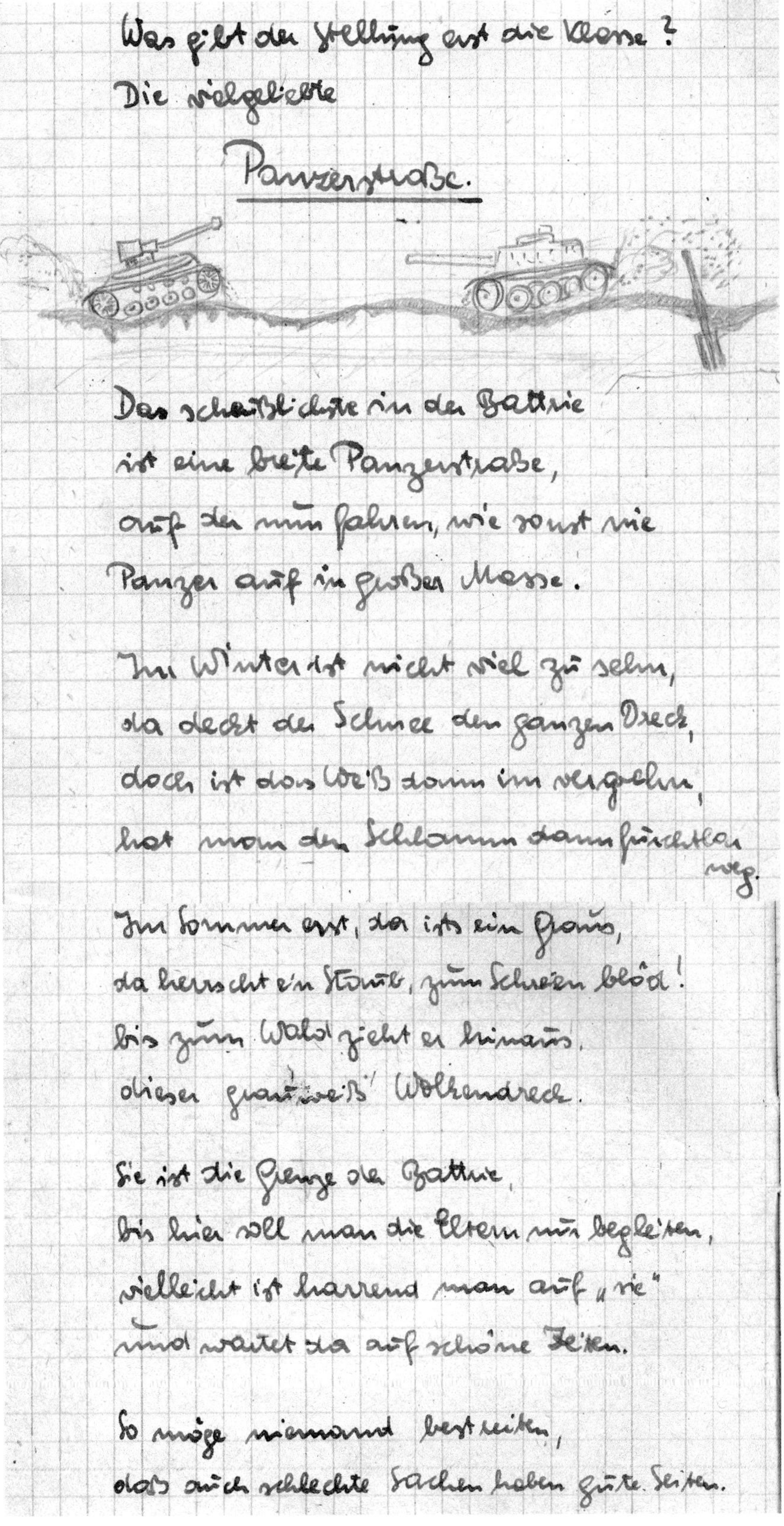

„The Panzerstrasse"; an example from the author's sketchbook

Letter written by the author to his cousin Erich

Envelope and first page of a letter written by the author to his cousin; quoted on page 103.

Other documentation and data

Markings of the American bombers

Two contemporary illustrations showing the squadron and group markings of the bombers of the 15th USSAF.

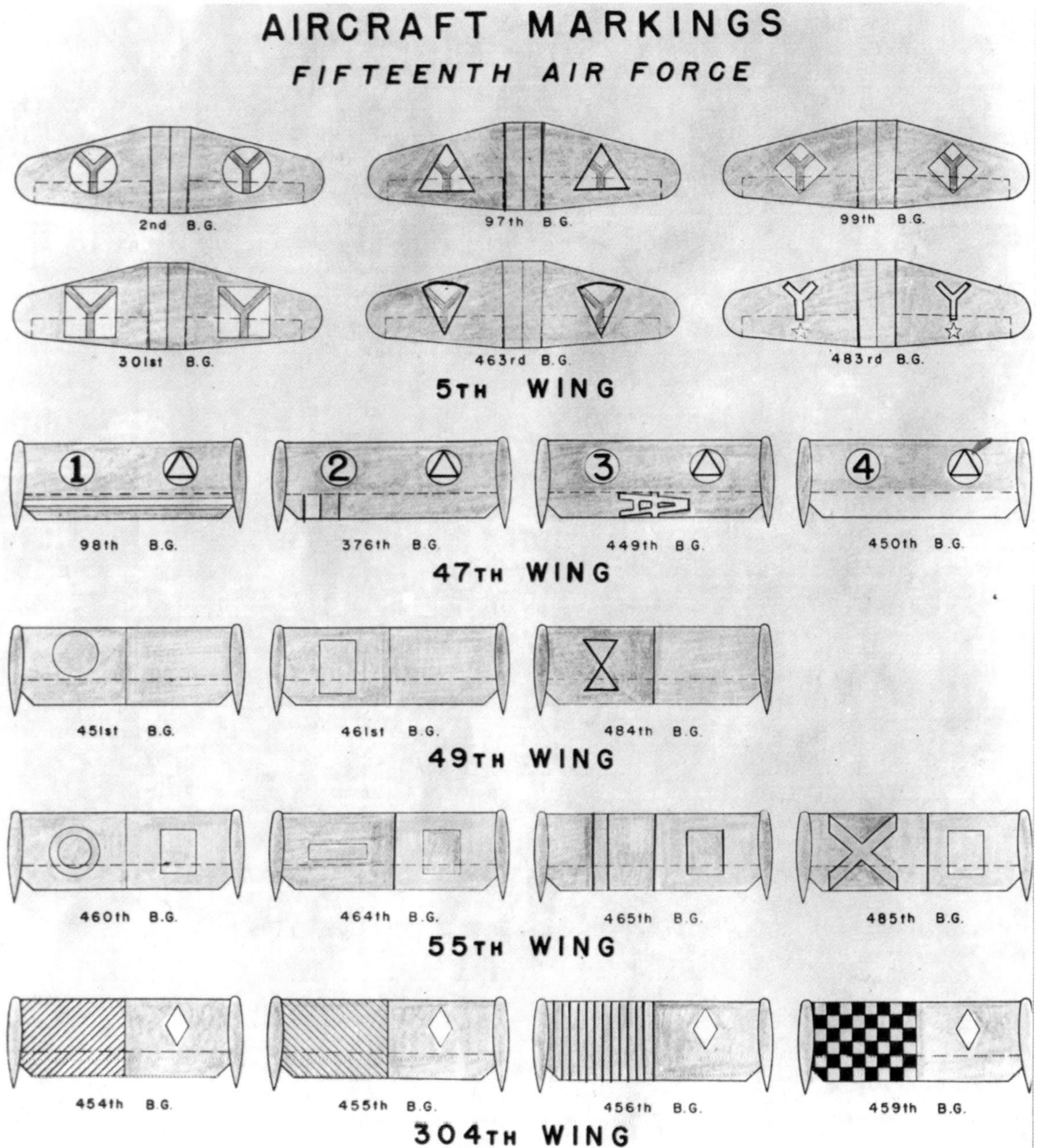

The sketch above shows the markings on the horizontal stabilizers (upper B-17, lower B-24) with their corresponding Bombardment Group markings; the sketch on the following page shows the vertical tail markings. (HF)

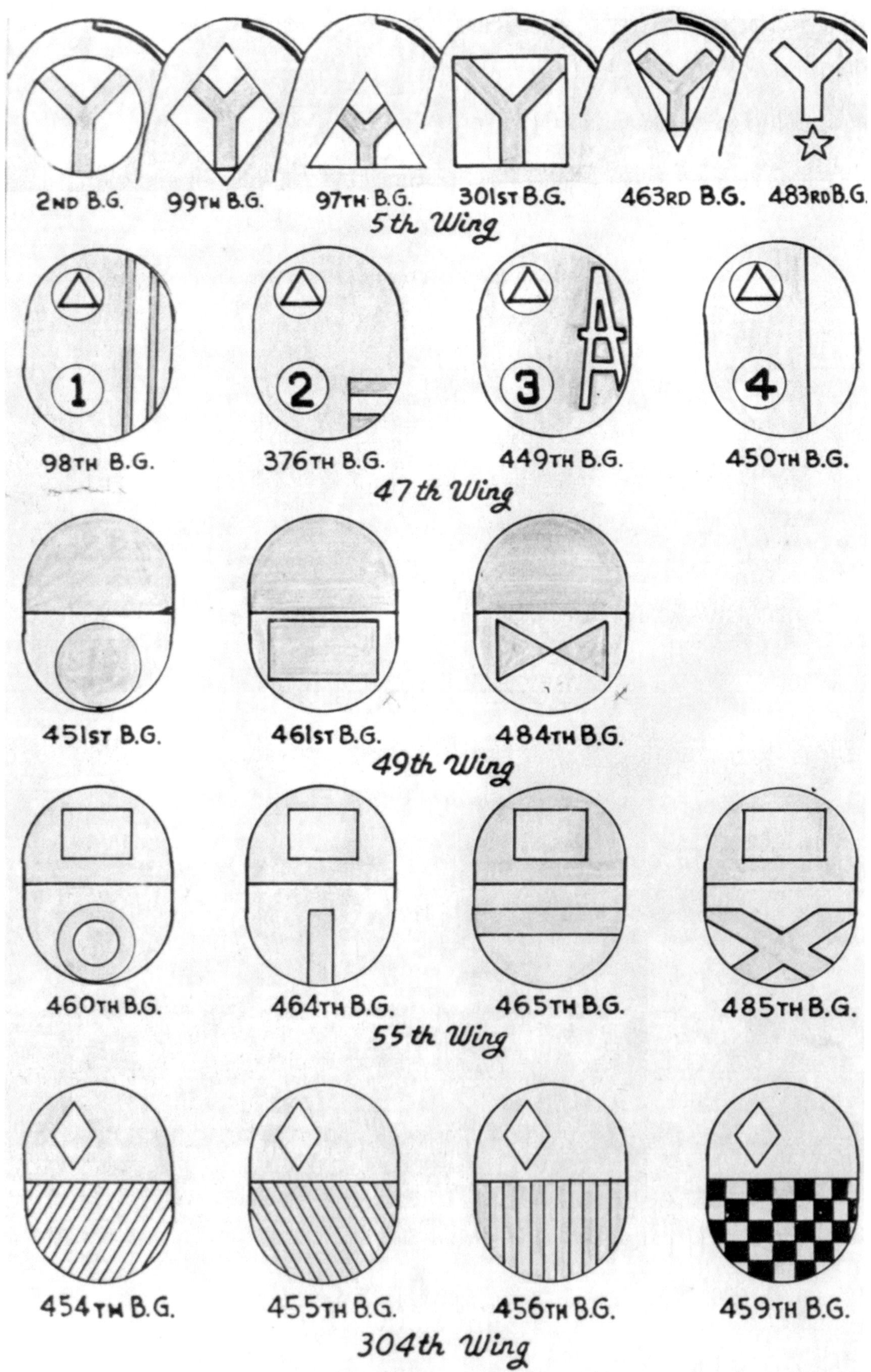

2ND B.G.
99TH B.G.
97TH B.G.
301ST B.G.
463RD B.G.
483RD B.G.
5th Wing
98TH B.G.
376TH B.G.
449TH B.G.
450TH B.G.
47th Wing
451ST B.G.
461ST B.G.
484TH B.G.
49th Wing
460TH B.G.
464TH B.G.
465TH B.G.
485TH B.G.
55th Wing
454TH B.G.
455TH B.G.
456TH B.G.
459TH B.G.
304th Wing

Hitler Youth festival parades

Harvest Festival 1944 in St. Valentin: a Nazi party event complete with parade – led by the Hitler Youth band marching behind an attractive outrider, followed by a cart piled high with harvested crops. Also seen are a few apparently disinterested onlookers and a number of strolling AA soldiers. (JK)

The parade led to the festival grounds complete with swastikas, speeches and choirs. The ceremony closed with the singing of the German National Anthem and the Horst Wessel Song with the right arm raised in the "German Salute". We were never required to participate in this sort of event. At the time, we were not even aware that such things were being held in our vicinity – after all, we had better things to do. (JK)

Report of a film unit on a movie show

Gerätehalter: *2. Battr. schw. Flak-947, 803*   *14.12.44*

Filmtrupp Flak-Brink/Mün.   Gerät Nr. *11 W 26.*

Durchführungsbestätigung für eine Filmvorführung.

Ort der Vorführung: *Stellung*

Bei der Dienststelle: *L 54347   2./803.*

Gezeigt wurde:	Länge m	Stückzahl bei Lehrbildreihen
Gemäß L.Dv. 983/1 u. /2 *NT 101*		*2 Rollen*
" 385		*1 Rolle*
" 66		*1 Rolle*
Beiprogramm:		*4 -*
Wochenschau Nr. (Ufa Nr.)		
Hauptfilm: *"Träumerei"* *für Wehrbetreuung*	Gespielte Filmlänge:	

Anfang: *19⁰⁰* Uhr, Veranstaltungsdauer *3.* Stunden.

Beteiligung: *145* Personen.

Besondere Bemerkungen: *Vorführung mußte wegen Stromstörung der Zuleitungsdrähte zum Lampengehäuse u. Blendenrahmen - 30 Min. unterbrochen werden.*

Filmvorführer: *Soramba Ogef.*   Spielleiter:

Datum: *14. III. 1944*

Bescheinigung der betreuten Einheit:

Dienstgrad und Dienststellung.

Rückseite beachten!

1936 — 42 — Buchdruckerei Bruno Bartelt (A. Trupp). Wien XVIII.

Statement of an Austrian POW captured by the Americans

1.   The following information was obtained from an~~Austrian~~ P/W
who, from June 1941 until March 1943, was employed at the Nibelungen
Werke at St. Balentin as a quality controller in the component man-
ufacturing section.

2.   This factory is known to be controlled by the Steyr Daimler
Puch concern which in turn comes under the Hermann Goering Corporatio
It is accordingly closely linked with the S.D.P. factories at Steyr
and Graz and also with the Hermann Goering works in Linz.

Layout

3.   The attached Sketh shows the layout of the factory and the
Key describes the functions of the various shops. Most of the
buildings were modern concrete structures erectdd in late 1940 and
early 1941 and they were paint camouflaged. Much of the plant was
beliebed to be of French origin.

Production.

4.   Throughout P/W's stay at the workd it was principally engaged
on the assembly and fitting out of Pzkw.lV and Tiger tanks, while in
February 1943 preparations were being made to assemble Panther tanks
also. In addition a number of tractors ("Ostschlepper") were also
turned out.

5.   The first tank built at the works was delivered in August 1941
and series production started in June 1942. By February 1943 output
was said to have reached a level of four Pzkw.lVs and two Tiger
tanks each week, but nothing was known of the destination to which
they were delivered.

Materials.

6.   P/W was aware that much of the necessary raw material was
supplied by the Hermann Goering Werke and the Wisenwerke Oberdonau
at Linz, but he was nevertheless under the impression that tank hulls
did not come from there but from the Krupps works at Essen. He had
no idea of the sources of the engines and armament.

7.   Some components for the Pzkw.lV such as gears, bogey wheels,
idlers and turret rings were menufactured on teh premises and ball
races were supplied by one of the S. D. P. factories. Work never
appeared to be held up on account of shartages.

Personnel.

8.   In March 1943 the managing director of the works was a Dr.
Justmann, the works manager was named Hochnausel and three of the
departmental chiefs were named respectively Tippe, Ruhe and Nemetz.

9.   It was estimated that between 6,000 and 7,000 workers were
employed including some 1,400 Austrians, made up of men and women
in equal proportions, and an assortment of foreigners such as
Poles, Dutchmen, Italians, and Russians; at one time there had even
been some Spaniards but these were subsequently sacked for bad work.

10.   Two 10-hour shifts were worked on six days a week, the times
being 0700 - 1800 hours (with an hour's break for lunch) and 1900 -
0500 hours. P/W himself earned Rm.300 per month as a quality controll
er.

<u>Security and A.R.P.</u>

11.   The workers were issued with blue passes bearing the holder's
photograph, name, number and signature and also an indication of the
type of work on which he was employed. The premises were guarded by
black uniformed werkschutz plice armed with revolvers by day and with
sub-machine guns. by night,

12.   The factory had its own air raid siren, but in P/W's
experience this was only sounded once a month for testing purposes so

he could not describe the action taken in the event of a genuine aler

13.   ████understood that underground P. A. D. shelters hadabeen
constructed in the woods near the factory, but he had never entered
these and could give no details of the type of accommodation provided

Missing Air Crew Report „Ship 33", 23.II.1944

This complete Missing Air Crew Report, including the postwar questioning, comprises 68 pages. A few are reproduced in the following:

2nd Lt. Benjamin B. Chase — Mrs. Evelyn B. Chase (wife), 2778 Herschell Avenue, Jacksonville, Florida

2nd Lt. Marwin J. Combest — Mrs. Twilla D. Combest (wife), Ransom, Kansas

2nd Lt. Edward M. Pine — Mr. James E. Pine (father), 4100 Saint Vincent Avenue, Shreveport, Louisiana

2nd Lt. Wayne E. Nesbitt — Mrs. Ethel M. Nesbitt (wife), Rural Free Delivery Four, Box 224, Greeley, Colorado

S/Sgt. Pasquale W. Agresta — Mr. Joseph Agresta (mother), 828 North Fourth Street, Newark, New Jersey

S/Sgt. David R. Fairley — Mrs. Winnie D. Fairley (mother), Johns, Mississippi

Sgt. Frank H. Perrin, Jr., — Mr. Frank H. Perrin, Sr., (father), 421 Del Amo, Artesia, California

S/Sgt. Freeman D. Smith — Mrs. Pauline Smith (mother), Jasper, Minnesota

Sgt. Martin Yerick — Mrs. Frances Yerick (mother), 730 East 157th Street, Cleveland, Ohio

Pvt. Russell P. Capogreco — Mrs. Lillian Capogreco (mother), 184 North Union Street, Rochester, New York

The list of addresses of the next of kin of the downed crew members to be informed – a distressing duty of the unit commander, even if the reported status was POW (prisoner of war). (HF)

AFPPA-14 (10 APR. 40)

MISSING AIR CREW REPORT   MACR NO. 2586

WAR DEPARTMENT
HEADQUARTERS ARMY AIR FORCES
WASHINGTON

IMPORTANT: This report will be compiled in triplicate by each Army Air Force organization within 48 hours of the time an aircraft is officially reported missing.

1. ORGANIZATION: LOCATION: San Pancrazio, Italy   COMMAND OR AIR FORCE 15th
GROUP 37th ; SQUADRON 512th ; DETACHMENT -

2. SPECIFY: POINT OF DEPARTURE San Pancrazio, Italy ; COURSE Inclosed
INTENDED DESTINATION Steyr, Austria ; TYPE OF MISSION High Altitude

3. WEATHER CONDITIONS AND VISIBILITY AT TIME OF CRASH OR WHEN LAST REPORTED:
Visibility - Good   Weather - Good

4. GIVE: (A) DATE 23 Feb. 1944 TIME 1214 LT ; AND LOCATION OF LAST KNOWN
WHEREABOUTS OF MISSING AIRCRAFT Steyr, Austria
(B) SPECIFY WHETHER (X) LAST SIGHTED; ( ) LAST CONTACTED BY RADIO;
( ) FORCED DOWN; ( ) SEEN TO CRASH; OR ( ) INFORMATION NOT AVAILABLE.

5. AIRCRAFT WAS LOST, OR IS BELIEVED TO HAVE BEEN LOST, AS A RESULT OF (CHECK ONLY ONE): (X) ENEMY AIRCRAFT; ( ) ENEMY ANTI-AIRCRAFT; ( ) OTHER CIRCUMSTANCES AS FOLLOWS:

6. AIRCRAFT: TYPE, MODEL, AND SERIES B-24-J ; AAF SERIAL NO. 42-100255

7. ENGINES: TYPE, MODEL AND SERIES R-1830-65 ; AAF SERIAL NO. (A)
BP - 428612 (B) BP - 427557 (C) BP - 427127 (D) BP - 423293

8. INSTALLED WEAPONS (FURNISH BELOW MAKE, TYPE AND SERIAL NUMBER) Attached.
(A) (B) (C) (D)
(E) (F) (G) (H)

9. THE PERSONS LISTED BELOW WERE REPORTED AS: (A) BATTLE CASUALTY X
OR (2) NON-BATTLE CASUALTY

10. NUMBER OF PERSONS ABOARD AIRCRAFT: CREW 11; PASSENGERS - ; TOTAL 11
(Starting with pilot, furnish the following particulars: If more than 11 persons were aboard aircraft, list similar particulars on separate sheet and attach original to this form)

CREW POSITION	NAME IN FULL (LAST NAME FIRST)	RANK	SERIAL NUMBER	STATUS
(1) PILOT	Chase, Benjamin B.	2nd Lt.	O-797470	KIA
(2) CO-PILOT	Combest, Morwin J.	2nd Lt.	O-684263	RMC
(3) Navigator	Pine, Edward M.	2nd Lt.	O-739495	KIA
(4) Bombardier	Nesbitt, Wayne R.	2nd Lt.	O-679206	RUS
(5) Engineer	Agresta, Pasquale W.	T/Sgt.	12135050	RUS
(6) Radio Opr.	Fairley, David R.	S/Sgt.	18217536	KIA
(7) Asst. Engineer	Perrin, Frank H., Jr.	Sgt.	39541583	RUS
(8) Asst. Rad. Opr.	Smith, Freeman D.	S/Sgt.	37451719	RUS
(9) Tail Gunner	Yerick, Martin (NMI)	Sgt.	35513438	KIA
(10) Armorer Gunner	Capogreco, Russell P.	Pvt.	12198242	KIA
(11) Nose Gunner(AEC)	Phelan, Arthur T.	Sgt.	3233795	RUS

11. IDENTIFY BELOW THOSE PERSONS WHO ARE BELIEVED TO HAVE LAST KNOWLEDGE OF AIRCRAFT, AND CHECK APPROPRIATE COLUMN TO INDICATE BASIS FOR SAME:

NAME IN FULL (LAST NAME FIRST)	RANK	SERIAL NUMBER	CONTACTED BY RADIO	LAST SIGHTED	SAW CRASH	SAW FORCED LANDING
(1) Burton, David C.	2nd Lt.	O-742678		X		
(2) Keator, Clyde J.	2nd Lt.	O-683716		X		
(3)						

12. IF PERSONNEL ARE BELIEVED TO HAVE SURVIVED, ANSWER YES TO ONE OF THE FOLLOWING STATEMENTS: (A) PARACHUTES WERE USED 3 ; (B) PERSONS WERE SEEN WALKING AWAY FROM SCENE OF CRASH ; OR (C) ANY OTHER REASON (SPECIFY)

13. ATTACH EYEWITNESS DESCRIPTION OF CRASH, FORCED LANDING, OR OTHER CIRCUMSTANCES PERTAINING TO MISSING AIRCRAFT. Inclosed

14. ATTACH AERIAL PHOTOGRAPH, MAP, CHART, OR SKETCH, SHOWING APPROXIMATE LOCATION WHERE AIRCRAFT WAS LAST SEEN. Inclosed

15. ATTACH A DESCRIPTION OF THE EXTENT OF SEARCH, IF ANY, AND GIVE NAME, RANK AND SERIAL NUMBER OF OFFICER IN CHARGE. None

25 February 1944   /s/ /t/ GERALD S. BROWN,
(Date of Report)   (Signature of Preparing Officer)
1st Lt., Air Corps,
Operations Officer.

REMARKS: (Use additional sheet if necessary)

Processed by Memorial Division (QMG).

Final evaluation with definitive status of the crew members. (HF)

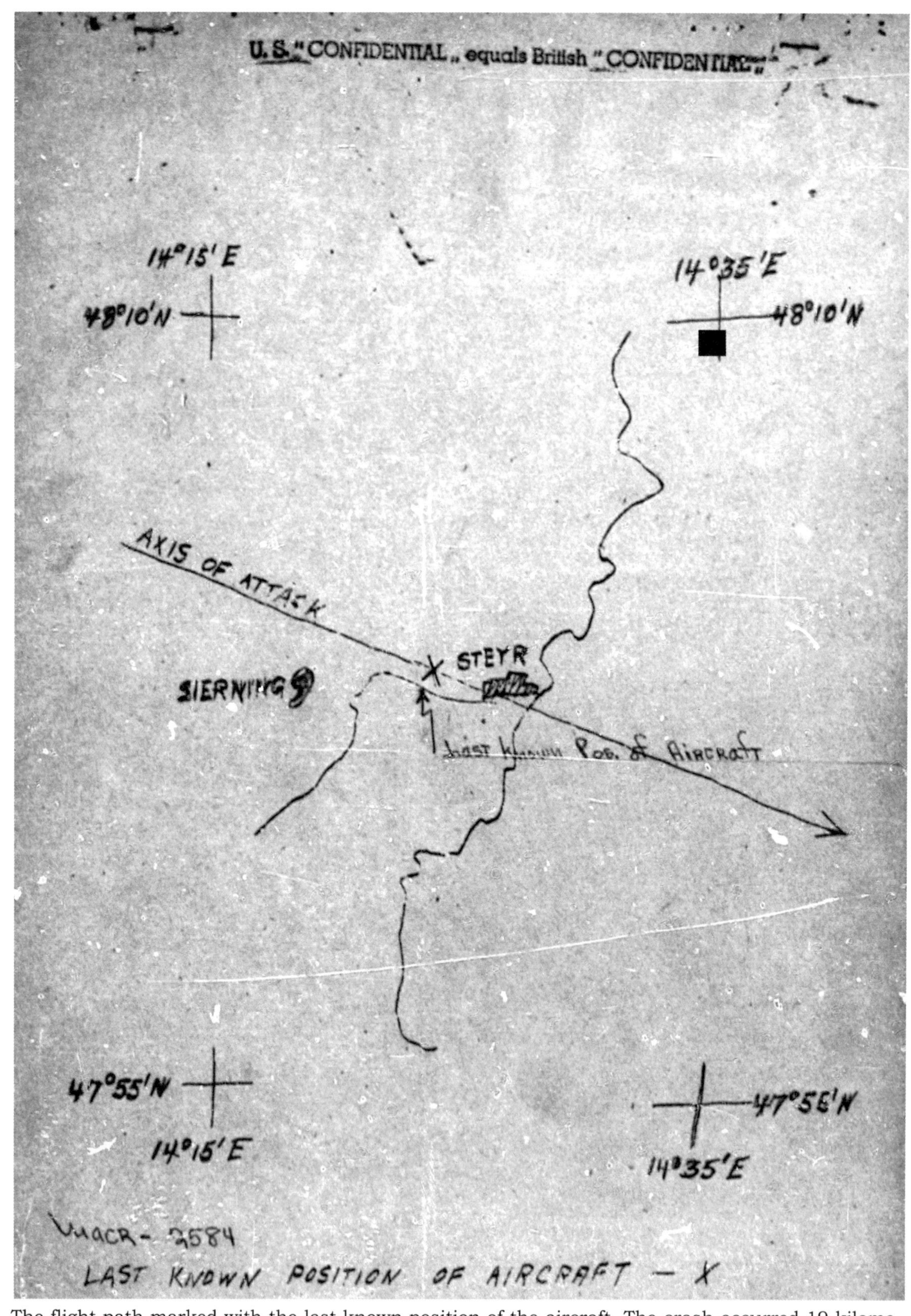

The flight path marked with the last known position of the aircraft. The crash occurred 19 kilometers north-northeast of Steyr, see the inserted black square. (HF)

MACR: 2584

24 February 1944

S T A T E M E N T S

The following is a statement of 2nd Lt. Clyde J. Keator, Serial Number O-683716, on plane number 31. Mission dated: February 23, 1944.

My tail gunner, Sgt. H. R. Hall saw ship 33 which flew directly behind us fall out of formation to the rear. The plane was smoking. Three chutes appeared and ship then went into a vertical dive and disappeared.

/s/ /t/ CLYDE J. KEATOR
512th Bomb. Sqd. (H)
Serial No. O-683716
2nd Lt., A. C.

*   *   *   *   *

24 February 1944

The following is a statement of Lt. David C. Burton, ASN O-742678 on Plane Number 24. Mission dated: February 23, 1944.

My waist gunner, Sgt. Harold Furney, sighted a plane pull out of formation and was smoking. It went so far and nosed over in a vertical dive. Three chutes appeared to open and one was on fire. The co-pilot saw the same ship. It is believed to be Lt. Chase and crew on Plane #33.

/s/ /t/ DAVID C. BURTON
512th Bomb. Sqd. (H)
Serial No. O-742678
2nd Lt., Air Corps.

Witness statements of the tail gunner Sergeant Hall of Aircraft No. 31 (above) and the waist gunner Sergeant Furney of Aircraft No. 24 (below) concerning the loss of Aircraft No. 33. (HF)

Missing Air Crew Report 42-95285, 8.I.1945

A few pages of this Missing Air Crew Report are also reproduced:

512th Bombardment Squadron (H)

376th Bombardment Group (H)

APO 520   U.S. Army

The following is a statement of S/Sgt Everett Webster,
12238702 on plane #28 AAF # 44-41216, mission dated 8 Jan 1945:

I was flying as tail gunner in A/C #44-41216, Snip # 6
in the second box of the formation. Some time after having left
the target and after we were well on our course, I noticed that
A/C 42-95285 #7 ship, type B-24 (H), in the second box, was in
trouble of some sort. We had been flying over the sea, and about
fifteen (15) minutes after passing the coast, while flying over
land, I noticed that A/C 42-95285 had one engine feathered.
She began dropping back from the formation, slowly losing altitude
and I later saw her disappear in the undercrest. This was the last
I saw of her.

EVERETT H. WEBSTER
S/Sgt 12238702

Statement of a tail gunner who witnessed how Aircraft No. 7 dropped out of the formation and, losing height, fell behind. (HF)

Harden, Gerald·L. S/Sgt 13141641
KIA 8 Jan 45   Air Corps Historical Records

16500

376th Bombardment Group
8 January 1945

B 24's took off at o845 to bomb the Linz North Main M/Y in
Germany Route: to San Vito di Normanni to caorle (4536N 1253E) to
Aviano (4604N 1236E to Reischach (4819N 1339E, th IP, to the target.

Total losses 1 A/C (Ser. No. 42-95285), previously reported
to have landed at Vis, now reported as missing. This A/C was last
seen at 1425 hour at 4448N 1500E, dropping behind the formation
Navigator or was given a course to Vis. #1 engine was out, 2 run away
props, 1 controlled and 1 uncontrollable.

Report on the missing aircraft on the day of the attack, assuming that the crewmen are all dead; here, page 2 of the statement made on 2nd Sergeant Harden. (HF)

MISSING AIR CREW REPORT — 16500

WAR DEPARTMENT
HEADQUARTERS ARMY AIR FORCES
WASHINGTON

IMPORTANT: This report will be compiled in triplicate by each Army Air Forces organization within 48 hours of the time an aircraft is officially reported missing.

1. ORGANIZATION: LOCATION, San Pancrazio, Italy; COMMAND OR AIR FORCE 15th Air Force
GROUP 376th Bomb Gp.; SQUADRON 512 Bomb; DETACHMENT
2. SPECIFY: POINT OF DEPARTURE San Pancrazio, Italy; COURSE *
INTENDED DESTINATION Linz, Austria (Noth M/Y); TYPE OF MISSION High altitude bombing
3. WEATHER CONDITIONS AND VISIBILITY AT TIME OF CRASH OR WHEN LAST REPORTED:
7/10 Cumulus tops at 8000 feet
4. GIVE: (a) DAY 8 Jan 45 TIME 1425; AND LOCATION OF LAST KNOWN WHEREABOUTS OF MISSING AIRCRAFT 4445N 1500E - Adriatic Sea (44 45N 1500E)
(b) SPECIFY WHETHER ( ) LAST SIGHTED; ( ) LAST CONTACTED BY RADIO; ( ) FORCED DOWN; ( ) SEEN TO CRASH; OR ( ) INFORMATION NOT AVAILABLE.
5. AIRCRAFT WAS LOST, OR IS BELIEVED TO HAVE BEEN LOST, AS A RESULT OF (CHECK ONLY ONE): ( ) ENEMY AIRCRAFT; ( ) ENEMY ANTI-AIRCRAFT; ( ) OTHER CIRCUMSTANCES AS FOLLOWS: Mechnical trouble
6. AIRCRAFT: TYPE, MODEL AND SERIES B-24; AAF SERIAL NO. 42-95265
7. ENGINES: TYPE, MODEL AND SERIES; AAF SERIAL NO. (a) CP-308320 (b) BP-454887 (c) BP-52362 (d) BP-447355
8. INSTALLED WEAPONS (furnish below make, type and serial number): All savage
(a) RT 1184244 (b) LW 1184307 (c) LT 1184542 (d) RW 1184581 RT 1187708
(e) RN 1187882 (f) LB 1185426 (g) LN 1188145 (h) RB 1184997 LT 1187787
9. THE PERSONS LISTED BELOW WERE REPORTED AS: (a) BATTLE CASUALTY; OR (b) NON-BATTLE CASUALTY
10. NUMBER OF PERSONS ABOARD AIRCRAFT: CREW 11; PASSENGERS 0; TOTAL 11
(Starting with pilot, furnish the following particulars. If more than 11 persons were aboard aircraft, list similar particulars on separate sheet and attach original to this form.)

CREW POSITION	NAME IN FULL (LAST NAME FIRST)	RANK	SERIAL NUMBER	STATUS
(1) PILOT	Scott, Phillip R	2nd Lt	0-827978	RTD
(2) CO-PILOT	Martin, Kenneth F	2nd Lt	0-830880	RTD
(3)	[redacted]			
(4) Nav	Dumm, Richard C	2nd Lt	0- 558805	RTD
(5) Bomb.	Walker, Robert C	2nd Lt	0-2056749	RTD
(6) Eng.	Snipes, Oscar	T/Sgt	14097788	EUS
(7) Rad Oper	Holt, Jack D	T/Sgt	39209660	KIA
(8) Arm Gnr	Harden, Gerald L	S/Sgt	13141641	KIA
(9) Arm Gnr	Messing, Gerard	S/Sgt	12227303	DOI
(10) Arm Gnr	Walker, Colby G Jr	S/Sgt	31398055	EUS
(11) Arm Gnr	McDermott, John E	S/Sgt	36961968	KIA
Photo Gnr	Loewenthal, Ralph H	S/Sgt	18153946	RTD

11. IDENTIFY BELOW THOSE PERSONS WHO ARE BELIEVED TO HAVE LAST KNOWLEDGE OF AIRCRAFT, AND CHECK APPROPRIATE COLUMN TO INDICATE BASIS FOR SAME:

NAME IN FULL (LAST NAME FIRST)	RANK	SERIAL NUMBER	CONTACTED BY RADIO	LAST SIGHTED	SAW CRASH	SAW FORCED LANDING
(1) Everett H Webster,	S/Sgt	12238702		X	(statement attached)	
(2)						
(3)						

12. IF PERSONNEL ARE BELIEVED TO HAVE SURVIVED, ANSWER YES TO ONE OF THE FOLLOWING STATEMENTS: (a) PARACHUTES WERE USED; (b) PERSONS WERE SEEN WALKING AWAY FROM SCENE OF CRASH; OR (c) ANY OTHER REASON (SPECIFY)
13. ATTACH EYEWITNESS DESCRIPTION OF CRASH, FORCED LANDING, OR OTHER CIRCUMSTANCES PERTAINING TO MISSING AIRCRAFT.
14. ATTACH AERIAL PHOTOGRAPH, MAP, CHART, OR SKETCH, SHOWING APPROXIMATE LOCATION WHERE AIRCRAFT WAS LAST SEEN.
15. ATTACH A DESCRIPTION OF THE EXTENT OF SEARCH, IF ANY, AND GIVE NAME, RANK AND SERIAL NUMBER OF OFFICER IN CHARGE: No search

14 January 1945 (Date of Report)
/s/ Donald L. Lacy (Signature of Preparing Officer)
Captain, Air Corps Adjutant

The final report dated 14.I.45 with the definite list of the lost crewmen. The statement that „technical troubles" (5.) were the cause of the crash is incorrect. (HF)

512th Bombardment Squadron (H)
376th Bombarment Group (H)

APO 520, c/o Postmaster
New York City, N. Y.
21 January 1945.

Mrs. Cecile K. Harden
St. Thomas Lane
Owings Mills, Md.

My Dear Mrs. Harden:

The War Department has no doubt notified you of the passing away
of your son, Staff Sergeant Gerald L. Harden, ASN 13141641, who was
killed in action on 8 January 1945 in the Adriatic Sea.

I feel it a sense of duty to inform you of the sincere sympathy
the entire squadron feels for you at this most trying of times.

Gerald was very well known among many members of the squadron
besides the men in his own crew, and these people are able, to a
certain extent, to understand your loss. When your son failed to
return the cheer and good will which was part of him left an
empty place in the hearts of his comrades,

Still we are truly unable to consider it as such. We are consoled
who hope and pray that you might be also, in the knowledge that
those we love are never lost. Gerald is waiting for you, we are sure.

May I state with sincerity the hope that this thought will
help to lessen your grief.

Sincerely yours,

DONALD L. LACY,
Captain, Air Corps,
Adjutant

The Letter of Condolence written by the Adjutant of the Bombardment Group to the mother of Staff
Sergeant Gerald L. Harden, killed in action. (HF)

American Aerial Combat Report of February 24, 1944

The following report graphically describes how an entire squadron of B-17s was shot down by German single-engine and twin-engine fighter aircraft during a bombing raid on Steyr. It was extremely difficult for the Americans to evaluate the aerial combat because most of the potential witnesses had been shot down themselves. The German fighter pilots displayed utmost aggressiveness in plucking one enemy aircraft after another from their formations, generally attacking from behind and then jointly shooting them down. A separate report was generated for each aircraft; the section reproduced here is common to each report.

```
                CONSOLIDATED EYE-WITNESS DESCRIPTION
                          COMPOSED BY
                  THE INVESTIGATING OFFICER


        FINDINGS AND CONCLUSIONS RE: LOSS OF SIX (6) B-17'S (ENTIRE SQUADRON),
   COMPRISING THE THIRD SQUADRON OF THE SECOND WAVE, WHICH WAS FLYING ON A
   COMBAT MISSION TO STEYR, AUSTRIA ON 24 FEB. 1944.

        THIS GROUP WAS HEAVILY ATTACKED BY E/A FROM 1215 HOURS TO 1315 HOURS.
   FROM 75 TO 110 E/A TOOK PART, COMING IN VERY AGGRESSIVELY TO AS CLOSE AS
   50 YARDS, FROM AROUND THE CLOCK, BUT MOSTLY FROM 5 O'CLOCK, CONCENTRATING
   ON THE REAR ELEMENTS.  B-17 F NO. 42-29638 COMPRISED PART OF THE THIRD
   SQUADRON OF THE SECOND WAVE, AND WAS IN AN EXPOSED POSITION.  BECAUSE OF
   FIGHTERS ATTACKING THE WHOLE GROUP WITH UNUSUAL AGGRESSIVENESS, CAREFUL
   INTERROGATION THROUGHOUT THE RETURNED CREWS SHOWED THAT ATTENTION WAS SO
   ENGROSSED, EACH IN MEETING THEIR OWN ATTACKERS, THAT COHERENT ACCOUNTS OF
   JUST HOW NAY ONE OR MORE OF THE PLANES IN THIS SQUADRON WERE LOST, WERE
   UNOBTAINABLE.

        FROM INTERROGATION AND CAREFUL STUDY OF NAVIGATORS LOGS, IT WAS AS-
   CERTAINED THAT THIS SQUADRON WAS ATTACKED REPEATEDLY BY FORMATIONS OF
   SINGLE AND TWIN ENGINE E/A, WHICH SEEMED TO SINGLE OUT AND CONCENTRATE ON
   ONE AFTER ANOTHER OF THE B-17'S IN THIS SQUADRON, UNTIL ALL SIX HAD BEEN
   ELIMINATED.  ATTACKS ON THIS SQUADRON WERE MADE AT ALTITUDES OF FROM
   19,200 FEET TO 21,000 FEET, AND FROM 45-35N, 14-32E TO 4729N,14-28E.


                          R.W. WUHRE, CAPTAIN, AIR CORPS,
                          INVESTIGATING OFFICER.
```

NB: E/A= Enemy Aircraft. (HF)

Bibliography and other useful reference sources

- Chronik der Stadt St.Valentin

- Ast, Oskar; Tesar,Eva : Jugend unterm Hakenkreuz : Wien 1988 : Verlag Jugend und Volk : ISBN: 3-224-1-0692-1

- Banny, Leopold : Dröhnender Himmel – Brennendes Land . Der Einsatz der Luftwaffenhelfer in Österreich : Wien 1988 : Österreichischer Bundesverlag : ISBN: 3-215-06272-0

- Bedürftig, Friedemann; Zentner, Christian (Hrsg.) : Das große Lexikon des Zweiten Weltkrieges : München 1988 : Südwest : ISBN: 3-517-00903-2

- Bailey, Ronald H. : Der Luftkrieg in Europa : Hamburg 1981 : Time-Life : ISBN: 9-06-182-432-X

- Dülk Franz; Fickentscher Fritz : Feuerglocke . Luftwaffenhelfer-Schicksale : Kitzingen/Main 1993 : Verlag Feuerglocke

- Grund, Josef Karl : Flakhelfer Briel . „und sie werden nicht mehr frei ihr ganzes Leben." : Ravensburg 1972 : Otto Maier : ISBN: 3-473-39271-5

- Edmunds, Paul (Hrsg.) : Mit fünfzehn an die Kanonen . Ein Versuch zur Zeitgeschichte : Aachen 1975 : Selbstverlag der VIa des Kaiser-Karl-Gymnasiums

- Müller, Werner : FLAK im Einsatz 1939 – 1945 : Wölfersheim-Berstadt 1996 : Podzun-Pallas : ISBN: 3-7909-0562-3

- Müller, Werner ; Die Geschütze, Ortungs- und Feuerleitgeräte der schweren Flak : Friedberg 1981 : Podzun-Pallas 1981 : ISBN: 3-7909-0331-3

- Nicolaisen, Hans-Dietrich : Die Flakhelfer . Luftwaffen- und Marinehelfer im Zweiten Weltkrieg : Wien 1981 : Ullstein : ISBN 3-550-07949-4

- Nicolaisen, Hans-Dietrich: Der Einsatz der Luftwaffen- und Marinehelfer im 2.Weltkrieg . Darstellung und Dokumentation: Büsum 1981 : Selbstverlag

- Nicolaisen, Hans-Dietrich: Gruppenfeuer und Salventakt : Band I und II : Büsum 1993 : Selbstverlag

- Nöstlinger, Ernst : Martin Wimmer und der totale Krieg . Fünfzehnjährige als Lufftwaffenhelfer : Wien 1985 : Dachs : ISBN: 3-7002-0572-0

- Oberleitner. Gerhard : Geschichte der Deutschen Feldpost 1937 – 1945 : Innsbruck 1993 : Steiger : ISBN: 3-85423-111-3

- Rauchensteiner, Manfried : Der Krieg in Österreich 1945 : Wien 1984 : Österreichischer Bundesverlag : ISBN: 3-215-01672-9

- Schätz, Ludwig : Schüler-Soldaten . Die Geschichte der Luftwaffenhelfer im Zweiten Weltkrieg : Darmstadt 1974 : Thesen : ISBN: 3-7677-0012-3

- Schmeling, Franz Josef :Vom Krieg ein Leben lang geprägt . Ehemalige Luftwaffen- und Marinehelfer antworten 50 Jahre danach : Osnabrück 1997 : Selbstverlag : ISBN 3-87898-358-1

- Schörken, Rolf : Luftwaffenhelfer und Drittes Reich . Die Entstehung eines politischen Bewußtseins : Stuttgart 1984 : Klett-Cotta : ISBN 3-608-91124-3

- Speer, Albert : Erinnerungen : Frankfurt/Main – Berlin 1969 : Ullstein

- Tessin, Georg : Verbände und Truppen der Deutschen Wehrmacht und Waffen-SS 1939 – 1945, Osnabrück 1979 : Biblio : ISBN: 3-7648-1170-6

- Wiesinger, Günter : Wels im Kriege : Artikelserie im Informationsblatt der österreichischen Flugzeughistoriker : Wien 2000-2002

- Winninger, Michael : Das Nibelungenwerk 1939 – 1945 . Panzerfahrzeuge aus St.Valentin : Erfurt 2009 : Sutton : ISBN: 978-3-86680-490-6

About the author

The author, MSc Eng. Gerhard Oberleitner, was born in Ybbs an der Donau, Austria, on April 7, 1928, the younger son of a Master Carpenter. He attended grade school in Ybbs, and the first to fourth years of high school in Vienna 19. He was supposed to attend the fifth to eighth high school years in Amstetten, but after the first trimester of the 6th grade, he was drafted as a Luftwaffe Anti-Aircraft Assistant. Almost up to the end of World War II, he served with a heavy AA battery in St. Valentin. After the war, he completed his studies at the Waidhofen High School, graduating with his Matriculation Certificate on June 6, 1946.

Subsequently, he earned a Master's degree in civil engineering and architecture at the Technical University of Vienna, graduating in 1956. After his journeyman years gaining practical experience in various architectural offices, and then as Construction Manager with Metallwerk Plansee, he became a freelance architect and judicially chartered consultant for architecture and structural engineering.

Married for the second time, Gerhard Oberleitner has four children and six grandchildren. He alternates between homes in Ybbs a.d.D. and Reutte in Tyrol. He holds a private pilot's license and counts modern history and philately among his pastimes.

Gerhard Oberleitner has written numerous professional articles and is the author of the book "History of the German Field Postal Services 1937 – 1945" (published 1995 by Steiger Verlag, Innsbruck, Austria), this volume and a manuscript titled "Der Ziegenkopf von Dabrowica" ["The Goat's Head of Dabrowica"].

History Facts' publications

Published by History Facts

Peter Müller : Heinkel He 162 "Volksjäger" · Last-Ditch Effort by the Luftwaffe : ISBN: 978-3-9522968-1-3

Peter Müller · Wolfgang Zimmermann : Assault Gun III · Backbone of the German Infantry : Volume I, History : ISBN: 978-3-9522968-4-4

Peter Müller · Wolfgang Zimmermann : Assault Gun III · Backbone of the German Infantry : Volume II, Visual Appearance : ISBN: 978-3-9522968-5-1

Mansal Denton : Battle for Narva, 1944 : ISBN: 978-3-905944-01-3

Thomas Anderson : Vorwärts immer, Rückwärts nimmer! · An Illustrated Guide to History and Fate of the German Assault Artillery in WW II : Volume I – The Early Years : ISBN: 978-3-9522968-9-9

Gerhard Oberleitner : You Up There – We Down Here · Anti-Aircraft Assistants vs. Allied Bomber Crews : ISBN: 978-3-9522968-7-5

In preparation at History Facts (working titles)

Michael Winninger : The "Toy Factory" · History of the Nibelungen Tank Works in St. Valentin : ISBN: 978-3-905944-05-1

Peter Müller : Tank production in the Third Reich · From Conceptions to Deliveries : ISBN: 978-3-905944-03-7

Peter Müller · Wolfgang Zimmermann : Panzerkampfwagen IV · Warhorse of the German Panzer Troops : Vol I - ISBN: 978-3-905944-07-5 / Vol II - ISBN: 978-3-905944-09-9 / Vol III - ISBN: 978-3-905944-11-2

Peter Müller : The Armament Minister's Files · Minutes, Memorandums, Speeches (probably published in German only)